HERE'S LOOKING AT US
Celebrating Fifty Years of CBC-TV

HERE'S LOOKING AT US

Celebrating Fifty Years of CBC-TV

Stephen Cole

M&S

National Library of Canada Cataloguing in Publication

Cole, Stephen
      Here's looking at us : celebrating fifty years of CBC-TV / Stephen Cole.

Includes index.
ISBN 0-7710-2251-4

1. Canadian Broadcasting Corporation—History. 2. Television broadcasting—Canada—History. I. Title.

HE8700.9.C3C62 2002   791.45'0971   C2002-902345-9

We acknowledge the financial support of the Government of Canada through the Book Publishing Industry Development Program for our publishing activities. We further acknowledge the support of the Canada Council for the Arts and the Ontario Arts Council for our publishing program.

Typeset in Bembo, Fairfield, ITC Century and Berthold Akzidenz Grotesk by PageWave Graphics Inc., Toronto

Printed and bound in Canada

McClelland & Stewart Ltd.
The Canadian Publishers
481 University Avenue
Toronto, Ontario
M5G 2E9
www.mcclelland.com

1 2 3 4 5   06 05 04 03 02

Front jacket (from left to right, top to bottom):
Percy Saltzman, Anne Murray, Ernie Coombs, Megan Follows (SULLIVAN ENTERTAINMENT INC.), *Brian Williams, Timothy Findley, Lorne Greene, Al Waxman and Fiona Reid, Tommy Hunter, Kevin Conway and Aidan Devine, Eleanor Collins, Gordon Lightfoot, Catherine O'Hara, Pat Mastroianni and Amanda Stepto* (PLAYING WITH TIME INC.), *Luba Goy* (AIR FARCE PRODUCTIONS INC.), *Norman Jewison, Toby Robins, Don Messer, Don Harron, Peter Mansbridge, Juliette, Joe Schlesinger, Adrienne Clarkson, Knowlton Nash, Mary Walsh* (SALTER STREET FILMS LTD./CHRIS REARDON), *Harry Rasky, Bruno Gerussi, Bob Homme, Barbara Frum, Ian Hanomansing.*

CONTENTS

HAPPY FIFTIETH, EVERYBODY!

CANADIANS LOVE TELEVISION. In 1952 we huffed when gas hit twenty cents a gallon, but when CBC-TV went to air that September people were more than happy to spend two months' salary on sets that, in some parts of the country, weren't yet operational.

"In Winnipeg," reports George Einarson, former long-time employee of CBC Manitoba, "all the spanking new TV consoles were in the windows of the department stores downtown — all tuned to the test pattern because TV hadn't arrived yet. But people still went to stare at them, and bought them, then waited for CBC to go to air."

Evidently, we were thrilled by what we finally saw. By 1954 a million TV sets had been sold in Canada. "I can't explain how exciting the arrival of television was," future TV performer and producer Lorne Michaels recalls. "It was all we talked about at school. We literally raced home to watch TV."

Note the "we." Early television was an explicitly collective experience, as *The Plouffe Family*, *Hockey Night in Canada*, and *Don Messer's Jubilee* were greeted with block-party enthusiasm across the country.

Canadians remain ardent TV viewers. And even with more than a hundred channels to choose from, we continue to flock together when events of supreme national interest are televised. How else to explain twenty thousand Vancouver citizens jamming GM Place to watch a jumbo-screen telecast of CBC-TV's "Hockey Afternoon in Utah" men's gold medal Olympic game in February 2002?

Now celebrating fifty years of service, CBC-TV has always been dedicated to the proposition that Canada deserves — no, *requires* — a national television service that allows all of us to see, understand, and distinguish ourselves. This book is both a pop chronicle and a celebration of that undertaking. It's also very much a toast to who we are and where we've come from.

Former *This Hour Has Seven Days* host (then later network chairman) Patrick Watson caught the essence of the tangled relationship between the Corps and Canada in a televised birthday salute that was delivered two decades ago (but is perhaps even more appropriate today):

"[For many years now the CBC] has tracked our times and touched our lives. It both reflects us and is a reflection of us — interesting, sometimes infuriating — but ours. Too bland for some, too controversial for others, but always there, at the centre of things Canadian. An evolving compromise — a bit like the country itself.

"As Canada grew up, became older, more complicated, through it all, in the middle of it and part of it all, was CBC-TV. In the thick of things — something to swear by, or at, or both. You're entitled to celebrate it — it's yours — you pay for it."

Yes, by all means, happy birthday to you, the network's shareholders. And welcome to an illustrated collection of reminiscences, profiles, and oral histories by and about more than one hundred performers, on-air personalities, and behind-the-camera talents who have provided us with five decades of adventure and achievement.

Please, feel free to mingle. Robert Goulet is in the first chapter, advising us how he used the CBC to beat traffic tickets in the '50s. Later in the book, we have Don Cherry and Ron MacLean discussing, what else? *Hockey Night in Canada*. And Rusty and Jerome (puppeteer Rod Coneybeare) are there in the '60s chapter, talking about life in the Friendliest place on television. Are you ready? As the Friendly Giant used to say – *here's our castle*.

Above: A cameraman films outside the studio, a rare event in the first year of CBC-TV.

Left: John Mestrey shoots the opening of the Manitoba legislature in 1956.

TOMORROW FINALLY COMES

THE ARRIVAL OF television was the party that signalled the real end of the Second World War. No one had the gang over to listen to the Grey Cup on radio. TV somehow changed our relationship to the world. Suddenly, the crowning of monarchs or sports champions was no longer an event — it was an occasion!

"The idea that you could press a button and see something happening, live, three thousand miles away was astonishing," remembers early CBC producer–director Norman Jewison.

Ask Canada's first TV buyers when they purchased their sets and you'll always get a story: "Well, everyone was talking about *The Plouffe Family*," a Quebecer might say. "Edmonton was in the Grey Cup and I just had to splurge," an Albertan will tell you.

Splurge is right. Units were $429 back then and the average working man earned $3,500 a year. Didn't matter. Once TV was here, the race for sets was on. Orders for televisions doubled in Toronto when

CBC went to air in the fall of 1952. A 1955 issue of *Canadian Broadcaster & Telecaster* reported a besieged retailer in Rimouski, Quebec, snow-mobiling units to snowbound customers prior to the Montreal-Detroit Stanley Cup finals.

By 1957, Canadians were watching forty-eight hours a week of programming on 2,490,000 sets.

Perhaps it's easiest to explain our rush to buy TV sets as pent-up demand. In 1943, *Maclean's* promised a coming apparatus that would provide "a front-row seat in your home for theatre, movies, sports, and news events." Five years later, "Mr. Television" Milton Berle turned TV from a toy into an industry in the United States.

The federal government finally authorized a national service in 1948, but for the next four years, consumer excitement over the coming medium was outstripped by bureaucratic dithering and institutional dread.

Alphonse Ouimet, who had helped design the first Canadian television set (in 1932!), was put in charge of establishing parallel services in English and French. "Toronto and Montreal wouldn't allow each other to have CBC head-quarters," recalls Mavor Moore, CBC-TV's first executive producer. "So it ended up in Ottawa, hundreds of miles from our production centres and well beyond the signal of American networks. Border cities knew all about TV. But not Ottawa. Which may explain why government was years behind the public on TV."

The print media, fearful of losing advertising to a new rival, were openly antagonistic. The

"Our Pet" Juliette — Juliette Augustina Cavazzi.

Chalk-tossing weatherman Percy Saltzman (left) was the first person to appear on English-language Canadian television. He was joined by puppets Uncle Chichimus and Holly Hock (right).

Globe and Mail suggested that "TV would make thinking obsolete." Our cultural elite were equally dismissive. In his memoir, *Reinventing Myself,* Moore recalls meeting his old University of Toronto philosophy professor in the early '50s.

"Well, Moore! What are you up to these days?"

"I'm putting a television network on the air, sir."

"Oh, Moore," the educator groaned, "when are you going to quit screwing around."

One of CBC's first executives, Fergus Mutrie, put the then-raging TV debate into perspective when he moaned, "The topics most talked about today are the atom bomb and television — the difference between the two being that we know how to use the bomb."

In retrospect, the forty-one-month delay-debate on television was the best thing that happened to CBC-TV, for instead of rushing to air with imitative fare, the network had time to formulate an inventive response to the phenomenon of television. "We didn't have the resources to compete with American TV," Moore says. "But what we could show Canadians better than the U.S. networks was, of course, Canada itself."

Many CBC programs were Canadian in content and style. The network's first game show, *Fighting Words,* featured sparring poets and short story writers. "We wanted to generate light, instead of the usual heat of American game shows," Moore says. Stephen Leacock's *Sunshine Sketches of a Little Town,* starring a young Timothy Findley, became television's first miniseries. Producer-director Norman Campbell presented the National Ballet dancing *Swan Lake,* a feat no one thought possible.

The rush to reinvent television even as we were learning the medium produced a giddy energy that would sustain Canadian TV through its first decade. Our earliest efforts included a slyly subversive puppet show for adults (*Uncle Chichimus*) and a news package (*Tabloid*) that was to public affairs shows what Salvador Dali was to traditional painting.

It seems a miracle, in light of the debate and worry that marked the birth of Canadian TV, that architects Mavor Moore and (head of programming) Stuart Griffiths managed to get the model for a public broadcaster right at conception. For two characteristics that marked early CBC-TV programming — socially relevant, distinctly Canadian fare and rule-bending commentary — are traits that can be found in all the best subsequent network shows, from *Wojeck* and *This Hour Has Seven Days* to *Seeing Things, The Journal, Hockey Night in Canada, This Hour Has 22 Minutes,* and *Canada: A People's History.*

Of course, Moore and Griffiths had a distinct advantage over the men and women who followed them. The CBC was the only TV game in town in the '50s. Or as Don Harron's Charlie Farquharson, who made his TV debut in a 1952 episode of *The Big Revue,* once put it, "The CBC had your TV tubes tied up back then."

Opening night jitters

SOMETIMES YOU can be too careful. For weeks, staff had been rehearsing and nursing their parts for opening night of the CBC English-language service. Then seconds before the network went to air, a technician decided to polish the logo slide.

"Don't do that!" cried producer Murray Chercover.

Too late. The switch was pulled at 7:15 p.m., on Monday, September 8, 1952. And just like a family slide show, the first image that blazed alive on our TV screens was upside down.

"I can't remember what we did, or if we shot the poor guy responsible," remembers Norman Jewison, then a twenty-five-year-old floor director sweating through his first day on the job. "It was live, remember, and all we were concerned about was what happened next."

Which was a three-puppet sketch, featuring soon-to-be-familiar Uncle Chichimus, advising viewers of the evening's entertainment. While the puppet prepared us for an imminent visit from pianist Glenn Gould, supervising producer Mavor Moore prepared to duke it out with his bosses at the stage door.

"CBC chairman Davidson Dunton and the board of governors, along with federal minister Dr. J.J. McCann, a former dentist, were supposed to arrive at 7:30 at our Jarvis Street studio," Moore remembers. "And I was to usher them to their seats."

But the visitors weren't there at 7:30. Or twenty-five minutes later, when Moore ordered the Toronto studio's double doors closed and the red ON AIR sign switched on. A few minutes after that, the group finally arrived. "I'm sorry," Moore informed his guests. "So are we," was Dunton's apologetic response. "Dinner, I'm afraid. Can you sneak us in?"

Moore tactfully refused the request. The dignitaries would have to wait for a commercial break. At which point McCann boomed, "Who the hell is he?" Dunton then introduced Moore, who obviously failed to make much of an impression on the Ottawa visitor.

"Do you know who we are, Moore? We're *yurr bahhsses!*" McCann brayed.

"Today, I have trouble believing it's true," Moore chuckles, "but I've been quoted by a number of people who were there as then saying, 'This broadcast is going out live to a million Canadians, Dr. McCann, and at this moment they're even more important than you are.'"

Fortunately, the evening and broadcast immediately got better, as a diplomatic Dunton spirited his group away until the studio break. Meanwhile, on air, Uncle Chich had given way to the news and CBC-TV's first scoop, the escape from Toronto's Don Jail of the Boyd Gang, a group of notorious bank robbers. After a few official words of greeting from Dr. McCann, the promised variety show followed.

Opposite: CBLT billboard in Toronto.

Above: Director Drew Crossan (standing left) and supervising producer Mavor Moore (reading paper) give "notes" to the opening night cast, including (front row, left to right) Peggi Brown, Jan Rubes, Barbara Hamilton (hidden), and Glenn Gould.

Left: The control room at CBLT on opening night. Just over a hundred thousand Canadians had televisions when CBC went to air. The first show received an 80 percent share of Toronto viewers.

Alfie Scopp, star of *Stopwatch and Listen*, dynamo producer Ross McLean's bold satire, was on hand to promote his new show. And he reports that by 8:30 that night everyone on set and in the studio audience had forgotten about the upside-down logo.

"Mistakes happened, then they were gone," he says. "Geez, you couldn't think about your last mistake. You were too busy worrying about your next one. To tell you the truth I can't remember anybody making anything about the upside-down logo, or whatever it was, the next day."

CBC's opening night ended with a repeat of the news and a few teaser scenes from *Call It a Day*, a domestic comedy. The preview went off without a hitch. But when the live teleplay was presented in total, two nights later, terror once again seized the Jarvis Street studio.

"Everything was going smoothly; you were almost tempted to relax," remembers Moore, "when all of a sudden one of the cameramen fell out of his mount like he'd been shot. He'd fainted, apparently. Well, everybody had been working so hard rehearsing, something like that was bound to happen.

"Anyway, there we were with one camera," Moore continues. "But the hero of the day, Peter McDonald, our director, managed to cover the play with one camera while our next brave soldier, the cameraman's understudy, assumed his position. Then Peter led the new fellow shot-by-shot through the play.... I'd like to think nobody even realized what had happened."

Below: The view into the studio from the control room. Opposite: TV was still a gala affair on CBC's second night, when Joel Aldred and Laddie Dennis performed live commercials for The Big Revue. *Yes, those are washing machines.*

Bandwagons and hay bales

Cross-Canada Hit Parade's Phyllis Marshall, Wally Coster, and Joyce Hahn belt out a pop song. The show featured all the hits of the day. If a song remained at the top of the charts for months, it had to be sung each week but in a different way. Jim Lowe's "Green Door" required eighteen interpretations.

VARIETY SHOWS RULED Canadian television in the '50s. In crowded CBC-TV studios and in private affiliates across the land, emcees, gag men, canaries, hoofers, jazzbos, and fiddlers stirred alive every weeknight between 7 and 10.

Three singing Tommys — Hunter, Ambrose, and Common — became household names. There were also two Joyces (Hahn and Sullivan) and as many Jacks (Duffy and Kane), Juliette of course, a Jackie (Rae), and a Joan (*The Joan Fairfax Show*).

And that's just the T's and J's.

A few performers, like *Holiday Ranch's* Cliff McKay, formerly of the Happy Gang, were familiar from radio. But mostly TV made its own stars. And predictably, many viewers wanted to get in on the act. *Maclean's* reported that in 1957, eight thousand Canadian singers and dancers auditioned for television.

And why not? Hadn't Robert Goulet, the Hames Sisters (*Country Hoedown*), and Paul Anka, pining for babysitter Diana — "I'm so young and you're so old, this my darling I've been told" — been discovered on the popular mid-'50s talent contest, *Pick the Stars?*

Some talent was easy to spot. Chiselled baritone Goulet had the looks and carriage of a matinee idol. But you couldn't always tell who was going to make it. Or how. Future Canadian broadcast journalist Lorraine Thomson was the first dancer hired for *The Big Revue* (1952-54), CBC's first variety showcase. She remembers how *Country Hoedown* singer-dancer Gordon Lightfoot would try to impress loiterers in the CBC cafeteria, telling all who would listen, "I'm going to be a big, big star someday."

"And the girls would look at him and say, 'Dream on, fella, dream on,'" Thomson says.

The eighteen-year-old Thomson dreamt of being swept away by Fred Astaire as she swirled through production numbers. And she remembers loving every minute of a performing career that saw her adorn guest Duke Ellington's piano — "I'm going to tickle the ivories and I hope to tickle you," Duke purred — and leap from *The Big Revue* to *CGE [Canadian General Electric] Showtime, Cross-Canada Hit Parade, The Denny Vaughan Show, The Barris Beat, Here's Duffy,* and *The Jack Kane Show.*

Well, maybe not every minute. One *Big*

Canada's young family magazine:

LIBERTY

10 cents

February 1958

TV IN CANADA ISSUE

This season's most beautiful TV singers

CBC's "canaries," or band singers, in 1958.
Top row (left to right): Sylvia Murphy, Joyce Sullivan, and Juliette. Bottom row:
Gloria Lambert, Joyce Hahn, and Joan Fairfax. Back when variety shows were king (and,
obviously, queen), one of these singers was on TV virtually every night. LIBERTY CANADA

Norman Campbell, the producer of The Big Revue, *pretends to ignore the sunny smiles of the show's dancers for an early publicity photo. Future broadcast journalist and producer Lorraine Thomson heads the chorus line.*

Revue sketch threw a feather-wrapped Thomson in front of a camera, a gleaming pigeon in each hand. When she began moving, the birds mutinied.

"We're on live and I'm hanging onto these pigeons, my feathers are swaying and I'm walking down a staircase," she recalls. "Then the pigeons start pooping all over my hands."

Perhaps the birds should have been trained by another guest on *The Big Revue*, a hypnotist whose spell — *you are getting sleepy* — put host Peter Mews into an unreachable slumber. When the hypnotist snapped his fingers, Mews regained half-consciousness, weaving in front of the camera like a muttering drunk. Mavor Moore (pinch-hitting for an ailing director) had to cut to a commercial and sort things out. Worse news soon arrived, as CBC

learned that many viewers had also been KO'd by the magician's spell. (An act of Parliament later that year banned hypnotists from plying their trade on television.)

The Big Revue lasted two seasons, which was standard for variety shows of the era, although *CGE Showtime* lasted seven, from 1952 to 1959.

As far as Norman Jewison is concerned, we rarely saw what made variety shows work in the '50s. "It was the background musicians — the bands," he says. "There was a fertile music scene in Toronto with all the TV and radio being produced. Each show had an orchestra or band. And they were all really professional when the rest of us were still trying to figure out what we were doing."

Two shows devoted entirely to music were *The Jack Kane Show/Music Makers* (1957-61),

Award-winning television and movie director Norman Jewison
began his career at CBC-TV directing and producing such shows as *The Big Revue*,
Country Hoedown, **and** *Jazz with Jackson*.

"We were crazy with excitement"

TV SEEMED PERFECT for me coming out of the University of Toronto, where I was active in theatre. So I got a meeting with Stuart Griffiths, who was running CBC-TV. This was 1950. Stuart told me, "We're not ready, go to New York or London." He recommended London, which he felt was ahead of the States. Don't forget, the BBC had been doing TV since before the war.

So I raised enough money to go. Acted, drove a cab. In London, I hooked up with another Canadian, Bernie Braden, who had a popular show, *Bedtime with Braden*. Bernie took me in. I did a bit of acting and writing for him and kept my eyes open, learning the business. With that job and the money I earned babysitting for Don Harron, I somehow made ends meet.

Then Stuart called me home. Told me CBC-TV was gathering the best young Canadian talent from theatre, radio, dance, and music.

A few weeks later, I was in a training centre on Jarvis Street. We had cameras, and Pat Weaver at NBC — yeah, Sigourney's dad — sent some advisers. I remember being in a room with Ross McLean, Norman Campbell, all of us supposedly learning how to put on a TV show.

The weeks before we went to air were terrifying. They were still pouring concrete. Our studio wasn't finished, for heaven's sake. And there was no recorded film for us to use, right? It was all live. So how did you know if you were improving? We were crazy with excitement and fear.

Opening night, I was a floor director. All I remember was running around in total chaos. After that, I got on an hour-long variety show, *The Big Revue*. I started working with comedy

Norman Jewison, photographed here in the mid-'50s, was one of 296 original employees of CBC English-language television.

writers. Eventually Don Hudson let me handle all the comedy.

When people asked why I directed the 1980 Academy Awards, I told them I wanted to experience terror one more time before I died. Live TV was an adrenalin rush like nothing you could imagine. You had four or five people in the booth. On set there was a stage manager, floor director, and people pulling cables and cameras around. Maybe twenty-five people tied together by headphones, trying not to bump into each other. Backstage, writers are cutting things, last minute. Your orchestra leader is working on arrangements until air time. Actors are throwing up.

Then you're live. The things I saw! Directors losing their cool, screaming like lunatics. Sets collapsing. People falling down. Cameras getting lost. But when it worked, the high was incredible. And the talent back then! Everybody talks about the actors, but how about the writers and directors? My stage director was Ted Kotcheff [future director of *The Apprenticeship of Duddy Kravitz*]. Only stage director I ever had who quoted Proust.

Why did we leave? Some say money, but I disagree. Artists don't leave for money. Artists want affection. People telling them they're worth something. It was the negativity of the press and public that got to us. "Canadian" was a pejorative back then.

And you know what, within ten years, BBC drama was being run by a CBCer, Sydney Newman. Bernie Slade had a big show on Broadway. I remember sitting in Los Angeles in the '60s and thinking, 70 percent of American television is being produced, written, or directed by people I worked with at CBC.

Tony and Grammy award-winning singer Robert Goulet hosted
CGE Showtime and made many appearances on CBC-TV in the '50s.

"*I never got a police ticket in Toronto*"

I CAN'T REMEMBER the first thing I ever did for TV. It may have been a guest spot on someone else's show. Or a dramatic piece. But someone must have heard me sing because when Don Garrard left *CGE Showtime*, they hired me.

It was a half-hour show, which was twenty-eight minutes then, not twenty-two like it is now. And we didn't have an audience. We didn't even have cue cards. Don Hudson, the producer, didn't believe in them. So you'd just get up and do it. Really, it felt like an audition or another rehearsal, except it was live, and you were on TV, so you did it the first time and that was it. But I wasn't nervous for some reason. I couldn't tell you why because I should have been.

I hosted *CGE Showtime* from 1956 to 1959, first with Shirley Harmer then Joyce Sullivan. I was in love with Shirley Harmer; she was a sweet, sweet, sweet lady. The Howard Cable Orchestra backed us up.

Once I got a bit of money, I bought a black Corvette with red upholstery. I would race all over town. And the police would stop me and say, "What about that show you do? Any chance of coming to see it?" Well, we didn't have an audience, like I said, but I'd sneak them in and let them stand at the back. I'll bet I snuck in every policeman on the force over the three years I hosted that show. Never got a ticket. Then I moved to New York in 1960 to do Broadway and got two tickets my first week. So I sold the car.

I am so grateful to the CBC because they were growing up in those days and allowed us to grow up with them. Every week they made sure at least one, but usually two, of the songs we sang were written by Canadian artists. I was a quick study, so I would learn the songs through the week, but come Sunday night and with no cue cards, I didn't always remember all the lyrics. On several occasions I would have to make up lyrics. And nobody seemed to notice, except for the poor guy in Winnipeg who wrote the song.

I'm trying to get my Canadian citizenship back, you know. Did you ever notice how Canadians in the States never really give up their heritage? Like Alex Trebek on *Jeopardy*. He always tries to get Canadian content on his show and gets so mad when no one knows the answer. "No," he'll say, "it's GRANDE PRAIRIE!"

Robert Goulet starred in variety shows and dramas, and even played Trapper Pierre on Howdy Doody *before* Camelot *on Broadway made him an international star in 1960.*

which employed the regular services of Moe Koffman and guests the calibre of Artie Shaw and Maynard Ferguson. *Jazz with Jackson* (1953-55), with pianist Cal Jackson, was also a dependable venue for bracing, straight-ahead jazz.

"Oh man, Cal was great," enthuses Jewison, the show's producer. "We used to get musicians dropping by just to watch. I remember sitting in the production booth with the Modern Jazz Quartet. They loved Cal."

As Jewison intimates, variety shows took a while to find their dancing feet. But maybe the occasional stumble only heightened the sense of high-wire excitement that was live television. Like the moment on producer-director Don Hudson's *The Big Revue* when a showgirl froze in front of a zooming camera and stammered, "...ah-ah I'm sorry, Don."

Live weekly extravaganzas eventually took a toll on companies. *The Big Revue*'s Don Harron remembers that some performers couldn't take the grind: "We had a great physical comedian on the show named Doug Romaine. He came from a music hall tradition and had what we thought was an endless bag of tricks. His best routine was a drunk trying to post a letter. Very, very funny.

"Then one night," Harron continues, "Doug shocked us all by announcing he was quitting. He simply said, 'I've used up all the material I've ever invented. I have nothing left. Goodbye.'"

Instructively, it was the performers who tried to be themselves (or at least ordinary Canadians) as opposed to stars who had the longest runs on CBC-TV. The featured performers on *Country Hoedown* (1956-65) and *Don Messer's Jubilee* (1959-69) were always called "regulars." And their shows attempted to be no more than end-of-a-hard-week reprieves for ordinary working folk.

"I've been across Canada a hundred times, and I've entertained Canadian troops all over

Manufacturers couldn't meet the swelling demand for TVs in the '50s. In September 1954 Canadians ordered 82,000 sets, while only 64,000 units were manufactured.
GENERAL ELECTRIC

the world," *Country Hoedown* host Gordie Tapp says today, "and when people meet you, fans I mean, and try to compliment you, they say, 'Gosh, you're exactly the same in real life as you are on TV.'"

Which is another way of saying that Canadians enjoy watching real, unvarnished people on television. "I think a lot of people want to think that's a friend of theirs up there on TV," Tapp says. "They want to feel that you're part of their crowd or life."

And the regulars on *Don Messer's Jubilee* and *Country Hoedown* were exactly who they seemed. Who can remember Don Messer saying anything? He was a fiddler. He fiddled. (King Ganam, the handsome, rail-thin fiddler on *Country Hoedown*, was bolder. He sometimes responded to a close-up with a wink.) *Country Hoedown's* Hames Sisters really were sisters. Gordie Tapp and Tommy Hunter went fishing together when they did the Medicine Hat Rodeo, Red River Exhibition, and Calgary Stampede summer tours. "Yeah, Tommy and I, we caught a lot of fish," Tapp reports. "We'd eat 'em right there, too; cook them up in a frying pan on shore."

Oh, *Country Hoedown* had as many flubs and frolics as *The Big Revue*. But, tellingly, their war stories come from rehearsal.

"King Ganam liked to snooze in a big chair in his dressing room," Tapp remembers. "One day, we saw him there dead to the world, and wrapped him in tape like a mummy, then we went to theme music and had the announcer yell out, 'And here he is, King Ganam!' King jumped awake screaming. He thought he was paralyzed."

In another rehearsal, crooner Tommy Common, who specialized in velvety Marty Robbins numbers, was to deliver the song "Gotta Travel On" while sitting on a trunk. A cute kicker had Tapp emerging from the trunk to deliver the final verse. But in the last dress rehearsal, a stripper Tapp had hired popped out

Two shots of Canadian wry

Wayne and Shuster used to joke that they met back "when there were only four provinces and twenty-two letters in the alphabet." In fact, they were friends from grade school who wrote their first comedy sketch for fellow Scouts in 1931.

After graduating from the University of Toronto, they found work on a local radio station. By 1951, the pair had their own CBC Radio show. They had done a TV special for CBS in 1950, but remained cool to the medium until 1954, when they signed to do two specials a month for CBC-TV. One of their earliest sketches, a burlesque of Russian politics and American game shows, called "The 64,000 Ruble Question," anticipated the Canadian tradition of freewheeling television satire.

The comedy team credited the Canadian public for getting them their shot on *The Ed Sullivan Show*, broadcast on CBC-TV Sunday nights. "Every time Sullivan was in an airport, Canadians would run up and suggest, 'Why not put Wayne and Shuster on your show?'" Wayne once told a reporter.

For their first appearance on *Sullivan*, in May 1958, the boys repeated a sketch they'd scored with on British TV. "Rinse the Blood Off My Toga," an investigation into the death of Julius Caesar conducted by a hard-boiled modern detective, was an immediate success. The detective's response to the announced arrival of Senator Martinus — "If I want two martinis, I'll ask for them!" — was so widely quoted that Manhattan bartenders began serving four-ounce "Martinus" that week.

Johnny Wayne (right) gets goosed while Frank Shuster looks on in amusement in a 1957 sketch.

instead. After dropping her robe, the naked woman cozied up to the startled Common while the Hoedowners threw themselves into a sizzling bump'n'grind routine.

Although they once dumped a bale of hay into a fan behind Tommy Hunter while he delivered a collar-up, walking-in-the-wind ballad, the *Country Hoedown* crew didn't joke much with the Country Gentleman who appeared on CBC-TV for twenty-seven years. "Oh, Tommy was mad when we sprayed all that hay over him, because he took what he did very seriously," Tapp remembers. "He wanted everything he did to be perfect."

Hunter's emergence as one of the CBC's most successful variety artists confirms the suspicion that seeming natural on television does take work. (When Hunter guested on Arthur Godfrey's CBS show during the '50s, he read

Top (first row, left to right): Country Hoedown's *King Ganam, the Hames Sisters, Tommy Hunter, Tommy Common, Lorraine Foreman, and Gordie Tapp. Second row: The Sons of the West. Above: "You'll stop paying the elbow tax when you start your cleaning with Ajax."* COLGATE PALMOLIVE

In his sixty-six-year entertainment career, **Don Harron** has succeeded in a variety of fields. He is the co-creator of the stage musical *Anne of Green Gables* and the author of twelve books.

"*I admitted I was Canadian*"

I HAD A radio show before the war: *Lonesome Trail*, the story of two boyish adventurers up in bush country. This would be 1936.

Shortly after high school I joined the RCAF, where I delivered my first bombs, you could say. After that, I did service shows and more radio. Then on a hunch, in 1950, I flew to London and, to my utter astonishment, found work in twelve hours. Vivien Leigh was leaving *Streetcar Named Desire*. They were recasting. So I stood in this long line of actors outside the theatre. Then this fellow popped out and shouted, "Only Americans, rest of you go home!"

Three stayed. Once I got inside, I admitted I was Canadian. "What's the difference?" the guy said. I got a small part as a bill collector. Later, I found work in BBC television.

I returned to North America with a touring play in 1952, which is how I came to be in Toronto the summer before TV arrived. I distinctly remember rehearsing the Jean-Paul Sartre play, *Red Gloves*, with Honor Blackman and Lorne Greene for CBC Radio that summer.

But the first thing I did on CBC-TV was Charlie Farquharson. That would be September 1952, on *The Big Revue*. I'd created Charlie earlier that year for *Spring Thaw*, the theatrical revue. This was a farmer I'd met ten years earlier, the summer I worked on the Farm Service Force, harvesting crops for $20 a month. He had Charlie's peaked cap, roll-top sweater, and glasses. And he also had that rural Ontario twang, kind of a lowland Scottish accent, five generations removed.

Don Harron as Charlie Farquharson gets in the swim of things on a 1952 episode of The Big Revue.

My farmer always got a reaction, so I decided to try and place him in a comedic situation, and I wrote a five-minute sketch about a farmer looking for a friend named Charlie Farquharson at the CNE exhibition in Toronto. Same look and dialect, only I introduced a few malapropisms. The character just seemed to flow.

The next time I did the farmer — he was Charlie now — was on *The Big Revue*. All I remember about that night was that I didn't have a costume. So I borrowed Norman Jewison's hat and a sweater Norman Campbell was wearing. I still have the sweater, although it's more holes than sweater now.

People liked Charlie right away. Except my daughter, Martha Harron. She's an accomplished film director now. Made *American Psycho* a few years ago. But when we did *The Big Revue* she would have been only two, I guess. She saw me on TV as Charlie one night and was horribly distressed. Her mother had to bring her down to the studio to prove I was all right.

One night in 1956 I was doing Charlie Farquharson and Norman Campbell came to see his sweater, I guess. I asked how he was doing. Not good, he said. I have ninety minutes of air time to fill; any suggestions? Well, I said, I've been reading something to my daughters they're quite enjoying. I told him the story. He kept nodding. Finally, he said, give me an outline. And a few months later we had the first broadcast of *Anne of Green Gables* on the air.

five papers every day, just in case the chatty emcee asked him a topical question.)

"Well, you gotta remember that at the beginning of the show, Tommy was raw, I mean he was nineteen," Tapp comments. "And he was back in the chorus. Nobody thought he'd make it, except Tommy. But he worked and he worked. And look what he did for himself. Well, good for him."

The art of *Country Hoedown* and *Don Messer's Jubilee* is that all the cast members were recognizable, sympathetic, and seemed to enjoy one another's (and their loyal audience's) company. They performed each show with obvious enthusiasm and little evident strain.

Tapp says his old show's popularity never ceased to amaze him.

"I remember once I was doing a show for the

Canadian Armed Forces and we were in the Middle East," Tapp recalls. "Now my father was a strict Baptist, and when we got to the Sinai Peninsula I remembered from Leviticus that that was where Esau sold his birthright. So I wanted to get him a souvenir. And I had a jeep take me into the desert to collect some castor beans.

"All of a sudden we came upon some Israeli troops," he continues. "Now they were all women. So naturally I wanted to talk to them. Well, I got up in the jeep there and I started talking. And one of the Israeli soldiers, an officer I guess, shouts out, 'Who are you?' And I say, 'Well, I'm an entertainer, my name is Gordie Tapp.'

"There's a silence for a couple of seconds, then somebody in their ranks mutters back, *Country Hoedown!*"

Future anchorman Lloyd Robertson (top, middle), the host of CBWT Winnipeg's Saddle Songs, *is flanked by two singers and members of Vic Siebert's band, the Sons of the Saddle.*

A talent rush took place on Canadian television in the '50s. Between 1953 and 1959 three hundred different CBC-TV shows went to air, including a wide range of music and variety series. A dancer could leap from CGE Showtime *to* Cross-Canada Hit Parade *and* The Denny Vaughan Show *in a single week.*

Right: Butterflies are free on an episode of Cross-Canada Hit Parade.

Below: A leopard woman on the prowl on The Denny Vaughan Show.

Above: Dancer, director, and choreographer Alan Lund (centre) and his wife, Blanche, were CBC-TV's first contract players. Here Lund counts off instructions to a camera crew for a Patterns in Music *special*.

Left: Three dandelion-sleeved caballeros in a 1956 edition of The Denny Vaughan Show.

Peter Appleyard, **one of the world's best-known vibraphonists, has a long history with the CBC and has performed with many top entertainers and orchestras.**

"*Good vibes*"

I PLAYED DRUMS and piano in England. I guess I combined the two when I arrived in Toronto in 1951. I started playing vibes.

My break came in 1953, playing CBC Radio with Calvin Jackson's quartet from the Park Plaza [Hotel]. Calvin also had a TV series, *Jazz with Jackson*. Terrific big band. The audience just lapped it up. I remember Ella Fitzgerald coming on and Calvin, who was an adventurous arranger, did a high-powered arrangement. She was nervous. She held her throat and took a hanky out and mopped her brow.

That was the first jazz show on TV. Norman Jewison produced. Stan Harris directed. It was live and very exciting — you could smell show business in the air. I remember once Cab Calloway guested. He had Caucasian hair and used to jive and roll his eyes. Calvin, who was real black, came up to him and said, "I see you're still totin' and fetchin'."

First show I soloed on was *CGE Showtime*. One night the host, Bob Goulet, asked where I was working next. Bermuda, I said. "Oh," he said, "I'd love to go, call the guy." You kidding? I said. He couldn't afford you. But I called my friend and he said, "Who? Bob Goulet? Never heard of him." Guy's great, I say. Besides, I need a golf partner. Finally he says, "I'll pay him $50 for five nights, free hotel and return fare."

We drove to New York, left the car at La Guardia. And on the last day of the trip, Bob was getting ready to tee off. "Hey, just a minute," he said, "I'm supposed to be in New York today to audition for Lerner and Loewe." This was for *Camelot*, which made him a star. So he rushed off to the airport in his Bermuda shorts.

Oscar Peterson and I did several shows together. On one of them I played piano with him; me at the top end of the piano. I play with two fingers. Same as vibes. And I can move pretty rapidly, which you have to do to keep up with Oscar.

Once Oscar and I had to be fitted for straw boaters and crazy jackets for CBC publicity shots. We're standing around waiting for the photographer and I threw the hat up in the air. Costume guy rushes over and says, "Don't crush the hat — they're authentic boaters." I looked inside and the label said Jermyn Street, London. "We sent somebody over last weekend to pick them up," he explained. They flew them over! That's when the CBC had a lot of money, I guess.

I did all kinds of stuff for the CBC: *Front Page Challenge*, *Wayne and Shuster*, *Mr. Dressup*. Used to do *The Friendly Giant* occasionally. Everyone must've seen me, though. People still come up to me and say, "I remember you, you played on *Friendly Giant*. Was he really big?"

Above: Peter Appleyard (centre) and Oscar Peterson (right). "One time, working live on camera, I had to hit a triangle on cue," remembers Appleyard. "'Peter, make sure you smile and look at the camera,' they said. So I smiled and looked at the camera and missed the triangle." Opposite: Moe Koffman and Sarah Vaughan perform on Cross-Canada Hit Parade.

Brainings

CANADA'S FIRST GAME show, which was hosted by rumpled *Toronto Star* drama critic Nathan Cohen, always felt like a university faculty club dust-up.

Take the December 9, 1956, episode of *Fighting Words*, featuring a panel of authors Morley Callaghan and Ted Allan, poet Irving "I'm not Jesus, I don't have to love everybody" Layton, and academic Douglas Grant. The show began, as always, with cartoon figures duking it out as Cohen (off camera) advised viewers who had sent in quotations what classical albums and history books they might win if their citation stumped the panel.

The gloves came off (and cigarettes out) with a quote from D.H. Lawrence suggesting that the novelist was God's greatest achievement. "There is no such thing as being more than a poet!" shouted Layton, whose tousled hair was wild with untamed thoughts that night.

The program's final quote, "The opinion that Montreal has a dazzling intellectual life is a myth," was from Callaghan, who further provoked Montrealers Layton and Allan by comparing English Montreal, both in size and spirit, to Hamilton. The two turned forcefully on Callaghan, ending the show with the TV equivalent of a screeching three-car pile-up.

The best moment came when a steamrolling Layton shouted, "Fashionable writers come and go, Layton goes on forever!" To which host-bouncer Cohen interjected, "Not on this program."

Although it lasted from 1953 to 1962, *Fighting Words* never attracted more than a small but loyal following. "Don't expect too much unless you happen to be an egghead who lives in an ivory tower," groused Gordon Sinclair. Sinclair's own quiz show, *Front Page Challenge*, took *Fighting Words'* concept three sections of a newspaper forward and lasted almost forever.

Right: Nathan Cohen hosted Fighting Words, *which was cancelled in 1955, then brought back after a vigorous, presumably eloquent letter-writing campaign.*

Opposite, above: Former U.S. First Lady Eleanor Roosevelt appeared as the mystery guest on Front Page Challenge *in 1958. Panellists were (left to right) Gordon Sinclair, Toby Robins, Pierre Berton, and Margerite Higgins.*

The most beautiful woman on television

Pierre Berton called her the most beautiful woman ever to appear on Canadian television. And indeed it was her flawless complexion and violet eyes that landed her second panellist's chair on *Front Page Challenge*'s first show, playing Beauty next to Gordon's Sinclair's Beast.

But if producers thought Toby Robins would be satisfied playing a giggling ingenue, they obviously didn't know the Toronto-born actress, who had completed a degree from the University of Toronto while pursuing a drama scholarship at Northwestern by having her twin sister, Ellen, sit in on classes and mail her lecture notes.

"The remarkable conversion of Toby Robins the expert ornament into Toby Robins the ornamental expert," as journalist June Callwood put it, began after she won the *Front Page* job in the middle of 1957. Every afternoon for three summers Robins sat in a library and read newspapers going back to before she was born.

There were flubs. She asked Rich Ferguson, third-place finisher behind Roger Bannister and John Landy in the 1954 British Empire Games, "Who was a better runner, Roger or Bannister?" But the actress smiled through her mistakes, and by season's end had solved as many challenges as Sinclair or Berton.

"She outgraced Grace Kelly," performer Larry Mann says. "She had this great inner beauty. People saw that she was a lovely, caring woman. That shone through."

Makeup artist Margaret Epp and Front Page Challenge *panellist (1957-61) Toby Robins.*

A bright ray of sunshine

The control room as an episode of The Plouffe Family *drama goes to air.*

TIMOTHY FINDLEY KNEW his audition for a small role in CBC's first dramatic series, a twenty-six-week adaptation of Stephen Leacock's *Sunshine Sketches of a Little Town*, had not gone well.

"You know as an actor when it's not working and so, usually, does the producer," the award-winning author and playwright recalls today. "I smiled and thanked the producer, a very nice man named Robert Allen. He in return thanked me. Then I wandered out of his office into the hall, feeling somewhat dejected, I suppose."

Findley had come to CBC-TV from the International Players repertory theatre company in Kingston early in 1952. It was late summer now, and all the twenty-two-year-old Toronto actor had to show for his efforts was a string of unsuccessful tryouts, mostly for musical comedy shows like *The Big Revue*, where he "sang, tried to move around, and told jokes."

Findley was almost out the door that afternoon when a bright voice called from down the hallway, "Ah, Mr. Findley, could you come in here a moment?" Hurrying back inside, Findley found Allen wrestling with a thought. "There was something that you did just a minute ago that made me think of another character," the producer finally said. A few minutes later, Findley had the coveted role of Peter Pupkin, a daydreaming bank clerk with boundless energy and limited intellectual resources.

"I don't want to think too much about what Mr. Allen saw in me that made him think of Leacock's Pupkin," Findley laughs, "but I was thrilled to get the part. Everybody loves comedy and Pupkin is such a marvellous juvenile — so stupid and filled with hope."

It's somehow appropriate that our first TV series was a loafing stroll into a world intimidated by change. For like the flustered characters in Leacock's turn-of-the-century comedy, the actors in *Sunshine Sketches* were immediately undone by a contrivance of the modern age — live television.

"I remember everybody being terrified opening night," Findley says of his company's appearance on CBC-TV's gala preview. "The problem at the beginning was we'd never had a proper run-through on the production stage.

"We would rehearse three or four days in what we used to call the Kremlin, a big, always cold building next to Havergal College on Jarvis Street. Then, the day of shooting," Findley continues, "we went into the yellow brick building down the road. I always thought of the CBC studio as very grand, with the lights so high up in the air. Of course, so much of the space would disappear when the cameras, cables, and equipment were brought in.... It was like weaponry from an invading army."

Many actors dried up below the hot lights. But after two or three shows Findley found himself enjoying the new medium. "When the red light came on, your stomach would turn over," he says, "but fear provides a great deal of energy. And after a while I didn't find television drama that different from theatre. Halfway through each show something would click, and you would gain confidence and begin to enjoy the material, which in this case was very good indeed."

The completion of every half-hour episode, Findley remembers, was punctuated by congratulations and curses, then actors raced to dressing-room sinks to wash away makeup.

"We hurried out of the studio because we couldn't wait to get to the Chez Paree, a bar on Bloor Street," he says. "The entire TV and arts industry in Toronto would be there. Those nights I remember being quite wonderful. All the excited conversation, the laughter. People falling in love. I remember watching Kate Reid and Austin Willis fall in love there one night. He had a head of brilliant white hair that made him seem older than he probably was. And a warm, engaging voice. And she was happy. We all were. It was a wonderful time."

Sunshine Sketches was a resounding hit in Toronto, beating NBC's *The Milton Berle Show* on Tuesday nights to capture a 63.6 share (63.6 percent) of the city's estimated sixty thousand sets. Findley enjoyed his turn as Canada's first TV star, even if his brilliance didn't extend much past southern Ontario. "I remember a lot of fan letters," he says, "and people recognizing me. It was all fun — I was very young, don't forget."

He also recalls the first time he saw himself on television. *Sunshine Sketches* was almost always shot live — once a show aired, it disappeared forever — but occasionally a pre-recorded kinescope was broadcast. (Kinescopes were made by putting a motion picture camera in front of a TV monitor and filming the live program off the monitor's screen.) Findley was at home in Toronto with his family the first time producers used a kinescope. Just prior to the show going on air, he felt a stab of curiosity: he wanted to see his show.

"But my family didn't have a TV," he recalls. "We used to go next door occasionally, where very gracious neighbours had a set and frequently hosted [television] parties, with everyone drinking draft beer and having loads of fun. Well, I didn't feel like going over and intruding when my own show was on, so I dressed up in a disguise and went over with my brother, and we watched the show, all of us drinking, enjoying ourselves."

Then, during a commercial break, Findley gave in to a mischievous impulse and threw off his costume to reveal his true identity, astonishing everyone. They had all assumed they were watching a live performance.

"I gave them all heart attacks," Findley laughs. "Who knows why you do those sorts of things when you're young?"

Author Timothy Findley was English Canada's first TV drama star, playing Peter Pupkin in Sunshine Sketches of a Little Town. *He gave up acting, cold turkey, in 1962 after fulfilling the ambition of playing Tom in a theatrical production of* The Glass Menagerie.

Every man had two mothers

On Ash Wednesday in 1955, a priest in Montreal's St. Stanislaus parish was conducting a Lenten retreat when he noticed a woman tiptoeing from her pew. "My sister," the priest cried, breaking from the service, "you can miss the Plouffes this one evening. I must miss them four times [this month]."

Based on Roger Lemelin's best-selling novel, *The Plouffe Family* began on radio and branched out to French, then English TV. In its mid-'50s heyday, the series aired Wednesday night in Quebec and Friday night on ten English channels across the country.

Although the show was a hit in some parts of English Canada, particularly Winnipeg, it was literally a way of life in Quebec. Come Wednesday night at 8:30, no hockey was played in Quebec City. Diners closed up in Montreal. And in the province's villages, general stores boasting a TV set were crowded with alternately laughing, shushing townsfolk.

The cause for all the furor was a working-class soap set in a boxy tenement in Quebec City. Mama Plouffe was an efficient disciplinarian of a family of dreamers, a group that included Ovide, an aesthete working in a shoe factory; Cécile, a skittish spinster; and Guillaume, an amateur hockey player certain he'd soon be raking it in like Béliveau. Meanwhile, Papa Plouffe (Paul Guèvremont) drank himself to sleep every night on distant memories of cycling championships.

Simply by folding her arms and pursing her lips, Mama Plouffe kept the extended family of thirteen Plouffes in line, although Guillaume sometimes required a "Maudit hockey!" to straighten up. Actress Amanda Alarie was so convincing as the show's ruling matriarch that it was said in Quebec that every man had two mothers — his own and Mme Plouffe.

The Plouffe Family cast did two shows a week, one in French and one in English. Author Roger Lemelin worked with a friend from Canadian Press, Bill Stewart, on the English script. Singer Anne Murray fondly remembers that whenever her own family piled into an overflowing car, someone would say, "We look just like the Plouffe family!"

William Shatner, who is best known for his role as *Star Trek*'s Captain Kirk, served his acting apprenticeship in live CBC-TV dramas.

"*I loved the camera*"

THE FIRST THING I did at CBC-TV in the '50s was write scripts. Three, I think. The CBC bought one, which was wonderful because the lead actress, whose name was Gloria Rand, became my wife and the mother of our three children.

CBC was filled with romance in those days — romance and passion. Both between people, and between people and work. It was a honeymoon, a time of exploration. We were getting to know what made good television drama. At first, down on the floor, we knew nothing. Nothing. We only knew we were theatre actors and we were doing it live.

Billy Budd was one of my first TV performances. I remember clearly that the fellow who played Sherlock Holmes, Basil Rathbone, was cast to play the malevolent lead, Claggart. And I was in awe of him, this famous movie star, because secretly that's where I wanted to be, in movies. So I dogged his footsteps.

What did I learn from him? I learned that even the largest stars have feet of clay. When he made his big entrance, he stepped into a bucket. Remember we were live on the air. He's stomping around with this bucket stuck to his foot. It was like a burlesque gag. We all broke up, but because you can't break up on stage, we tried to stifle it, which led to uncontrollable hysteria.

Julius Caesar was another memorable play we did. Paul Almond, a friend from my Montreal youth, directed it. The funny thing about that piece of work that I'll always remember is that I borrowed a bit from the McCarthy hearings [broadcast in 1954 on CBC via a feed from a U.S. network]. I remembered McCarthy kept saying, "I have the names of the Communists right here" and he would pat his pocket as if he had a note in there with all the names on it and could produce it at any time. When I got to the part in the big speech "Friends, Romans, countrymen, lend me your ears," I patted my pocket as if I had a list. Just like McCarthy.

Between live dramas at CBC, I would do Stratford. I once toured the U.S. in a Stratford production — Marlowe's *Tamburlaine the Great* — and was noticed by some agents and offered TV work. I think I was successful at that juncture because I had this wealth of experience with CBC. I knew cameras and hitting marks. In fact, I didn't just know cameras, I loved the camera, which was unusual for a lot of stage actors because cameras were huge, bulky things then. They whirred and made sounds like they were breathing. For close-ups, this big machine's light went on and it came moving right in on you. You felt as if it might swallow you whole. But I came to look at the camera as a beloved pet.

All stars on deck. Left to right: Patrick Macnee (later Steed on TV's The Avengers*), Basil Rathbone (Sherlock Holmes in the 1939 film,* The Hounds of the Baskervilles*), and William Shatner in a 1955 production of* Billy Budd.

Live, tonight

*Pillow talk —
Lorne Greene
"loving not wisely,
but too well" in
Othello.
Peggi Loder is
Desdemona. The
1953 special was
CBC's first
production of
Shakespeare.*

FEW WEEKS WENT by in the '50s when there wasn't at least one live drama on CBC-TV. By mid-decade, the drama department was producing more than thirty one-hour dramas and fifty-eight half-hour dramas a year. Most teleplays came under the auspices of a few flagship anthologies: *CBC TV Theatre* (1953) begat *General Motors Theatre* (1953-56), while *Scope* (1954-55) turned into *CBC Folio* (1954-60). *On Camera* (1954-58) also produced a number of memorable dramas.

The breadth of what was shown is impressive — Canadian dramas from Robertson Davies, Morley Callaghan, Ted Allan, and Leslie McFarlane (author of *The Hardy Boys*) were presented.

Producers Sydney Newman and Norman Campbell were everywhere. Directors Harvey Hart, Paul Almond, Daryl Duke, and Ted Kotcheff, along with performers Kate Reid, William Shatner, Leslie Nielsen, and Barry Morse, all made their debuts. (One critic suggested that Morse received more work than the network's test pattern.)

The first wave of producers and many early stars were British, which prompted English actor Gerry Sarisini to observe, "Oh to be in England, now that England is here." But by 1956, Canadian television drama was being exported to Britain, and Granada had hired CBC producer Newman to revitalize its drama department.

Attack of the killer salmon

"Open up, open up, you're losing height too fast, watch the air speed, lift the nose up, open up quickly or she'll stall. OPEN UP, MAN, OPEN UP!"

Arthur Hailey was flying from Vancouver to Toronto when the former RAF pilot was asked by a stewardess if he wanted fish or meat. Which got him thinking, what if the pilots ordered bad fish, they became ill, then someone else had to fly? Someone like him! "It was pure Walter Mitty daydreaming," the best-selling author once said. He wrote up the daydream in a week and was astonished when CBC's *General Motors Theatre* offered him $600 for his first try at writing.

An immediate sensation, *Flight into Danger* (1956) was later sold to U.S. and British television, then made into the movie *Airport*.

James Doohan (later Scottie in Star Trek*) at the controls.*

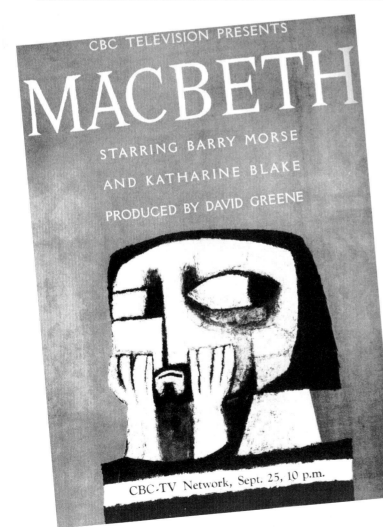

Above: Toby Tarnow played the first of many CBC-TV Annes in the 1956 musical Anne of Green Gables.

Left: A poster advertising the network's 1955 production of Macbeth.

The weatherman was always sunny

THERE IS NO better illustration of the boundless sense of optimism and adventure that permeated Canadian television in the '50s than our first public affairs show, *Tabloid*.

Producer Ross McLean adapted to TV like a kid takes to the best toy under a Christmas tree. Just twenty-seven when his program began in March 1953, McLean played with the nightly, half-hour series until the show's batteries finally ran dead in 1963.

"We needed young people with ideas like McLean," Mavor Moore says today. "We were new; we saw what other people [in the United States and Britain] had been doing. And we thought, well, we'll have to do some of those things, people will expect it, but let's experiment, mix things up, and see what works."

For McLean, who came to TV from the oddly titled CBC program *Radio Cartoons*, what worked *was* experimenting and mixing things up. Viewers who snapped on the set expecting to watch the news might find correspondent Lister Sinclair interviewing a groundhog. When a fussy scientist, Dr. Hans Selye, was brought in from Montreal to talk about stress, McLean, fearing a lecture, decided to pair him with black vaudevillian Stepin Fetchit.

But it was when the weatherman showed up that we were most frequently surprised. For that's when meteorologist Percy Saltzman, who played Zorro with chalk across a blackboard every night, would finally appear. Who knew what would happen next?

Tabloid's Ross McLean was always full of surprises. In 1960 he was approached by Peter Gzowski, then-assistant editor at Maclean's, *who said he hoped to capture the broadcaster's wit for a profile. McLean reached into his pocket for a handy list of prepared ad libs, handed them to Gzowski, then walked away.*

"One time Ross had me dressed up like Charles Boyer in a silk smoking jacket," Saltzman remembers. "He told me to do the weather like I was making love to a beautiful woman."

Even Saltzman's signature sign-off — tossing up and catching a piece of chalk, then shouting, "And that's the weather!" — came about as a response to one of McLean's bits of business.

"Ross thought the weather was getting boring again," Saltzman says. "Out of the blue he decides he wants to do the weather Keystone Cops fashion. So he and the camera guys figured out how to speed up film, like in the old days. One night I stayed late and did my forecast a second time. Only this time they used this special film that would have me racing around like I was in a silent movie.

"So me being a bit of a ham," Saltzman continues, "I tried to figure out what I could do to make this joke a little bit funnier. What physical movement could I do that would look funny? I know, I thought, I'll throw the chalk in the air."

Everyone on set howled when *Tabloid* used the speeded-up film the following day. Except McLean, who grew serious while analyzing the fast, squealing footage. "You know, Percy," he told Saltzman seconds after the mock weathercast, "Let's keep using that chalk thing."

Incredibly, McLean and Saltzman's playhouse was the setting for Canada's first nightly newscast. But late in 1953, CBC management

Opposite: Percy Saltzman gets a real close-up of Tabloid *co-host Joyce Davidson when the playful supper-hour show took its act on the road to CFCM in Quebec City. Saltzman's glasses were a prop.*

Joyce Davidson and Tabloid *host "Mr. Relaxation" Dick MacDougal. Each show opened with the words: "A program with an interest in anything that happens anywhere, bringing you the news at 7."*

wisely decided it would be safer to cordon off the news between 6:45 and 7:00. *Tabloid* came on afterwards, usually with a self-deprecating teaser.

"*Tabloid*! meeting place for millions!" announcer John O'Leary shouted in greeting one particular show. Saltzman, who was on camera, sadly shook his head in disagreement.

"*Tabloid*! nightly habit of nearly every ..."

Saltzman again indicated his displeasure.

"*Tabloid*, where the unexpected is ..."

Another shake of the head.

Two tries later, the defeated O'Leary finally resorted to "*Tabloid*, a convenient way to get to 7:30."

Predictably, not everyone made it that far. In early 1956, Dr. E.E. Robbins, of Montreal, sent McLean a critical letter. The correspondence was read on air and the doctor's name and address were flashed twice on the screen, perhaps because the producer wanted to have "E.E. Robbins" bob-bob-bobbing across our TVs. As a result, Dr. Robbins received hundreds of letters and abusive phone calls. His consulting practice dropped by 50 percent. He later sued *Tabloid* and was awarded $3,000.

At the time, *Tabloid* was receiving a great deal of attention for introducing glamorous hostesses to television. Both Elaine Grand (1953-56) and Joyce Davidson (1956-61) were the kind of women bachelor McLean liked, according to Saltzman. "They were

attractive, warm, intelligent, but not afraid to speak their minds. Well, who wouldn't like that?"

Well, there were some. In 1959 Davidson horrified many Canadians by suggesting on NBC's *Today Show* that, "like the average Canadian," she was indifferent to the upcoming royal visit. Eventually, she was hounded off the air for telling Pierre Berton in an interview that a woman who was still a virgin at age thirty was "unlucky."

Still, the program's cold-water wit and jarring mix of guests — American TV celebrity Faye Emerson, famous for her plunging necklines, was once yoked to two grunting wrestlers — attracted a large following. (The network's long-time in-house magazine, *CBC Times*, suggests that a quarter-million Toronto viewers watched the show in its prime.) Critics invariably liked it, too — a very real accomplishment in the early days of Canadian television. "Night in and night out you won't find a better television program," Trent Frayne wrote in the *Globe and Mail*.

The show's biggest draw was Saltzman. After a year, McLean elevated Saltzman's status to featured entertainer, throwing him into the ring with more professional wrestlers in one famous bit, and letting him do nightly interviews. Like Gordie Tapp and Don Messer, Saltzman probably appealed to many viewers because they sensed he was one of them. In his case, he really did have an ordinary job like everyone else and was simply moonlighting as a TV star. By day, the weatherman toiled for the "Dominion Government" as a meteorologist.

"Then at 4:30," Saltzman remembers, "I hopped on my bike and pedalled down to the CBC studio to do my bit. Afterwards, I went home. I had a wife and two kids. If there was socializing on the show afterwards, I wasn't a part of it. I was too busy."

He and McLean got along fine, Saltzman says. "We were professionals and respected each other. I certainly liked my job. And the days I didn't, I didn't complain too loud because the money was damned good." The only real source of conflict between man-about-town McLean and man-about-the-house Saltzman was time. Percy always thought the weather deserved more time than the two or three minutes he was allotted. Fed up with the incessant grousing of his star performer, McLean plotted his revenge.

"There I was doing my little bit at the board one day," Saltzman recalls, "and all of a sudden I turn around and notice everyone has gathered around behind the camera and is looking at me, kind of half-smiling. Then I come to the end of the weather, but nobody moves. The camera is still on me. Uh-oh, I'm up for the chop, I say to myself. McLean is out to get me.

"Now fortunately for me," Saltzman continues, "I had developed a real interest in space travel around this time. This would have been when Sputnik was in the news. I read up on the subject whenever I could. So I just started talking about space travel. And I explained what zero gravity was. And I explained what escape velocity was. On and on I went. I was really getting going by about the seventeen-minute mark when McLean finally threw his hands up and said, Enough! So they cut to something else. But me, hell, I was still fresh, I could have gone on for another hour or so."

Joyce Davidson, who started in TV working as a chef's assistant on a Hamilton cooking show, had many fans. This 1957 fabric crest was sent to her by Lee Tasher of Toronto.

When the news was new

IT COULD BE argued that CBC–TV is now best known for its news and current affairs, documentaries and information programming, but in its early years news was something of an afterthought. *Newsmagazine* appeared in the early evening, but it wasn't until 1954 that a ten-minute newscast called the *National Edition* was added to the broadcast schedule at 11 p.m., just before sign-off. Former actor Larry Henderson took over from Lorne Greene on *Newsmagazine*, then anchored *The National* to become the "face" of the news from the mid-'50s until 1959 when Earl Cameron was hired. Henderson was assisted by correspondents, including Morley Safer, Michael Maclear, Norman DePoe, James Minifie, Stanley Burke, and Charles Lynch.

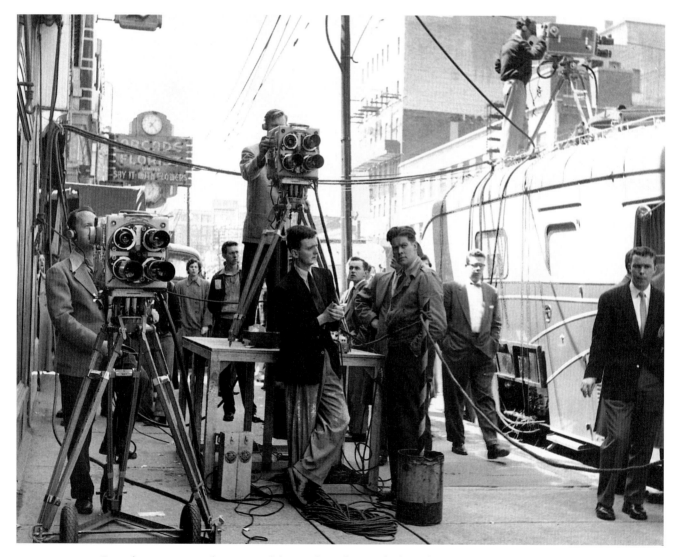

Several cameramen and a CBC mobile unit (a studio on wheels, with cameras, cables, and monitors) take up most of the sidewalk at the corner of Yonge and Bloor in Toronto in 1953.

Above: CBC reporter Kingsley Brown conducts an interview at the Springhill Mine disaster in 1958. Anne Murray grew up in Springhill. "I [stood] at the pit heads with the other kids, waiting for fathers to be brought up either dead or alive. It's a vivid memory for me. In the cold, standing there for hours, waiting." Seventy-five miners perished.

Right: Larry Henderson anchored the CBC national news from 1954 to 1959.

Television

A.M.

10.00—F-OF—Fon fon
11.00—F-OF—Concert pour la jeunesse

P.M.

2.00—M—Camera Three
2.15—O—Today on CBOT
2.30—L-O-M—Speaking French
3.00—O—Cowboy Corner
      L—Bowling
      M—Feature Film
3.30—O—Grand Ole Opry
      L—Speaking French
4.00—L-O—NBC-TV Opera
      World premiere of La Grande
      Breteche by Stanley Hollingsworth
4.30—M—Under the Sun
5.00—L-O-M—Count of Monte Cristo
      Today: The Island

F-OF—Tic tac toc
5.30—L-O-M—Wild Bill Hickok
      F-OF—Pepinot
6.00—F-OF—Beau temps, mauvais
      temps
      L-O-M—Oh Susannah
      With Gale Storm as entertainment
      officer on a luxury liner
6.30—L-O-M—Mr. Fix-it
      Hints for the handyman. Today: Peter
      works on a recreation room
      F-OF—Ce soir
6.45—L-O-M—News and Weather
      F-OF—A votre service
7.00—L-O-M—Radisson
      The story of Canada's illustrious
      frontier fighter, Pierre Esprit Radisson.
      Tonight: Escape—from the Indians
7.15—F-OF—Tele-journal
7.30—F-OF—Cinefeuilleton
      L-O-M—Holiday Ranch
      Music in the western style with Cliff
      McKay and the Holiday Ranch Gang.
      Guests tonight: harmonica player Brian
      Terry and singer Sheri-Lee Hall

7.45—F-OF—Quelles nouvelles
8.00—L-O-M—Perry Como Show—NBC
      With the Ray Charles Singers and
      Mitchell Ayres' orchestra
      F-OF—Aventures
8.30—F-OF—Chacun son metier
9.00—L-O—Hockey
      Detroit at Toronto
      M-F-OF—Hockey
      New York at Montreal
10.15—L-O—King Whyte
      For the sportsman
10.30—L-O-M—Wayne and Shuster
      Canada's comedy craftsmen
      F-OF—A la romance
11.00—L-O-M-F-OF—CBC News
11.10—L-O-M—Juliette
      Musical show with Juliette, George
      Murray and Bobby Gimby's orchestra
      F-OF—Nouvelles sportives
11.15—F-OF—Feature Film
11.30—L-O-M—Wrestling

The Schiefners, a farm family living outside Milestone, Saskatchewan, toss aside a newspaper to watch television in 1956. After the news, according to the schedule above, they may have spent their Saturday evening watching Holiday Ranch *with* Cliff McKay *and* Hockey Night in Canada.

NATIONAL ARCHIVES OF CANADA, PA 111390

Harry Rasky, an acclaimed producer, director, and writer,
has received more than two hundred international prizes and citations
for his documentary film work.

"*Learning as you go*"

I WAS THERE in 1952 with the pioneer group that founded CBC-TV. It was just myself and one other person that made up the news department. I produced a show every week for three years. That's how *Newsmagazine* started. We learned as we did it, and we did it as we learned.

The arrest of the Boyd Gang after their escape from the Don Jail was the first big story we covered. I had a police radio in my office and heard they were trapped in a farmhouse, so I jumped in a car with a cameraman. We were able to film the police as they arrived. But once we had the film, we had to figure out how to project it. There was just a kinescope and we were still learning to operate it. So while we were waiting for the film to be processed, we went on air and just talked.

Looking back, it's amazing just how primitive conditions were. We used an Aurecom camera. Sometimes it worked, sometimes not. We had limited staff. Forget about correspondents. Sometimes I would be interviewing, and with my right hand I would be operating the sound level. We had no sound engineer.

Everything was new. There were no rules. I remember doing a story on shock therapy and we filmed someone getting shocked. I was young and stupid. I offered to take electric shock, but fortunately the doctor wouldn't let me. But we were willing to try all those things.

Then all of a sudden management started paying attention. One time, we filmed inside a union hall, where there was bad language, as there is in union halls. The censor came

Harry Rasky started as a reporter and eventually became producer of Newsmagazine. *The show always began with the line, "These are the sights and sounds of our time."*

to see what we'd done. I knew where all the swear words were and asked the engineer and cameraman to cough when the words came up. That's how I got the first swear words on TV.

We had one person, Lorne Greene, reading *Newsmagazine* at the time. We aired Sunday night at seven o'clock and repeated the same show the next day. Both times, we were top ten in the country. There was a craving by Canadians to find out what was happening.

People don't remember, but for a brief period the news was bilingual. We were idealistic. We thought we could change the country by allowing us to understand French Canadians and have them love us. Didn't work out that way, I guess. We would also take newsreels to Montreal and translate them into French.

I left for America in 1965. Edward Murrow had seen a *Newsmagazine* profile I'd done of Winston Churchill and invited me down to CBS. Even though I won an Emmy down there, American TV just wasn't making the documentaries I was interested in. Also, I was a father by then, and when I was in Vietnam, a grenade had been thrown at my feet. It didn't go off, fortunately, but it made me think about what I was doing. So when Thom Benson at CBC called me to come home — this would've been in 1970 or '71 — I did. The climate was just better here.

Since then I've made one film a year for thirty years. All those documentaries — Chagall, Karsh, Leonard Cohen, Tennessee Williams. For years, Thom had a budget item that read, Something from Harry Rasky.

God save the queen's film!

Viewers could buy this program for the 1953 Coronation news special. CBC correspondent and future Quebec premier René Lévesque reported from London's Trafalgar Square.

THOUSANDS OF CANADIANS bought or rented their first television sets to watch the coronation of Queen Elizabeth on June 2, 1953.

"People were curious about TV," remembered Dalton Camp. "And there was this historic event. I bought my first set just before the coronation. I thought it was something my children should see."

CBC figured the coronation was something all Canada should see — on CBC, not a U.S. border station. So a small contingent, including cameraman Oscar Burritt, was flown to London for the event. Get the kinescope film and beat the Yanks home was their mission.

Your Guide to Coronation Broadcasts
RADIO AND TELEVISION
CBC TIMES—PROGRAMS FOR THE WEEK OF MAY 31-JUNE 6

10c

E II R

The Coronation - 1953

They got a break when the NBC aircraft, which had left Heathrow first, developed engine trouble and returned to London. CBS's plane was also delayed for some reason. But whatever advantage the Canadian TV crew enjoyed was lost upon landing to refuel in Gander, Newfoundland, then still an American air base. The base's commander, presumably in cahoots with the U.S. networks, refused to let the crew reboard.

Cameraman Burritt phoned his boss, Stuart Griffiths, in a boiling rage.

"Oscar, how many of them are there?" Griffiths wondered.

"Three."

"And how many of you are there?"

"Four."

CBWT Winnipeg's first mobile studio heads to Ottawa (by rail) to cover the 1957 royal visit.

Above: On October 14, 1957, Queen Elizabeth became the first reigning monarch to open the Canadian Parliament. More than 4.5 million Canadians watched the event live on TV, and another 2.2 million saw a kinescope replay that evening. NATIONAL ARCHIVES OF CANADA, PA111420

Right: A CBC camera crew has a bird's eye view of a tickertape parade held for the royal couple in Toronto during a 1959 visit.

"Then rush them."

Griffiths correctly presumed that the American commander would be unwilling to risk losing his Canadian base by holding the CBC personnel against their wishes. So Burritt's crew was allowed passage to Montreal, where the film was flown by helicopter to the roof of the CBC building. Hours away from running its own footage, NBC decided to buy CBC's feed.

"There was then this unique moment," Mavor Moore remembers in his memoir, "when the CBC signal ... went out over all of North America."

Cue Diefenbaker

Populist firebrand John Diefenbaker appears on air March 5, 1958. Dalton Camp, who helped Dief use television to get elected, later used the medium to stage his downfall.

N O ONE HAD seen a politician perform on Canadian television before John Diefenbaker.

"Prime Minister St. Laurent loathed the new medium because he wasn't good at it," remembered Dalton Camp, Diefenbaker's campaign manager in the 1958 federal election. "Mackenzie King before him, we barely saw in newsreels. In the States, President Eisenhower kept out of sight."

While Eisenhower saw campaigning as a bothersome, necessary means to government, Diefenbaker experienced elections as a deep, personal vindication of self.

"He'd grown up with a German name in two world wars," said Camp. "And lost [five] times before getting elected." Always an outsider, even in his legal career, and continually vilified first by his own party hierarchy and then by the hated Grits, Diefenbaker looked to ordinary Canadians for approval.

And in 1957, when he won a slim minority, then in 1958, when he triumphed with an unprecedented 208-seat victory, Diefenbaker did much of that looking into a TV camera lens.

"Television was still a phenomenon and so was Diefenbaker," Camp said. "They intersected. And I think there may have been a steamroller effect.... Diefenbaker was a performer. Not to get too McLuhan-esque, but audiences wrote his speeches. He'd give two, three a day. And if he didn't get a cheer right away, he'd switch to something that worked before. When he had a sense of the crowd, he'd really pour it on."

Right: Norman DePoe stands beside a machine used to keep track of polling returns in the March 1958 federal election.

Below: Dief looms large in a 1958 pre-election newscast from CKBI-TV, Channel 5, a private affiliate in Prince Albert. Jim Spooner is the newscaster.

Kidding around

LARRY MANN AND Don Harron somehow managed to get to know each other when they were the only two boys in a class of forty-eight typing students at Toronto's Vaughan Road Collegiate.

So when the actor was out of work in early 1953, he decided to visit Harron.

"I walked into this room at the CBC and saw the back of Don's head," Mann remembers. "He spun around and shouted, 'Hey Larr!' Then turned to this other fellow and said, 'There's the guy — he'll be great!'"

The other fellow, Norman Jewison, immediately offered Mann the job that Harron had declined. "We're doing this show called *Let's See*," he said. "And we need someone to talk to dummies, you know — puppets. Can you do it?"

Mann said yes, then asked for a week to get his life in order. He spent that week at the TV puppet show *Kukla, Fran, and Ollie* in Chicago, where he studied the work of hostess Fran Allison.

Opposite: Puppeteer John Conway has his hands full with Uncle Chich *and* Holly Hock. *Beside him, host Larry Mann is caught changing hats.*

Right: Uncle Chich puttering around. Who knew he was green?
CANADIAN MUSEUM OF CIVILIZATION

The NBC show struck Mann as a frantic affair. The set was no bigger than a washroom. And the puppeteers seemed, well ... *disconnected*. "This isn't easy," Allison confided. "Puppeteers are crazy."

Crazy wouldn't be a problem in Toronto. By decade's end, the CBC would have created two of the most tender, nurturing kids' shows ever, *The Friendly Giant* and *Chez Hélène*. But in the early '50s, CBC programming was still dedicated to the idea that viewers — kids, adults, everybody — should be challenged by furiously original programming.

It was Mavor Moore who decided *Let's See* was to be a kids' puppet show, adult commentary, weather forecast, and program guide. All in fifteen minutes, right before the news, six days a week.

Norman Jewison still chuckles at the bluff required to pull the show together. "A bunch of us would get together and write fifteen minutes of whatever came into our heads," he says of the show that became *Uncle Chichimus*. "Then when we got on air we'd mostly wing it. We had puppeteer John Conway on roller skates racing around the set. He handled real phones and props. He even had his own network, the Chichimus Broadcasting Corporation, which was a satire of our employers."

Chich was a benign eccentric with countless obscure interests. One show was devoted to his marine misadventure, "Twenty Leaks Under the Waterline." The horseshoe-bald puppet was always joined by his niece, Holly Hock, who in author Hugh Garner's words "had the hatchet-shaped visage of a retired private secretary and a horsetail hairdo made from a string mop."

At first, the puppets' human foil was Percy Saltzman. "But I was a weatherman and didn't have time to figure out all the games that were going on," Saltzman says. That's when Jewison turned to Mann of a thousand voices. "Every show I changed characters, hats, accents," the actor remembers. "*Chich* was my acting school."

Although the show lasted only two seasons, *Uncle Chichimus*

attracted a cult audience who responded to the show's loopy playfulness. "Everybody in the business used to ask, 'How did you get away with this or that bit?'" Jewison remembers. "Well, we were doing a puppet show, we could get away with anything."

The Canadian version of *Howdy Doody* (1954-59), CBC's next kids' show, was more conventional and better attended by children. But adults who watched *Howdy Doody* were occasionally surprised by some of the things that spilled out of Dilly Dally and Mendel Mantelpiece Mason. Which isn't surprising when you consider Doodyville was by then the residence of the incorrigible Larry Mann (Cap'n Scuttlebutt).

"I was reading the voice-over to … a charming little fairy tale," cast member Barbara Hamilton once remembered. "Something to do with a witch and a princess who had been turned into a horse. Anyway, at the end I read, 'And then the handsome prince mounted his new bride and rode her all the way home.'"

Lost in studio

*"Gee, I thought for sure there would be more than two
planets around this sun."*
"Ah well, two planets are better than none."
— *Space Command*, November 3, 1953

An early attempt to capture youngsters and sci-fi fans, *Space Command* was set in a distant future where men used incredible amounts of hair gel and every spaceship had a cord phone. In other words, the series was unmistakably set in the early '50s. The XSWI, manned by three pilots, including an unrecognizable James Doohan (later Scotty on *Star Trek*), travelled the galaxy to, according to the opening narration, "pierce the vast blackness of interstellar space."

Easier said than done on a shoestring budget. Most of the action was confined to two sets. In between we saw a hurtling spaceship that resembled a steam iron powering through a darkened closet. The show, produced by Murray Chercover who in later life became president of CTV, ran for a single season.

Austin Willis at the controls in Space Command. *CBC promised that the show would promote an understanding of science, so there were no "moon maidens, space-pirates and space-spies." James Doohan (far right) would later encounter all of those and more on* Star Trek.

Beth Morris was the first of three young actresses to play the role of Maggie on
Maggie Muggins. She was on the show from 1955 to 1956.

"*It's time to talk to Fitzgerald Field Mouse*"

I WAS DISCOVERED when I was four. Mom took me shopping at Eaton's and there was a photographer there who felt I could work as a model. Modelling led to acting lessons from Josephine Barrington. There were six of us in the class, which is a lot now that I think of it because there might have been a dozen children working in show business in Toronto.

From there I did local theatre summers — Melody Fair and Summer Stage. Oh, and lots of radio. *Jake and the Kid*, for instance. When TV came, well, that was heady stuff for a little girl. Paul Anka sang "You Are My Destiny" to me on *CGE Showtime*. I did *Wayne and Shuster*, *The Big Revue* — everything. I remember one night going to bed and hardly being able to sleep because I was going to dance next day with Alan Lund.

Then I auditioned and won *Maggie Muggins*. I was excited, of course. Mary Grannan, who created the show, was a heavy woman who wore colourful outfits, big, big hats, and enormous earrings. And she had this obvious, very simple love for children. To this day I wear big costume earrings, probably because of her.

Everyone thought *Maggie* must have been hard because I was only ten, but the show was fifteen minutes and I'd done theatre. Also, the cast was great. I had three Mr. McGarritys

— John Drainie, Frank Peddie, and Mavor Moore for a while.

I would concentrate hard and think systematically, Okay, you've talked to Grandmother Frog, now it's time to talk to Fitzgerald Field Mouse. If I forgot something, the puppeteers, John and Linda Keough, would whisper to me.

The only hard part was going back and forth between Maggie Muggins and Beth Morris. I was playing this sweet character on TV, wearing frilly dresses and trying to please adults. And at the same time, I was in school with kids who were twelve or thirteen — I'd skipped a grade — and that wasn't the kind of behaviour they necessarily appreciated.

So it was confusing. But maybe all girls feel that way. You're beginning to grow breasts and all of a sudden you're going to parties where you go down in the basement and kiss boys.

The way I look at life, everything is a gift, and it's your challenge to take advantage of what you've been given. And *Maggie Muggins* and everything else I did as a child actor gave me the knowledge that I could accomplish things in life. That's important. Besides, acting was probably a necessary outlet for me as a child. I sing in a choir here in Kingston. Rehearsal ends at ten o'clock, and everyone else is ready to go home, but I think, no, no, I'm just getting going.

CBC executive producer Mark Starowicz once attended a wedding where the star guest was Alfie Scopp: "[Everyone] of my generation — myself included — fell over one another to get a glimpse of him and shake his hand."

"*There's a people in there*"

Alfie Scopp as Clarabell visits the Howdy Doody *Peanut Gallery.*

IN THE WAR I was stationed in Gander, Newfoundland. I did some stand-up comedy. Pretty soon, I found myself working with a thirty-piece orchestra.

My routine? Well, I'd say, "Hey, I visited a burlesque house on furlough. Most dancers went da-da-*bump*, throwing out a hip, but this one girl, she went da-da-*bump-bump-bump*. I went backstage, asked what was wrong. She said, "C-c-can I h-help-p it-t if-if I st-stut-tt-ter?"

Well, the guys liked it.

Moxie Whitney, who used to lead a band at the Royal York Hotel, told me to go to Toronto after the war. When I got there, I joined The Academy of Radio Arts, Lorne Greene's radio school. Met a trumpet player from Ottawa, Fred Davis.

I was on the first cover of Canada's *TV Guide* for *Stopwatch and Listen*. Show lasted six weeks. Wayne and Shuster were smart, they didn't jump into TV right away. They wanted TV to work the kinks out. But I needed a job.

I did everything, early on. One day, I was up at a cottage, writing a show for Normie Jewison. I phoned my service and found out they needed a clown on *Howdy Doody*. I drove into town, got into a clown costume, and sprayed everyone with water. Day later, I had the job.

Playing Clarabell the clown was the most rewarding job in my career. Clarabell never spoke, so I had freedom to fool around. And we had a guy playing organ, Quentin Maclean, an English fellow, who was fantastic. One sketch, I was taking socks off a line, and every sock I touched, he made a sound like I was playing a xylophone.

Everyone was on *Howdy Doody* at one time or another. Robert Goulet, I used to play poker with Tuesday nights. He was broke, just married. We got him the job of Trapper Pierre. Then there was Larry Mann and Barbara Hamilton, who were wonderful comedians. I remember doing a sketch with Larry on another show. We were supposed to be British. Someone brought a tea tray in and a painting of our stuffy father accidentally fell — *crash!* — on the service. This was live, right? Larry, without missing a beat, said, "Father appears to be in his cups again."

But, mostly, I loved the kids. The Peanut Gallery. I remember meeting two kids after one show. Little girl, maybe seven, and her four-year-old brother. Eyes big as saucers. When the boy saw my eyes behind the makeup, he shouts, "Hey, there's a people in there!" Kids loved Clarabell because kids enjoy knowing something adults don't. When they saw me sneak up on people they were delighted. We had a deal, the kids and me, you might say.

I kept my clown outfit in the back of the car, just for dropping into hospitals. One time in Montreal, where I grew up, something happened to my car. I went to a gas station. Mechanic opens the trunk and says, "What's this?" I said, "That's my job. I'm on *Howdy Doody*."

"Well then I can't charge you," he says. "If I told my kids I made Clarabell pay to get his car fixed, they'd kill me."

Left: Peter Mews as Timber Tom chats with Howdy Doody on the Canadian version of the popular program. Thirty-five children were invited to every show. A few celebrities also snuck in. "Barry Morse was on CBC every night back then," Alfie Scopp remembers. "But he couldn't convince his kids he was a star until we let him sit in the Peanut Gallery one day."

Centre: CBC's safety book for young viewers.

Right (left to right): Jean Cavell, Alfie Scopp, and Drew Thompson take part in a parade. All together now, "It's Howdy Doody time! / It's Howdy Doody time! / Timber Tom and Howdy Do / Say Howdy Do to you. / Let's give a rousing cheer / 'Cause Howdy Doody's here. / It's time to start the show / So kids let's go!"

children's programming   53

The heart of Saturday night

DANNY GALLIVAN WAS hockey's great lyricist. And our sport's first generation of TV fans, kids who grew up watching *Hockey Night in Canada* every Saturday night, sang his music on streets, schoolyards, and rinks from Corner Brook to Kitimat.

Play-by-play man for les Glorieux, the Montreal Canadiens, from 1952 to 1984, Gallivan's impassioned delivery and ecstatic wordplay informed how we understand hockey. More than anyone else, he taught us how to delight in the pleasures of the game. We'd mimic his delivery and repeat favourite Gallivanisms in describing our own efforts: a good goalie made "a larcenous save." Occasionally, when playing street hockey, we would lose the ball in "the paraphernalia" of galoshes and sticks.

After serving in the army during the war, Gallivan became a radio fixture in Halifax. He was discovered while in Montreal doing a game between his home team and the Junior Canadiens. When Montreal's play-by-play man, Doug Smith, became ill, a producer asked an assistant to bring in "that chap from the Maritimes." It's

The Canadiens' "Rocket" Richard and "Le Gros Bill" Jean Béliveau risk flattened faces by coming within flailing distance of Gordie Howe's elbows in mid-'50s hockey action.

hardly surprising that he remembered a play-by-play man who lived a thousand miles away. Former colleagues still marvel at how far Gallivan's voice would carry.

"To get to the English broadcast booth in the old Montreal Forum you had to travel past René Lecavalier in the French booth," remembers Gallivan's one-time broadcast partner, Dick Irvin. "And the thing I always remember about Danny is he was so loud I don't think I ever heard René, not even when I was passing right behind him.

"And once you got next to him, well, that's when the show began. Because Danny would swing over to the right if a long pass changed direction of play. Back he'd jump a few seconds later. And he'd leap out of his seat if something exciting happened…. He was right into the game."

And what a game the Canadiens played in the '50s! The team won the Stanley Cup the season Gallivan and TV arrived (1952-53) and made the finals the next seven seasons, winning five Cups in a row at one point. Many have

called this decade's Canadiens the best hockey team ever.

Surely they were the most exciting to watch on TV, with Jacques Plante, a skilled acrobat in net, and implacable Doug Harvey anchoring the defence. Butter-smooth Jean Béliveau and racing Henri Richard controlled the middle. And on the wings you had wily Dickie Moore along with Bernard "Boom Boom" Geoffrion, author of what Gallivan called "a cannonading shot." Then there was the star of the team, Joseph Henri Maurice "Rocket" Richard, whose eyes lit up as if he'd swallowed a candle when he cut in on goal.

"Only thing Danny was ever sensitive about was the suggestion he was a homer," says his first broadcast partner, Frank Selke, Jr. "He'd hear that from time to time and his answer was always the same: 'I have to be heard above the crowd and I'm doing play-by-play in Montreal. If the Rocket scores, I yell so people can hear me. But if Gordie Howe pots one for Detroit, you can hear a pin drop, so what am I going to do?'"

In fact, Gallivan made only two trips into the Canadiens' dressing room in thirty-two years, both times for player ceremonies. "He never wanted to feel bad about doing his job," explains Selke. "He figured if he knew and liked Doug Harvey or Jacques Plante, then it might bother him if he had to point out mistakes they made."

Gallivan's only allegiance was to the game, which he interpreted as a critic and performer. He turned irritable during sloppy play, then came alive when games grew feverish, shouting commentary in a voice that drew energy from the climbing expectancy of a roaring crowd. He was so good, so well liked, that he made his TV debut a year before he actually walked in front of a camera.

"You have to remember that when the CBC first came on air, in the 1952-53 season, Montreal only had a French hockey broadcast," remembers Selke. "So what everyone would do in English Montreal was turn on their set, turn off the volume, then turn on Danny's radio broadcast. He was big right away. People realized he was special."

Asked to comment on the impact television made on Montreal in the '50s, Selke, who was vice president of promotion with the Canadiens at the time, pauses for a moment. "The easiest answer to that," he says finally, "would be to say

that by 1955 if you owned a bar in Montreal that didn't have a television, your place would be empty Saturday night. Everyone else was at your competitor's watching hockey. Television turned our whole society upside down."

Montreal obtained an English-language station in 1953. And Gallivan joined Foster Hewitt in Toronto as a *Hockey Night in Canada* play-by-play man that fall. Selke says the new medium didn't intimidate Danny at all. He'd show up Saturday as always, with a pack of cigarettes in his jacket and a shirt board from the cleaners filled, both sides, with handwritten notes on that night's contest.

Selke doubts Gallivan would have scribbled potential Gallivanisms on that piece of cardboard.

Gallivanting

"Geoffrion creases the post with a cannonading drive ..."

"Oh, and Plante kicks his pad out in rapier-like fashion ..."

"With Richard's goal the Leafs now face a Herculean task ..."

"Oh, and Provost just fails to negotiate contact ..."

"Ferguson makes a visitation to the penalty box ..."

"Gadsby has put in twenty-one years of yeoman service ..."

"The puck is lost in Worsley's paraphernalia ..."

"Savard avoids him with a deft spinarama move ..."

"The Boston Garden is festooned in banners ..."

"Dryden stymies him with a scintillating save ..."

"Lafleur gobbles up the puck. And away he goes ..."

"A classic Robinsonian effort has tied the game."

Danny Gallivan 1917-1993
Former English teacher
Hockey's best ever play-by-play announcer
Montreal's Irishman of the century

In the 1950s Hockey Night in Canada used three cameras: one concentrated on the goaltending, one followed the play, and a wide-angle camera covered broad shots.

Opposite: "Rocket" Richard, Elmer Lach, and Canadiens' coach Dick Irvin, Sr., celebrate an early '50s win. (Dick Irvin, Jr., was the long-time Montreal Canadiens' analyst on Hockey Night in Canada.*)*

NATIONAL ARCHIVES OF CANADA, PA 142656

"No, they were notes on players, anecdotes maybe," he says. "Danny didn't put on an act with those colourful expressions. The Danny people saw on the screen was Danny in real life. When he relaxed with his real buddies, golfing or going down to the curling club where he played cards, he loved to talk, and his conversation was salted with the same talk you'd hear on the air."

At work, "Danny was always the quarterback," Selke continues. "He liked to direct traffic and call the plays. You never knew when he was going to ask you something on air. You just had to be ready. But his timing was always perfect. At the end of the game, you felt you'd done a good job. That was what he was in it for. He loved the game and he wanted to do it right. Just out of, I don't know, professionalism maybe."

And yet Gallivan was no martinet. It was he who changed how hockey was covered by succumbing to an impulse, then going with a new idea he sensed was working.

"At the time I used to be Danny's statistician," Selke remembers. "I'd sit beside him and feed him whatever information he needed. But he did the entire game by himself. There were no colour men in the booth then.

"Anyway, Danny and I were doing a playoff game between Boston and New York. And someone shot a puck that went right through the net. Play continued. Ten seconds later there was a whistle, and Danny turns to me and says, 'Frank, that puck went through the net, didn't it?' Without thinking, I replied, 'Yes, I think it did.'

"So we talked a little more," Selke remembers, "then later, Danny asked me another question, I answered him, and so it went through the game. And that was the first time there was conversation in a hockey booth on *Hockey Night in Canada* ... Danny just figured the time was right, I guess. And he must have been right because they've been doing it that way ever since."

Perhaps because he was as good a critic as he was a performer, Gallivan was the rare sports professional who left the game before the game left him. It was 1984 and the Canadiens had just lost a series to the New York Islanders. Gallivan and Irvin were to continue on to do the finals between Edmonton and the Islanders. The two men rode home on the charter flight after the game, exchanging small talk. Then in the parking lot, before climbing into their cars, they said goodbye.

"See you next Tuesday," Irvin said, alluding to the finals.

"No, you won't," Gallivan replied. "That's it. I've done my last game."

No warning. He just quit. Selke and *Hockey Night in Canada* executive Ted Hough raced to see Gallivan immediately after he gave notice, imploring him to reconsider. Danny wouldn't budge. He wouldn't explain exactly why to Hough, but later took old friend Selke aside and told him plainly, "Frank, my eyes aren't as good as they once were. And I catch myself having trouble with names. I'm missing things. Not often, but enough. I could do it for a while longer, I suppose. But I don't want to go out like that."

The great broadcaster then nodded and said, "It's time."

Fostering a tradition

ALTHOUGH HE HASN'T called a hockey game since 1972, Foster Hewitt's voice can still be heard on *Hockey Night in Canada*.

"Foster was my broadcast model," says current *HNIC* play-by-play man Bob Cole. "He was the best, and when I was breaking into radio in the '50s, Foster was kind enough to listen to one of my tapes, and he invited me into his office and closed the door."

For the next half-hour, the broadcast legend, who took over Maple Leaf TV play-by-play duties in 1952, broke down the game of hockey. Not as a coach, but as a dramatist.

"One of the first things he told me," Cole remembers, "is he felt uncomfortable if someone said, 'Hey, Foster, you called a great game.' To him the ultimate compliment was, 'Boy, that was a great game.' The game, he said, always came first."

Hockey, Hewitt believed, was best served by an announcer who understood that drama had a gradual ebb and flow. "Don't try and yell for a full sixty minutes," he told Cole. "There is a voice level for a game-winning goal, that's your top level, and you have to build to it."

Hewitt advised his pupil that every aspect of a broadcast had a different sound. "If a player swept behind his net with the puck on a rush up the boards, well your voice climbed with him as he travelled past the blue line then up through centre," Cole remembers Hewitt saying. "And a player hitting a goalpost late in the third period should be translated with a different sense of excitement than a player hitting a goalpost early in the game."

Upon returning to St. John's, Cole tried to implement his teacher's lessons. "I would tape the games I broadcast," he says, "then come in the following morning and listen for all the things Foster talked about.... Gradually, I developed my own style, and learned, I hope, to do what Foster suggested.

"'Don't get in the way of a game,' he said, 'embellish it, heighten the drama when you can ...but let the game play itself.'"

Opposite: Foster Hewitt is tickled to be flanked by Thom Benson, then-head of CBC-TV specials, and hockey star Sid Smith.

Left: Hewitt's script for a New York Ranger-Toronto Maple Leaf broadcast one month after Hockey Night in Canada *went to air.*

To *Hockey Night in Canada* viewers, actor Murray Westgate *was* the friendly
Imperial Esso dealer. He later appeared in numerous CBC-TV programs, including
Jake and the Kid and *Seeing Things.*

"*A smiling, nicely dressed man*"

I WAS BORN in Regina in 1918. When I graduated from high school we were in the Depression. No jobs. So I went back to art school, did some amateur theatre.

When the war came I joined the navy. I was lucky. I served on several escort ships that were sunk right after I transferred. So you could say these past sixty years have been a bonus.

After I was discharged, I went back to Regina where I did more amateur drama — I really had the bug — for a group called Little Theatre. One day I saw a tiny ad in the paper. Who knows where I'd be otherwise? Some Vancouver people were forming a company, which became Every Man Theatre. I wrote them a convincing letter, I guess, and they hired me. I acted there for three years.

But if you want to grow strawberries you have to go where they grow them. So in 1940 I got on a bus for Toronto. Took me four days. But things worked out when I arrived. Pretty soon I was doing work for Andrew Allan, in radio. Performed in the odd play and did a little modelling, too.

One day I got a job to do an Imperial Oil promotion film. I played a smiling, nicely dressed man, a gas station dealer on one side of the street. And another fellow played the bad dealer across the way. He was a slob, with no customers. They'd show this film to gas station dealers at conventions.

Then TV came along and, as I understand it, McLaren's Advertising were looking for someone to play an Imperial Oil dealer on *Hockey Night in Canada*. Apparently, they were having some trouble. Finally, someone at Imperial Oil said, "Well, why don't you use this bird we've been using in our films?"

And that's how I got the job with *Hockey Night in Canada*. Did it for sixteen years. At first, when we did commercials live, I'd work one week in Montreal, the next in Toronto. I'd rehearse two or three hours for my parts, which would be two or three commercials. And I'd introduce the Hot Stove League in the first intermission. What else? Oh, I also signed off at the end of the game. Foster would cue me.

Funny thing, I didn't meet Foster Hewitt until three or four years in, when we did a promotion for Imperial, opening a dealership in Calgary. That's because I was in the CBC studio on Jarvis, and he was around the corner at Maple Leaf Gardens on Church. But it was nice finally meeting him because of course I grew up listening to hockey on the radio. He was really big out West.

No, no, doing those commercials live wasn't hard at all. I was used to working on stage, don't forget. And everything was pretty simple. I was always smiling, and we always ended off with "Always look to Imperial for the best!"

Opposite, above: Murray Westgate wishes us "Happy motoring!" in an early '50s Hockey Night in Canada *broadcast.* IMPERIAL OIL ARCHIVES

Opposite, below: "Put a tiger in your tank" was an advertising slogan developed the following decade. IMPERIAL OIL ARCHIVES

Above: The Hot Stove League is in session. Front row, seated (left to right): Harold "Baldy" Cotton, Wes McKnight, Bobby Hewitson, and Elmer Ferguson. Standing: Dave Price, Murray Westgate, and Syl Apps. HOCKEY HALL OF FAME

Right: "Happy Motoring" song lyrics. IMPERIAL OIL ARCHIVES

HAPPY MOTORING
Music below keyed in the enclosed harmonica

When the tires are humming, and the mo . tor purrs, and your car is eager and the

Thought oc . curs that it's good to be a - live in this land of ours

Good to drive in this land of ours, what a great great feel - ing what a

**Popular songstress Juliette came on every Saturday night
after *Hockey Night in Canada* from 1954 to 1966.**

" *I never watched hockey* "

I MOVED FROM Vancouver to Toronto with my husband in 1954 because I'd been guaranteed six performances on *Holiday Ranch*. I got off the plane on St. Patrick's Day, and Cliff McKay — he was host of the show — met us and was all excited because he had hockey tickets. Hockey, I said, I don't watch hockey! I didn't go.

The first song I sang on TV was "Young at Heart." I brought a black velvet dress [to the studio] and had big platinum hair. They told me they couldn't light black. I should have worn blue. And my hair was a problem because white hair "haloed."

I also had laryngitis. But that was the best thing that ever happened. My voice was so soft, they had to put my microphone close, then pull the camera in so the mike wouldn't show. It looked as if I were singing right to people in their living rooms. I was recognized all over Toronto the next day.

Jackie Rae was the head of variety then. After my shows with Cliff, he told me I'd had my turn and would never work in Toronto again. The problem might have been Terry Dale, who was his girlfriend and also a singer. It was a silly thing for him to say, though. There were lots of us — Joan Fairfax, Phyllis Marshall, Sylvia Murphy, Joyce Hahn — we were all working. Fortunately, I knew Ira Dilworth from Vancouver. (We called him Pap Dilworth.) He was above Jackie. I told him the story and he made sure I was okay.

Then I went on Billy O'Connor's show. We clicked right away. We were the Kathy and Regis of that era. Later, though, he got a little upset — I started to get more letters than he did. He started saying negative things on air, about my weight and other niggly things.

One summer in the late '50s — by this time I had my own show — I returned to Vancouver and wasn't feeling very well. I saw the doctor and he told me to cut out all fat. So I did. I lost about forty-five pounds and then went back to Toronto. Well, everyone made such a fuss. I loved losing that weight because I still had terrific curves and a good bosom and waist.

You know what's funny? I never did get to watch hockey Saturday night. My show, *Juliette*, was live, after the game, and I was in the studio rehearsing while the game was on. I did have some players on the show, though, and they would try to sing. It was fun.

Everyone asks me about my "Good night, Mom" sign-off. That happened after Dad died. Mom went into the hospital in Vancouver and my sister put a television in her room. So I said "Good night, Mom" to her, just so she knew her daughter in Toronto was thinking of her. When Mom went home, I stopped. But then I started getting all kinds of letters, especially from moms who didn't hear from their daughters. From then on, I did it every week.

*When Juliette first appeared on black-and-white TV in the mid-'50s, she made a point of telling viewers
the colour of her dress. Something she didn't have to do in this 1967 special.*

Spaghetti Westerner

IN 1952, AN insubordinate cable prevented viewers from watching much of Toronto's 21-11 victory over Edmonton in CBC's first televised Grey Cup.

After that shanked kickoff, however, the Grey Cup became a Canadian institution in the mid-'50s, as the country gathered together to watch the Edmonton Eskimos defeat the Montreal Alouettes in three straight marvellously played and deliciously tense championships.

The hero in every one of the 1954-55-56 championships was Edmonton's two-way sensation, Jackie "Spaghetti Legs" Parker. Parker's exploits in the first of these affairs established the nail-biting tone for all three matches.

"Montreal was leading 25-20 late in the dying moments and were going in for an easy kill," remembers CBC play-by-play man Johnny Esaw. "They were on the Esks' ten-yard-line with time running out. All they needed was a field goal for the win. For some reason, coach Pinhead Walker told Sam 'The Rifle' Etcheverry to go for the pitchout. Sam went to Chuck Hunsinger, but he couldn't hand the ball off so he tried to pass it off to offensive lineman Ray Cicia, who was ahead of him and looking down the field. Referee Hap Shouldice ruled it a fumble. Jackie Parker picked it up and scampered ninety yards, as fast as his spaghetti legs would carry him for the winning touchdown."

In a way, the celebration concluding Edmonton's win never really ended. After that game, Grey Cup parties became annual events that were eclipsed only by New Year's Eve get-togethers. Starting the next year, the menu was always the same — flapjack breakfasts, potato chips and onion dip for lunch and dinner, with lots of brown stubbies in between. And we all woke up the next morning with pool-table tongues.

TV Quickie Suppers

VIRGINIA ATKINS

Opposite: Edmonton's favourite Eskimo, Jackie "Spaghetti Legs" Parker, in a classic "pro pass" publicity shot.
CANADA'S SPORTS HALL OF FAME

Above: CBC cameras follow a hand-off in a CFL football game.

Left: Liberty magazine follows the handing off of snacks at a television dinner party. "When it's your turn to entertain the TV crowd," the magazine advised, "here are hostess recipes to turn out with a casual flourish." Swanson invented frozen TV dinners in 1954. Stacking TV dinner trays quickly followed.

Let's rassle

WRESTLING WAS ON American TV every night except Sunday in the late '40s. The spectacle was a natural for television, given that the action was restricted to a small surface and could be covered with a single camera. Of course, in the '50s, CBC exhibited a little more couth, restricting the sport to Saturday late nights when presumably only sour bachelor types and confirmed delinquents could relish its gamy pleasures.

Wrestling "heels" of the day included Farmer Jones, who followed a pig into the ring; "The Human Orchid," Gorgeous George; and Windsor, Ontario's Killer Kowalski. The era's great "face," or hero, was Toronto's own Whipper Billy Watson.

Above: Whipper Billy Watson puts a gag headlock on CJIH Lethbridge's sports reporter, Stu Henderson. LIBERTY CANADA

Right: The title image of CBC's wrestling show, which came on at 11:30 Saturday nights.

... and in other sports

Below: CBC weekend afternoons became sports bonanzas by the late '50s as the network began covering curling, bowling, tennis, sailing, boxing, and horse racing, including the Queen's Plate.

WHEN TV CAME TO TOWN

TV MAY HAVE come to town in Toronto and Montreal in 1952, but for other places it took a little longer — 1953 for Sudbury, Ottawa, London, and Vancouver. In 1954 CBC opened in Winnipeg and Halifax, and private affiliates, carrying CBC programs, went on the air in Calgary, Edmonton, Regina, Saskatoon, Sault Ste. Marie, Windsor, Kitchener, Hamilton, Quebec City, Moncton, Sydney, Saint John, Port Arthur, and Rimouski. In 1955, eight more affiliates went to air — Lethbridge, Brandon, North Bay, Wingham, Barrie, Peterborough, Jonquière, and St. John's. In 1956, private stations emerged in Victoria, Charlottetown, Timmins, and Sherbrooke and, in 1957, Kamloops, Kelowna, Medicine Hat, Swift Current,

Red Deer, Noranda, and Quebec City. By 1958, the network had six CBC-owned stations, forty private affiliates (Prince Albert and Yorkton went on the air in 1958), and was accessible to 91 percent of Canadians.

On July 1, 1958, CBC-TV marked the completion of its 4,900-mile microwave facilities from Victoria to Sydney — making it the longest television network in the world — by broadcasting *Memo to Champlain*, the first coast-to-coast live television transmission. Prior to gaining full network service, CBC stations and affiliates had to wait for kinescopes of live network shows. In 1959 the microwave network extended to Newfoundland, uniting all ten provinces with a single, truly national television system.

The CBC grew from two stations to a national network in seven years. The 1961 census reported that more Canadian households had TV sets than had their own furnaces, flush toilets, or cars. Above: Two CJON St. John's employees show off their new mobile studio.

Above: Local stations covered scores of community events. Broadcaster Paul Soles (in the striped hat) attends a London hula hoop contest covered by CFPL. The craze began in California in 1957 and spread quickly. Kids competed by counting how many times they could twirl a hollow plastic hoop around their hips in a minute.

Right: CBWT Winnipeg's pioneers stand under their recently completed microwave tower in 1954, and a new camera is tried out at CKCW Moncton.

GETTING WITH IT

CANADA RECEIVED A fresh coat of paint in the '60s. First we got a new flag and anthem. Montreal dressed up to host the World's Fair — Expo — in 1967. Next came Centennial trees and gardens. Then, because we just couldn't stop ourselves, we learned a second national song: "Ca-na-da, one little two little three Canadians, we love thee ..."

Before you knew it we had a prime minister who did backflips and said things like, "What was Thucydides' lesson to the Greeks? 'Nothing lasts forever.'"

Not even black-and-white TV, apparently. Colour television, which arrived in 1966, meant that even our most venerable broadcasting institution, Foster Hewitt, required a make-over.

Hockey Night in Canada executive producer Ralph Mellanby took the legend to lunch and offered a few suggestions. Next game a makeup artist powdered Foster's face before he climbed into a snappy, sky-blue *HNIC* jacket and strode in front of the camera, gleaming. People thought he looked terrific.

Not every change in TV would come so easily this decade. Television's adolescence coincided with the emergence of a restless professional class who were eager for power and recognition. Show titles indicate the spirit of the time: *Quest, Let's Go* — even the name of CBC's potent new drama series, *Wojeck*, read like a cartoon-balloon sock in the jaw.

Television also left the studio in the '60s. Our news correspondents not only told, but *showed* what was happening in Vietnam and Moscow. In turn, CBC beamed Expo 67 to the world with the first live satellite TV broadcast. And on July 20, 1969, TV stepped off the planet

entirely with the *Apollo 11* moon landing.

"After the show I remember walking outside and looking at the moon, pinching myself," remembers former CBC anchorman Lloyd Robertson. "I felt so fortunate to be covering history."

Above: CBC's butterfly logo celebrated the arrival of colour in 1966.

Below: Toronto Maple Leaf Eddie Shack is surrounded by, among others, Barbara Amiel (far left) and Clarabell the clown (far right) in a surrealistic sketch for the 1966 arts program, Umbrella.

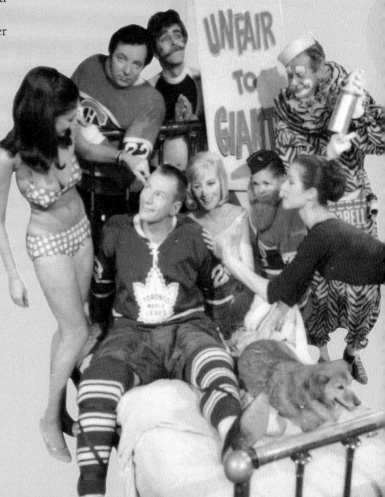

*The Maharishi and Shuster wear love beads in
a comedy sketch from the late '60s.*

The moon's Tranquillity base was one of the few peaceful spots travelled by man in the '60s, however. Perhaps the show that best symbolized the unruly nature of the time was the fabulous, infuriating *This Hour Has Seven Days*.

"We were brazen and sure we were good," co-creator Patrick Watson remembers. "We were told not to cover the queen's visit; we went ahead anyway. We exhibited no diplomacy and little tact in dealing with those in power. Probably, we enjoyed being difficult." In fact, Watson admits today that he wanted to end *This Hour* when management pulled the plug, but that "we were having too much fun fighting them to stop."

While there was a huge audience for *Quentin Durgens*, *Wojeck*, and *This Hour* — shows that acted as agents for social change — Canadians also welcomed programs that served as deceleration chambers. In a decade marked by war, protest, and strikes, it was sometimes easier to leave the challenge of front-page events to Pierre Berton, Betty Kennedy, and Gordon Sinclair.

Thankfully, Wayne and Shuster were always there as well to guide us through world events:

"Say, Johnny, what do you think of Red China?"

"Well, I always think it goes best with white linen."

Television was a wonderful portal through which to view the frequently jarring mystery of the '60s. And oh, the combinations of players who whispered us the clues. Here, on the CBC in 1961, Percy Saltzman interviewed Marshall McLuhan. Five years later, on the arts show *Umbrella*, then-CBC receptionist Barbara Amiel took her baby steps as a Canadian media celebrity by appearing as a gingham-bikinied temptress to Eddie Shack's puzzled seeker in the Fellini-esque fantasy, "Eddie Shack's Nightmare." And in 1969, Lloyd Robertson talked bagism, shagism, and rag-a-tagism with John and Yoko on their peace tour of Canada.

Then there was this TV encounter between well-known writer and broadcaster Pierre Berton and poet Leonard Cohen:

"Let's get this straight: Are you telling us that there's nothing that worries you? Nothing that bothers you? How can you write poetry if you're not bothered by anything?"

"Well, I'm bothered when I get up in the morning. My real concern is to discover whether I'm in a state of grace.... If I'm not in a state of grace, I'm better off in bed."

"What do you mean, a state of grace?"

"A state of grace is that kind of balance with which you rise to the chaos you find around you. It's not a matter of resolving the chaos, because there is something arrogant and warlike about putting the world in order that kind of ... it's like an escaped ski going through the ..."

"You've lost me."

Not so fast

THROUGHOUT THE FEVERISH, self-regarding '60s, Wayne and Shuster and Don Messer "did their own thing" by remaining true to the style of entertainment they had perfected in the '50s.

Not that Johnny Wayne and Frank Shuster believed their act wasn't always in need of some fine-tuning. Still searching for perfection after three decades as a comedy team, the pair had become as prickly as old marrieds who feel free to snarl and snipe, secure in the knowledge that their relationship will last forever.

"One rehearsal they got into an argument on set, so the director called a break," remembers veteran CBC writer-performer Alex Barris. "During the break they needed Johnny to stand in a spot on the set to line up a shot, so the director had him paged: 'John Wayne wanted on the set. John Wayne wanted on the set.' Out he walked on his little bow legs and went to the centre of the set where the microphone was. And he said, 'This is Johnny Wayne, not John Wayne. *Johnny Wayne!* John Wayne is fortunate enough to have a whole horse as a partner.'"

"Migawd, the yelling we did in our editing sessions!" Shuster once told broadcaster and journalist Frank Rasky. "There was blood on the floor." Sometimes the arguments were over a single frame. "I'd want to go a touch tighter, to get the show jumping. So I'd say, 'Let's cut two frames out of the scene.'

"'Over my dead body!'" Johnny shouted back.

But if the two men fought over style, they seldom quarrelled over substance. Both were bemused skeptics. Wayne commented on John Diefenbaker's fall from grace by saying, "Behind every prime minister stands not only a beaming mother but a Peter Newman [author of *Renegade in Power*] ready to reveal him to posterity

Wayne and Shuster crack up old stone face, Ed Sullivan. The comedians appeared on Sullivan's show a record sixty-seven times.

Wayne and Shuster parodied countless American shows throughout their careers, including the '60s hits The Man From U.N.C.L.E. *and* Star Trek. *Here they throw a comic torpedo into* The Love Boat *in the early '80s.*

and the Book-of-the-Month Club as a maladroit dunderhead."

And when in the mid-'90s Shuster was brought into CBC-TV headquarters to view the Wayne and Shuster Comedy Wall of Fame, he joked to old friend Rasky, "Well, I got one wall; if I get three more I'll get my office back."

Wayne and Shuster spent the '60s bouncing between the United States and Canada. In addition to regular appearances on *The Ed Sullivan Show*, they did two summer series for CBS. But they were never really comfortable among the suntans and smiles of Hollywood.

"Everybody would be telling us how great and fabulous we were," Shuster once remarked, "and I'd turn to Johnny and say, 'Translation — they thought we were fair.'"

"Frank distrusted success," comments friend and former son-in-law Lorne Michaels. "If he

said 'We got away with it,' that meant he was pleased with a show they'd done. I think that's because his standards were very high.

"He could break down for you how Jack Benny was a genius, and why Preston Sturges was so funny," continues the producer of *Saturday Night Live*. "For me he was a wonderful mentor because at the time comedy was mostly an oral tradition. There were no VCRs or repertory cinemas ...Wayne and Shuster had it all in their head ... and Frank could tell you, for instance, how to frame a two-shot to serve a punchline."

The '60s were good for Wayne and Shuster because there was so much for parodists to ridicule. Television proved an especially ripe target. Here, in a Wayne and Shuster special from March 1962, they take on the pretension of Hollywood medical shows, where self-important doctors like Ben Casey routinely

Opposite: Don Messer's Jubilee *began as a summer replacement for* Country Hoedown *in 1959. Clockwise: Don Messer, Waldo Munro, Charlie Chamberlain, Marg Osburne, Cecil MacEachern, Johnny Forrest, Julius "Duke" Neilson, Warren MacRae, Ray Simmons, Vic Mullin, and announcer Don Tremaine.*

played God with patients' lives. The Wayne and Shuster twist? They set up Ben and his intellectual conscience, Dr. Zorba, as garage mechanics:

"How many times have I told you never to become involved with a customer?"

"Mr. Zorba ..."

"You know it'll take four days."

"I can have that car ready tomorrow afternoon."

"And what if you fail, Sam Casey. *What if you fail?*"

"If I fail? Well, like we used to say at the Edsel factory, you can't win them all."

"You're a strange young man, Sam Casey. Someday I'd like to find out what makes you tick."

"I wish you would. The noise is driving me crazy."

Frequently the boys, who read four books a week in their formative years at Harbord Collegiate, would exhibit a linguistic grace that was impossible to find elsewhere on television. Who else but Wayne and Shuster could describe a baseball batter's slump in iambic pentameter ("Oh, what a rogue and bush league slob am I, who has ten days hitless gone")?

The wonderful irony about the

comedy team is that the same perspective that prevented them from being carried away by their own careers allowed them to be content in their private lives.

"Frank used to enjoy telling the story about their agent in Los Angeles," Michaels remembers. "'I can get you a sitcom here,' he'd tell them. 'Ah, we're not sure,' they'd say, 'We're pretty settled here.' And he'd say, 'I can get you twenty-five times more than you're making in Canada.' And Frank said, 'But we're happy here.' And the agent said, 'Hey Frank, there's more to life than just happiness.'"

Like *Wayne and Shuster, Don Messer's Jubilee* was a Not So Fast! braking mechanism for a speeding decade. Where else could you go to celebrate St. Andrew's Day, an annual theme show, but *Don Messer's* with regulars Don, Marg Osburne, and Charlie Chamberlain?

Jubilee singer Catherine McKinnon recalls Chamberlain, the Halifax show's singing lumberjack, with great affection. "When I came in for rehearsal, he'd always be leaning forward on a chair, watching whatever was going on, and he'd see me and his eyes would light up, and he'd say, 'Darlin', darlin', would ya go up to the canteen and buy me a packet of Beechnuts and a cuppa tea.'"

Above: Jubilee Centennial Tour booklet. FESTIVAL CANADA CENTENNIAL COMMISSION

Right: Halifax's Little Buchta Dancers, directed by Gunter Buchta, appeared on Don Messer's Jubilee *in 1963.*

McKinnon was more than happy to oblige because Chamberlain, an always-smiling giant with a baritone that seemed to come out of a deep cave, was ready to give anyone whatever he had.

"Oh, Charlie, he was such a simple man, bless him," she remembers. "And I mean that in the nicest, most respectful way. When he got paid, Charlie would keep his wallet filled with fives, ones, and twos. He had another job pumping gas, too. So he had money. For a while anyway. He'd just give it all away to anyone who asked."

Don Messer, on the other hand, who ran the *Jubilee* with a banker's brains and a father's watchful pride, once stopped in the middle of

rehearsal, put down his fiddle, and walked to the corner of the set, where he found a lost dime. Picking it up with a smile, he announced, "Every little bit helps."

"Messer's as tight as me own arse," Chamberlain used to say. "He wouldn't pay five cents to see the pope do the shimmy."

The other featured performer on the show was singer Marg Osburne, whose husband was frequently out of work. There were also health problems with her children. "But Marg showed up every day for rehearsal or a show, smiling," McKinnon remembers. "She wouldn't ever think of burdening anyone with her troubles."

It's impossible to exaggerate how popular the show was in its prime. Occasionally it was the top-rated show in the country, beating *Hockey Night in Canada* and *The Beverly Hillbillies*. In the Maritimes, the show regularly scored a 96 rating. Which is another way of saying that every *Jubilee* excited the same kind of interest as the moon landing.

"The show was who we were back then," McKinnon remembers. "And not just in the Maritimes. I can remember going on *Jubilee* tours where we'd sell out every place we played right across Canada. We'd get five thousand fans in hockey arenas in Manitoba. The only difference across the country was that west of Winnipeg, Marg would become Marge for some reason."

Anne Murray, who starred in *Don Messer's* summer replacement series, *Singalong Jubilee*, says the secret of the show's success was simple. "People identified with the characters," she says. "I remember taking Dad on set once and introducing him to Mr. Messer. Afterwards he said, 'You know, I just met him right there, but I felt like I already knew the man.'"

The *Jubilee* crew was "a family," remembers McKinnon. "We did things that I know no union would allow now. For instance, every week the crew would let me paint a portion of the set. Just to let me pitch in. And God help you if you picked on Charlie or one of the regulars. I can remember one week when a guest came on the show with a highfalutin attitude during rehearsals. Well, that particular show, every time he went to do his song he was just a little bit out of focus or cropped funny, if you know what I mean."

Jubilee's fans were just as protective of *their* show. And when the top-rated series was cancelled in 1969, a legion of step dancers and fiddlers descended on Parliament Hill, followed by three hundred placard-waving supporters. Inside the House of Commons, John Diefenbaker rose in a dark fury and suggested that "the Black Panthers and the like apparently have an inside track at the CBC."

An angry fan put the show's appeal in context when he complained in the *Toronto Star*, "I think some of the tripe that is showing on TV is not fit for man or beast and that *Don Messer's Jubilee* is one of the few programs that my family and myself are able to tolerate. It is a stabilizer in a time of unrest."

A better than average culture

Gordon Lightfoot was commissioned by the CBC to write "The Canadian Railroad Trilogy" for its Centennial tribute, *One Hundred Years Young*, which was telecast on January 1, 1967. (The program was just one of more than 130 CBC Centennial specials.)

Wearing a tie and a leather Ponderosa vest, Lightfoot debuted his classic folk tale, crooning the immortal words, "Oh, they looked in the future and what did they see? They saw an iron road running from the sea to the sea / Bringing goods to a young growing land / All up from the seaports and into their hands," while backed by a crew of bending, hammering railroad dancers.

Other highlights of the show included a group posing as the Fathers of Confederation singing one of founding father Sir George-Étienne Cartier's own compositions; appearances by Juliette and Wayne and Shuster; and an Alan Lund jazz ballet "inspired by the moods of Eskimo sculpture."

Don Harron's Charlie Farquharson also paid a visit, putting Canadian culture into welcome perspective. "Now you take yer average culture — that's mould," he told host Austin Willis.

Former Country Hoedown *dancer-singer Gordon Lightfoot sings on* One Hundred Years Young *in 1967.*

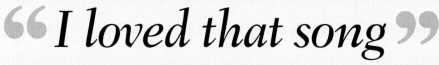

After her debut on *Singalong Jubilee*, Anne Murray never looked back. Countless hits, super specials, and guest appearances later, she is a true international star.

"*I loved that song*"

MUSIC IS PART of the culture down East. That's why so many singers and entertainers come from home. If you go to a party in the Maritimes, you sing. You don't sit around talking. I've been to hundreds of parties in Ontario; I've never sung once.

At fourteen I started singing in fairs. I used to think it was all for fun. But when you think about it, there I was getting up every Saturday morning to catch the 7:30 bus for a two-and-a-half-hour ride — that bus stopped everywhere!—to take me from Springhill to Tatamagouche for singing lessons. So I must have had some idea in the back of my mind.

My brother, David, was working at Victoria General in Halifax in the mid-'60s, and one of the nurses was on *Singalong Jubilee*. He asked her how I could get an application. So that's how I applied.

My first time on an airplane was the trip I took to Halifax. I went in to this audition and sang in groups, duos. Then they had solos. And I thought, well, I'm here. But they didn't pick me. They told me they had all the altos they needed. I was crushed. Mad, too. Because there was no one who was even close to me in talent.

But apparently musical director Brian Ahern and host Bill Langstroth liked me. One of them got hold of me and said, "Will you please come down and give it another try?" And I said, "Forget it." He could see I was mad. So he said, "Well, if I tell you it's just a formality?" So I went back and they hired me.

Unfortunately, at that time, I had cartilage removed from both my knees. So I ended up missing all but five shows that summer. *Singalong*, don't forget, was a summer replacement for *Don Messer's*.

Anyway, I was pretty surprised when I showed up for work that fall in Summerside, P.E.I., where I was a Phys. Ed. instructor. All the kids saw the show. I was a celebrity. End of the year, the school said, "Are you coming back or what?"

Well, at the time, I'd been offered a job on the late-afternoon music show, *Let's Go*, doing their Halifax segment. Bill thought I should do it. My parents agreed. I guess I thought so, too. I just wanted to hear other people agree with me. So I did *Let's Go*. I sang the charts — "Never My Love," "Daydream Believer." Everything.

Bill phoned me up one day and said there's this guy who is doing a guest spot on *Don Messer's* and he's written a song for you. So I went into a studio and met Gene MacLellan. And he did "Snowbird" and a few other songs. I was overwhelmed.

"Do you like these songs?" he asked.

"Yes," I said.

So he handed me the tape and said, "They're yours."

The Maritimes' other Anne sang barefoot in the '60s after a knee operation left her feet swollen.

I played "Snowbird" for everyone who would listen before it came out. I loved that song. I guess I was lucky because Canadian content rules had just come out, so that gave it a boost. Which in this case is somehow appropriate. After all, the song is so Canadian. Canadians who went to Florida in the winter had been called snowbirds for years. But now "snowbird" really seems synonymous with Canada. Now we even name our precision flying group the Snowbirds. Yeah, I feel a little proud knowing I had something to do with that.

The barefoot image was strange. I don't know what was going through my head. The first time I played *Singalong* I was barefoot because my knees and feet were still swollen from my operation. But even after, I went barefoot. I sang barefoot at the O'Keefe [Centre] in Toronto. Looking back, I think it must have been youthful rebellion. My way of saying that all that glamour, the long dresses, was a lot of crap. But that's just a guess.

When "Snowbird" took off the way it did, I felt I had the whole of Canada behind me. I'd go in to Toronto, where the critics are world-renowned for being caustic, and even they were in my corner. Across the country everyone thought I was the squeaky-clean girl next door. I don't know about squeaky clean, but I like to think I am the girl next door.

Above: Anne Murray's Ladies Night Show *special in 1978. Clockwise from left: Lisa Dal Bello, Colleen Peterson, Shirley Eikhard, Charity Brown, Phoebe Snow, Marilyn McCoo, Mary Anne McDonald, Salome Bey, Anne Murray, and Carol Britto.*

Left: Anne enjoys a duet with Barenaked Lady Steven Page in 1995.

IVAN OTIS

arts and entertainment   79

Guitar wars

Below: Joni Mitchell performs on The Way It Is *in 1967. Mitchell moved to Toronto from Saskatoon in 1964 and was soon playing coffee houses in Yorkville for $10 a night.*

THE MUSIC VARIETY show lost the "variety" tag in the '60s. Now programs had target audiences: kids (*Music Hop, Let's Go*); country and western music fans (*Red River Jamboree, The Tommy Hunter Show, Don Messer's Jubilee*); and folkies (*Let's Sing Out*).

Music Hop (1963-67) and *Let's Go* (1967-68) were weekday, late-afternoon affairs, from Vancouver, Winnipeg, Toronto, Montreal, and Halifax. Notable talent: early Toronto host Alex Trebek, frequent guest Bobby Curtola — "She sat four rows over-ah, and ah-two seats down-down-down" — and *Music Hop*'s cool-cat cardigan band, featuring future Gordon Lightfoot backup musicians Red Shea and John Stockfish. The Winnipeg segment boasted jazz guitar legend Lenny Breau, and later Guess Who patriarch Chad "Shakin' All Ov-ah" Allan. Halifax stars included Anne Murray and (future Murray producer) Brian Ahern and the Brunswick Playboys.

Without trying especially hard, the CBC did a better job interpreting American popular music in the '60s than its U.S. network counterparts. The decade's best jazz special produced in North America, for instance, was arguably Paddy Sampson's 1962 Duke Ellington program. And although host Noel Harrison's commentary on the 1967 *The O'Keefe Centre Presents: The Rock Scene — Like It Is!* was bong-full of hippie platitudes — "Tonight we're going to travel into the canyons of the young

Opposite: Folk singers Ian and Sylvia (Tyson) perform on In Person *in 1967.*

Below: Musical chairs. Singers Anita Bryant (left) and Bobbi Gibson (right) serenade host Alex Trebek on Music Hop *in 1964.*

Chad Allan, The Guess Who's first singer, hosted Let's Go *from Winnipeg. From left to right: Burton Cummings, Jim Kale, Garry Peterson, Chad Allan, and Randy Bachman.*

Below: Stu Phillips and Peggy Neville in 1960 on Red River Jamboree *out of Winnipeg.*

mind" — the show itself, which featured the Doors performing "The End" and Jefferson Airplane doing "Somebody to Love," was properly trippy.

The decade's great unknown treasure, however, is director Daryl Duke's March 1964 Bob Dylan special, *The Times They Are A-Changing*, which anticipated the folk-rock legend's Desolation Row period by having Dylan perform a bunkhouse concert for forlorn, chain-smoking lumberjacks (one has no arms). Dylan makes no announcements during the set, just sings, although he did talk to a *Globe and Mail* reporter before the shoot: "I love my guitar; sometimes I'd like to get inside and sing out the hole."

Another great period piece is the 1966 special, *The Blues*. "The show was director Paddy Sampson's idea," recalls host Barry Callaghan. "The night before we shot, we all went to Paddy's house. Muddy [Waters] told Paddy, 'I drink Chivas Regal.' Paddy did his homework. He had a bottle. But Muddy only had two drinks. He and Willie Dixon were like Captain Ahab, they kept everyone working the three-day shoot. Paddy's only direction was 'Get them talking and playing.' The men treated the show as history. This was the only time they talked about their art collectively, and they were glad to be recognized. One of Muddy's guys, who had never been out of a ghetto, was overwhelmed. 'I'm a barber when I'm not playing,' he said. 'Maybe I could be a barber here.'"

People of colour found easier acceptance here than on American networks. In the '50s, black performers like Vancouver singer Eleanor Collins and jazz pianist Cal Jackson had their own shows at a time when Nat King Cole failed to attract any sponsors to his NBC series. And *Take 30*'s Adrienne Clarkson became the first Asian in North America to host a national show in the '60s.

Above: Jefferson Airplane, backed by a psychedelic light show, performs on The O'Keefe Centre Presents: The Rock Scene — Like It Is! *in 1967. Below: The 1966 special* The Blues *featured (left to right) Willie Dixon on bass, pianist and singer Otis Spann, Muddy Waters on guitar, and singer Mable Hillery.*

Lifetime challenge

Former Ottawa trumpet player Fred Davis hosted the show that became a national institution.

WHO COULD FORGET how it worked? First, we were told the identity of the mystery guest. Then host Fred Davis would flash us a conspiratorial smile and advise the panel if the story was national or international in nature.

Looking back, maybe the secret to *Front Page Challenge*'s remarkable run (1957-95) was Fred's welcoming nod, a gesture that gave us a dramatic stake in the two-minute chase that followed.

"We'll start with you, Gordon," Fred might then say.

Gordon was Gordon Sinclair, of course, always farthest left on our TV screen. Dressed in a Parker Brothers game-board suit and full of mischief, Sinclair was the show's sparkplug. Once, he tangled with guest Kate Millett, a feminist who called brassieres "female mutilation." "They circumcise little boys in the hospital," Sinclair countered. A fight ensued.

When Millett advised Gordon off air that she had a Ph.D. in feminist studies, he responded with, "Okay, let's make up. If you show me your Ph.D., I'll show you my circumcision."

Immediately right of Gordon was panellist Betty Kennedy, a warm and personable broadcaster who in one season solved as many front-page challenges as Sinclair and Berton combined. Her job was to pull the show back into clement waters after Hurricane Gordon. Children who watched the show dreamed of having a mom like Betty to help with their homework.

The chair next to Kennedy was filled with the audience's surrogate, that week's guest panellist. They hardly ever got any mystery guests, and sometimes we wondered if they were there to keep us in our place — to make sure we understood that this TV game of twenty questions wasn't as easy as the show's regulars made it look.

Finally, at the far right sat the show's cleanup hitter, Pierre Berton, a veteran broadcaster whose probing intellect was most apparent in the post-quiz interview segments. Barbara Frum, an occasional *Front Page* guest panellist, once commented on Berton's work by saying, "*Front Page Challenge* has done more good raw journalism for the past twenty-five years than a lot of pretentious, expensive public affairs programs."

Over its thirty-eight years, *Front Page Challenge* guests included five prime ministers, billionaire media baron Roy Thomson (who insisted the show pick up the cost of a flight he was already taking), Linus Pauling, Sir Edmund Hillary, Indira Gandhi, Harold Wilson, Martin Luther King, Malcolm X, Mary Pickford, Duke Ellington, Groucho Marx, Helen Gurley Brown, René Lévesque, and Gordie Howe.

But it was the panellists who kept us coming back. And if you believed their press clippings, who could accept that they got along? From 1961 to 1985 the lineup was headed by Berton, the show's "villainous, bow-tied intellectual," and "curmudgeon" Sinclair. We knew they were nice, but how much patience did "sympathetic" Kennedy and "congenial" host Davis possess?

Former kids'-show star Larry Mann, who warmed up *Front Page Challenge* studio crowds in the early '60s, thinks the cast stayed together so long because, except for Kennedy, they were all *very different* from their onscreen personas:

"With rare exception, people on TV are the same off and on screen," Mann says. "But *Front Page* was the exception. Gordon was a pussycat, for instance. Do anything for you. Pierre, he was really a quiet, nice guy. And then you had calm, easygoing Fred Davis, who was actually a worrywart, pacing around before the show making sure everything was okay."

Betty Kennedy laughs at Mann's remark, but finds it hard to disagree with any of his assessments.

"Pierre is fundamentally a very shy man," she says. "He's so tall and self-assured, and very good in public, but that ease in front of a camera or crowd is something he's developed. One-on-one he finds it impossible to chit-chat. Work is his pleasure. At the same time, he's a loyal and

NDP leader Tommy Douglas is the mystery guest. Left to right: Regulars Gordon Sinclair, Betty Kennedy, guest panellist Charles Templeton, and Pierre Berton. The set for Front Page Challenge *stayed pretty much the same for thirty years. Only the length of Pierre Berton's sideburns ever changed, until Allan Fotheringham and Jack Webster became panellists following the death of Gordon Sinclair in 1984.*

generous friend. Once I asked him if he might do a voice-over on a film I was doing. I hesitated because I knew how busy he was. Well, I hadn't finished the question before he said, 'When and where do you want me?'"

Kennedy's voice softens when the subject of Gordon Sinclair is introduced. "I really loved him," she says. "He was so much fun. Oh, he'd be the cock of the walk when he strutted into a room wearing those outrageous clothes that were expensive but never quite matched.

"But he was more vulnerable than anyone thought," Kennedy adds. "He'd pretend letters people wrote didn't get to him, but they did.... And two or three times every year, he would go into a deep depression.

Christmas made him blue. His daughter died tragically when she was young; maybe Gordon thought of her. For two or three days, he would really be in the pits. Sometimes a producer would say to me, 'Betty, go talk to Gordon.'"

Sinclair's biggest crisis on the show came in 1969 when he asked swimmer Elaine Tanner if she had trouble training during her menstrual cycle. More than 3,100 Canadians wrote in to complain. Sinclair's offer to resign was refused by producer Don Brown.

"When Gordon said that I just thought, 'Oh Gordon, you're just showing you're from another generation,'" Kennedy recalls. "That was such an old wives' tale."

She adds that Sinclair often got into trouble for the sake of the show. "He was a born showman and sensed when a story was dying," she says. "That's when he stirred the pot."

On one show he rescued a lagging interview with '30s evangelist Aimee Semple McPherson's

The 1961 game show The Superior Sex, *hosted by Elwy Yost, pitted men against women in quizzes and non-contact sporting contests.*

retiring daughter by asking the challenger if her mom ever drank.

"No, never," she replied.

"Well, I've got news for you," Sinclair roared. "Over the years, your mom and I split many a jar together."

Betty performed the opposite function. Fred Davis would call on her when the show got out of hand — like the time Winston Churchill's daughter, Sarah, showed up to honour the hundredth anniversary of the statesman's birth.

"Before the show we were all in the green room," Kennedy remembers, "when the producer came in and said, 'Remember what you're wearing, we're having trouble with one of the guests and we might have to reshoot a segment tomorrow.'

"Five minutes later," Kennedy recalls, "the producer came in and said, 'This doesn't look good, our guest was just spotted directing traffic on Yonge Street. She's pretty drunk.'"

But the show did go on. And when Sarah Churchill finally weaved down from her mystery perch to be interrogated, the panellists all groaned inwardly. This wasn't going to be much fun. At which point, Fred Davis put on his very best broadcaster smile and began the interview session by announcing, "We'll start with you, Betty."

He could fix everything but the weather

"It could be said of him," producer Ross McLean once wrote, "that he sawed and hammered his way into the hearts of millions."

Mr. Fix-It's Peter Whittall could fix everything but the weather. A spry rooster with an obliging manner, Whittall won the Winnipeg flyweight boxing championship in 1924. But his mom disapproved of fighting. "The night I won my title," he once said, "my mother took it away from me."

His first CBC job was writing a radio soap opera for the noontime farm broadcast in Manitoba. Later he was transferred to Toronto. In 1954, McLean invited him to apply for the handyman's job on his new series, *Living*. His test project was a leaky tap, which he fixed with the calm, cheerful manner that was his trademark.

First on *Living*, then on his own fifteen-minute show, *Mr. Fix-It* (1956-65), Whittall showed us the ins and outs of home repair. His audience numbered two million. The show received 35,000 letters annually. Perhaps because he wore the same costume — plaid flannel shirt and jeans — on and off air, Canadians assumed he was always on the job. And Whittall was frequently called upon to change a flat tire and inspect faulty electrical wiring.

Mr. Fix-It's legacy is everywhere. There is likely not a rec room in the land that went up in the '50s and '60s that doesn't bear his thumbprints.

Mr. Fix-It *host Peter Whittall wrote a series of handyman's manuals in the '60s.* WHITTALL-FRAZER PUBLISHING

Heroes for a decade

IN 1968, GORDON Pinsent waltzed into a Calgary hotel and was quickly surrounded by well-wishers at the check-in desk.

"It was all very nice; I was signing autographs," Pinsent, then the star of *Quentin Durgens, MP*, remembers, "but out of the corner of my eye, I noticed a dusty-looking gentleman peering at me, trying to decide who I was."

The crowd finally dwindled to the one stranger. Pinsent turned to give the man his full attention.

"How long you in town?" the stranger inquired.

"Just overnight," Pinsent replied. "I have a flight in the morning."

"Oh, that's too bad."

"Why's that?"

"Well, I'd like you to come out to the farm and look at my dry wheat problem."

Pinsent was perplexed.

"Well, you helped the Indians last week, and the teachers the week before," the farmer said. "I figured you might do something to fix me up."

It's not surprising that an ordinary Joe looked to a TV character for help in the '60s, for at the time the CBC was stocked with gutsy ombudsmen who were looking out for the little guy. Typically for the period, these heroes all had short, sharp names that were meant to be hollered out loud: McQueen (Ted Follows) you called for consumer fraud (*McQueen*, 1969-70); Nick King (Stephen Young) tracked down trouble on the St. Lawrence (*Seaway*, 1966-67); racial and moral injustices were Quent's department (*Quentin Durgens, MP*, 1966-71); and, if all else failed, there was crusading coroner Dr. Steve Wojeck (*Wojeck*, 1966-69).

All these men answered Montrealer Galt MacDermot's call for social justice in the definitive '60s musical, *Hair*. "How can people have no feeling?" the plaintive crooner of "Easy to Be Hard" wanted to know. Morally righteous seekers who battled the system from within, Quentin and Wojeck cared about "strangers," "evil," and "social injustice."

"My crusading coroner was based half on real-life coroner Morton Shulman in Toronto and half on consumer advocate Ralph Nader in the States," remembers *Wojeck*'s John Vernon. "Every show had a different moral issue, and I was always fighting for someone or something. One show it was abortion. We also did homosexuality. What else? Drugs. Auto safety. You name it, we fought for or against it."

At the time, Vernon didn't mind being placed in the "protest bag." Sounding very much like a cool, committed '60s hipster himself, he told a *Toronto Star* reporter, "Indifference is really what the series is all about: indifference to the plight of others. I'm not scared about messages. Television needs a few."

Wojeck was gruff and always close to anger, but occasionally, when his wife kidded him about being "a Polack," there flashed the look of a wounded outsider in his eyes. Though equally determined, Pinsent's character was more vulnerable. With the ghost of his old man peering over one shoulder, Quentin Durgens's troubled idealist embodied the whole '60s experience.

"I was a young backbencher from Moose Falls, Ontario, who learned a painful life lesson nearly every show," Pinsent remembers. "Some crafty opposition member was always tricking me. Sometimes, I must confess, I wondered how Quent could always be so naive and still manage to get re-elected."

Opposite: Two towers of political virtue, circa 1967.

Below: CBC election poster for Quentin Durgens.

CBC
QUENTIN DURGENS MP
Vote X

CBC

Vote for Quentin Durgens MP! CBC-TV, Tuesday nights starting Dec. 6

"Quentin Durgens MP will try to show how difficult, challenging, and rewarding it is to be that much-maligned man in the federal hot seat—your Member of Parliament."

David Gardner, *series producer*

A series of hour-long dramas, built around the career of an idealistic and rebellious young MP, played out against the background of the momentous events that shape our nation. QUENTIN DURGENS MP brings to life the flesh-and-blood our individuals, the human conflicts, triumphs and errors behind the scenes in present-day Ottawa.

Introduced to a national CBC television audience on The Serial's Mr. Member of Parliament last season, Quentin Durgens received resounding acclaim from press and public.

Now, Gordon Pinsent returns in the role he created, and which made him a star to be reckoned with. 'Durgens' follows the highly successful Wojeck series, in CBC-TV's most ambitious dramatic venture to date.

Durgens, the naive, well-intentioned lawyer from tiny Moose Falls, Ont., has developed in the intervening year into a determined, realistic federal politician (he's also, in the new series, unmarried). But backbencher Durgens is still a maverick, given to hullheaded crusades that make him the despair of the House leader and the party organizer.

'Quent' doesn't win them all, but even when he loses a battle, he grows as a person and a politician. He fights hard for the causes and the people he believes in, but even when he's down, he never loses the salty rural humor that charms friend and foe alike.

Subjects of Durgens embrace:
• An investigation of obscenity and pornography laws . . .
• An amusing look, taped at Expo '67, at Canada's French-English relations problem . . .
• Human interest stories about a disabled veteran, and an immigrant from behind the Iron Curtain . . .
• A parliamentary sex scandal . . .

and many more . . .

Creator-writer George Robertson sought advice on script authenticity from a number of MPs; and producer Gardner has sent his videotape camera to Ottawa for many location scenes filmed around Parliament Hill and in the House of Commons itself (this, a TV first!).

"For some reason after Expo in 1967, we were all worried about our identity," remembers Pinsent. "I can distinctly recall sitting in Los Angeles one morning, reading Canadian magazines that had been sent to me. This would have been 1969 probably. And every one of them had something about Canada's identity crisis. And I turned to Charmion, my wife, and said, 'Charm, I know who I am, I'm a Newfoundlander.' So I started writing *The Rowdyman* shortly thereafter."

Stylistically, both *Quentin Durgens* and *Wojeck* benefited from remaining true to Canada's cinematic identity: the National Film Board tradition of social realism. *Quentin Durgens* writer-creator George Robertson's best friend was Liberal party whip Jim Walker, who provided much of the show's incidental colour. And the series was shot in and around Parliament.

"Every time John Diefenbaker had to step over one of our camera wires he muttered, 'Goddamn CBC,'" Pinsent laughs. "I spent so much time in Parliament that when I received the Order of Canada [in 1980] a few of the old security guards gave me a little wave as I went in."

The costliest Canadian series of its day, Seaway *starred Austin Willis and Stephen Young (above). The series was aimed at an international market, but black-and-white dramas were on their way out in 1966.*

ASP PRODUCTIONS

Like most '60s heroes, there was something of a willing martyr in Durgens. "They tapped his phone, withheld information from him, broke into his office, stole his recording equipment, searched his apartment, threw his pyjamas on the floor — it's enough to drive a man back to Moose Falls ... [why does he stick around]?" asked *Globe and Mail* reviewer Leslie Millin after one show.

Pinsent suggests that Quentin Durgens might have resonated with Canadians because, like Durgens, we were fighting depression. His problem was the ghost of a dead father who was better than him at politics. And by the late '60s we had a really bad hangover.

Vernon had a small part in NFB filmmaker Don Owen's moody high school lament, *Nobody Waved Goodbye* (1964), so he was accustomed to the kind of location shooting that sacrificed production values for ambience. (*Wojeck*'s principal lensman was hand-held camera ace Grahame Woods, who started out in documentaries.)

"I think a show like that, with a coroner running around trying to save the world, is obviously going to come off a lot better if you're shooting in the world, in the streets as they say, as opposed to a studio," Vernon comments.

The first ten black-and-white episodes of

Wojeck, which anticipate the work of a later, equally passionate CBC coroner, Dominic Da Vinci, represent an obvious high point in our drama history. All were written by Philip Hersch and produced by Ronald Weyman, a former NFB director-producer who helped liberate TV drama from the studio. (Weyman's '70s legacy would include the far-ranging docudrama series *For the Record*.) Directed with a real sense of purpose and place, and made real by John Vernon's grainy authenticity, *Wojeck* was justifiably called "the best television series being produced in North America" by the *Toronto Star*. *Quentin Durgens*, another Weyman production, was almost as good.

So whatever happened to the restless searchers who offered Canada striking role models for five seasons?

"Oh, I know what happened to them," says Gordon Pinsent. "I was there in the gallery in the House of Commons, studying for my part, when our replacement came into the House. He was wearing a rose in his lapel and his name was Pierre Elliott Trudeau. Compared to him, Quentin Durgens was not just black and white, he was grey."

pop up
Lorne Greene

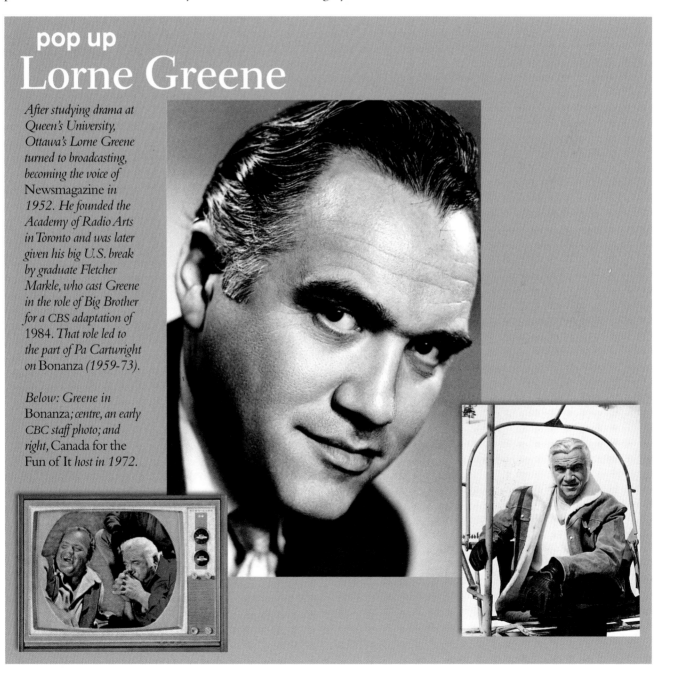

After studying drama at Queen's University, Ottawa's Lorne Greene turned to broadcasting, becoming the voice of Newsmagazine *in 1952. He founded the Academy of Radio Arts in Toronto and was later given his big U.S. break by graduate Fletcher Markle, who cast Greene in the role of Big Brother for a CBS adaptation of 1984. That role led to the part of Pa Cartwright on* Bonanza *(1959-73).*

Below: Greene in Bonanza*; centre, an early CBC staff photo; and right, Canada for the Fun of It host in 1972.*

**John Vernon, the star of *Wojeck*, has acted on the stage
and in many television shows and movies, including *Dirty Harry*, *National Lampoon's
Animal House*, and *The Outlaw Josey Wales*.**

"*Adolphus Raymondus Vernon Agopsowicz*"

I WAS BORN in Zehner, Saskatchewan, which in the '30s was a few grain elevators. My father ran the grocery shop and gas station. The place caught fire, so we said goodbye to Zehner and moved to Regina.

I played Scrooge when I was thirteen in a class play. I had terrible acne, so I needed a part that required makeup. After that I continued in amateur theatre all the way through high school. Now, I guess a little history lesson is in order here, because across Canada at the time, adjudicators were invited from New York and London to sample native efforts. Sometimes, invitations were made.

Someone asked would I be interested in coming to the Royal Academy of Dramatic Art in England. I was. This was in the early '50s. When I got there I changed my name from Adolphus Raymondus Vernon Agopsowicz to John Vernon. So I kept my name. Well, one of my names.

I studied with Peter O'Toole and Alan Bates. It's funny to think who made it. Not always the talented do. Sometimes it's the ones who have the most childlike need to scream, Pick me! Pick me!

I left England because a Canadian living there could be subject to the draft and I didn't want to go to Cyprus. Hell, I didn't even know where the bloody place was. By then my

Above: John Vernon and Patricia Collins in Wojeck, *the series that took Canadian TV drama out of the studio. This accident was staged on Toronto's Don Valley Parkway. Opposite: A caged Wojeck from "The Last Man in the World" episode.*

family was in Toronto. This was 1958, '59. And to my surprise there was work — radio, theatre, television.

It was a good time to be an actor. I did Ibsen, Chekhov, Shakespeare. Live TV, too. I was doing *The Royal Hunt of the Sun* on Broadway with Chris Plummer when George McGowan came to see me and offered me this part in a CBC-TV movie [*Tell Them the Streets Are Dancing*] he was making in Toronto. I'd been in the play for five months by then, and my kids were young, so I returned to Canada.

That became *Wojeck*. I was TV's first Polack. *Banacek* came later. Wojeck was in the spirit of the time. You know, impatient, wanted things done his way. We rode that crest for twenty shows. It made an impression. The director John Boorman saw me in it. He came up to Toronto and asked if I wanted to play in his movie *Point Blank*. I played a snivelling bastard in that one.

After that I was a cruel bastard in *Dirty Harry*. And a vicious bastard in *Animal House*.

Bastards became my specialty. I even played one on *Quincy*, with Jack Klugman. Both Quincy and Wojeck were based on Toronto coroner Morton Shulman. No, playing Wojeck didn't feel different or special. They wanted an actor for a part so I went in and did it. Acting is my job.

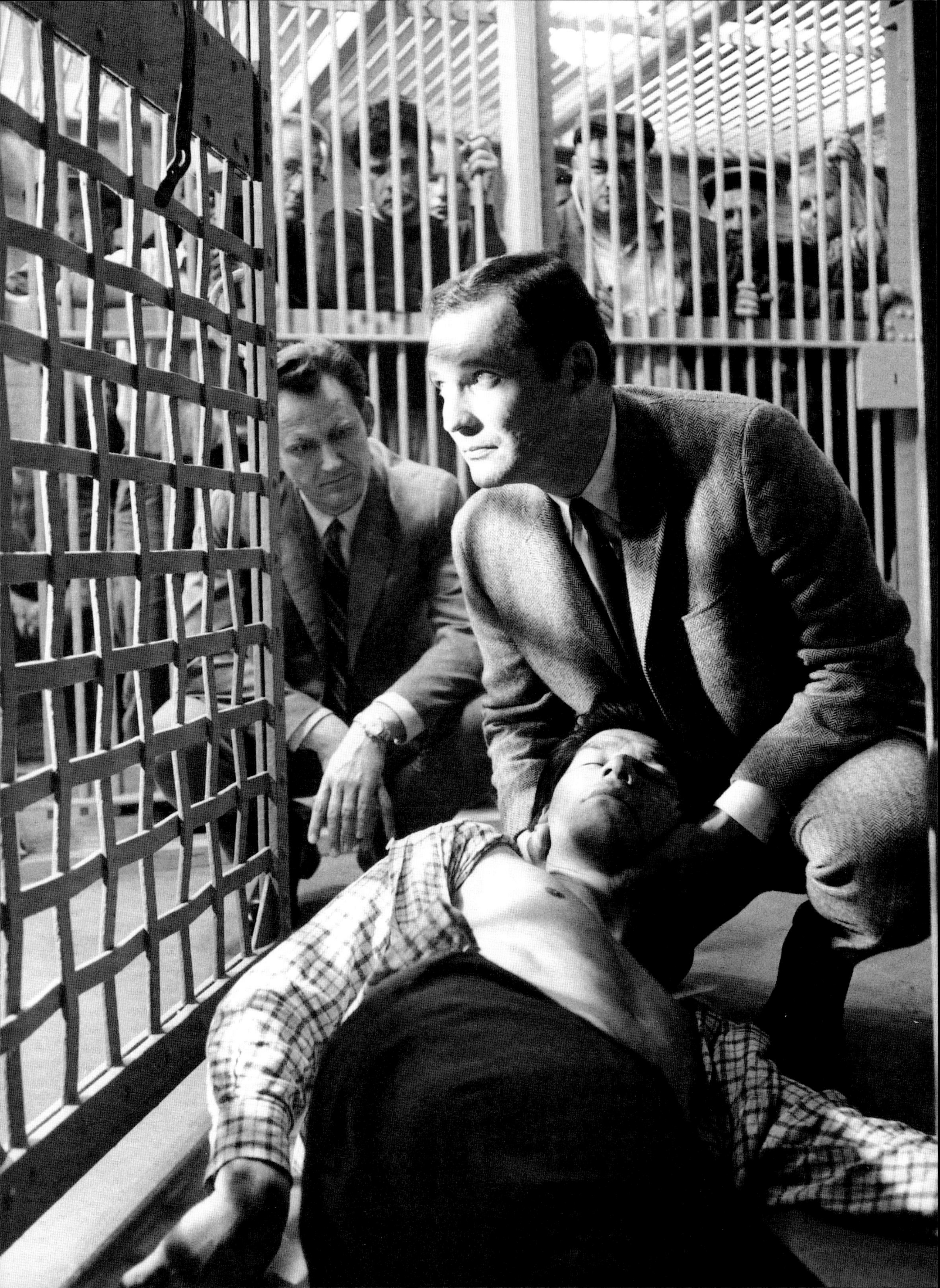

A national theatre

IN THE UNITED States, '60s TV drama consisted of shootouts between cops and cowboys, but in Canada dramatic anthologies thrived, both nationally (*Festival*, *Eye Opener*, and *Playdate*) and regionally (Vancouver's *Cariboo Country*).

Robert Allen's *Festival* (1960-69) perpetuated the CBC tradition of standard repertory theatre. Notable instalments included Paul Almond's 1966 *A Doll's House*, featuring a fragile, sexually alive Geneviève Bujold as Nora, and Eric Till's lyrical *Pale Horse, Pale Rider* (1964), with Joan Hackett and Keir Dullea. Stratford actor Bruno Gerussi introduced himself to TV audiences, offering up a conflicted revolutionary in *Riel* (1961) as well as a supporting role in Mario Prizek's *Galileo* (1963). (Brecht's widow asked for a kinescope of *Galileo* for the archives of the Berliner Ensemble.)

Perhaps the boldest drama to emerge from the period was Almond's droll TV satire *The Close Prisoner* (1964), the pseudo-documentary of a mental patient who becomes so fascinated with a pretentious filmmaker's interpretation of his predicament that he begins to lose interest in his own life.

John Colicos (left) and Bruno Gerussi (right) appear in a 1963 Festival *production of Bertolt Brecht's* Galileo.

Above: Another example of how TV escaped the studio in this decade was the 1966 dramatic special Julius Caesar, *which featured Budd Knapp as Julius Caesar, Christopher Wiggins as Cassius, and Peter Donat as Antony.*

Left: Geneviève Bujold starred in a Festival *production of* A Doll's House, *directed by future husband Paul Almond. Other specials in CBC's signature arts series, which ran from 1960 to 1969, included a Stratford production of Gilbert and Sullivan's* H.M.S. Pinafore, *directed by Tyrone Guthrie and adapted for television by Norman Campbell.*

This hour has three million viewers

LIKE CHARLES FOSTER Kane's the *Inquirer*, Patrick Watson and Douglas Leiterman's *This Hour Has Seven Days* began with a grandiloquent manifesto.

This Hour, the two executive producers promised in 1964, would be "a one-hour show of such vitality and urgency that it will recapture public excitement in public affairs television and become mandatory viewing for a large segment of the nation....We will probe dishonesty and hypocrisy. By encouraging leads from our viewers, we will provide a kind of TV public ombudsman to draw attention to public wrongs and encourage remedial action."

The comparison to Orson Welles and *Citizen Kane* is not made idly. Both Welles and Patrick Watson were child magicians who acted in radio as teenagers. Boredom was, for both storytellers, a constant enemy, and their creative instincts frequently led them to risk sensible narrative flow by indulging in bold dramatic flourishes.

"I can remember getting into lively editing room debates with our very knowledgeable production supervisor, Ken Lefolii," Watson recalls. "We'd be looking at an interview subject talking and I'd get restless and say, 'Cut that out, he's going on too long.'"

"You can't, Patrick, it's vital information," was Lefolii's inevitable response.

"It's dull."

"If you take it out, people won't understand the story."

"If you don't take it out, people will turn the channel and they'll understand even less of the story," replied Watson.

Right: Laurier LaPierre (left) and Patrick Watson (right) with Dinah Christie, who sang the show's theme song to the tune of "Worried Man Blues."

Opposite: This Hour's set during a public forum segment. "We rehearsed all day Sunday before going to air," remembers Patrick Watson. "It was important to get the flow of the show right."

the sixties

The owl and the tree toad

Comedian Rich Little delighted CBC-TV audiences throughout the '60s with impersonations of prime ministers John Diefenbaker and Lester B. Pearson. Here's how he captured both men:

"[John Diefenbaker] looks like a big white northern owl, and he has a voice that goes with it: a baritone, stern and rebuking — the Old Testament prophet in action. He keeps putting an 'aaah' prefix in front of words as if pausing to get the word exactly right. Of course, he emphasizes with a lot of head-shakings and jowl-quiverings. He puts his hand on his hip, glaring down at the floor as though he's hunting for something and is angry because he can't remember what it is.

"I portray [Lester Pearson] as a kind of flappy little mole or tree toad. His voice is a tenor. He doesn't have a lisp, though it often sounds that way. But he gets his tongue mixed up: it doesn't ride right in the mouth. The 'sp' sound in particular bothers him. It's sort of a mushy sound, with a lot of spray and splatter. Of course, I exaggerate his funny little walk, with one leg stiffer than the other. He smites himself on the forehead for emphasis and wipes his hands down his cheeks. But I don't see anything self-important in his posture; there's a chuckly shyness in the midst of it all."

Rich Little as the owl-like John Diefenbaker, one of nearly two hundred well-known people mimicked by the Ottawa-born impressionist.

Although Watson respected Lefolii, former editor of *Maclean's*, the one-time magician lived in fear that his "audience might take their eyes off the screen."

Few did. *This Hour* charmed and bullied its way into three million Canadian homes on Sundays at 10 with a fast-spinning combination of skits, documentaries, music, and always-intemperate news reports. Most often, the show focused on the forbidden topics of polite society: sex, drugs, religion, and politics.

When Queen Elizabeth visited Quebec City in 1964, CBC ordered *This Hour not* to cover the event. Watson immediately dispatched a crew. Asked today whether the story might have been handled some other way, Watson admits, "Sure it could have." Well, then didn't sending a crew represent a kind of death wish? "Absolutely, without a doubt," he replies.

A papal visit to Yankee Stadium prompted a skit where the pope's infallibility was called into doubt in a contest between the Yankees and Cardinals. Angry letters ensued. Management apologized. Leiterman called a press conference to reassert that *This Hour* wouldn't be deterred from pursuing "intelligent, pointed satire."

And so it went. For a while. To interview an inmate in the Ontario Hospital for the Crimi-

nally Insane, a *This Hour* crew posed as relatives carrying a picnic basket — loaded with camera equipment. Correspondent Larry Zolf knocked on junior defence minister Pierre Sevigny's door with impertinent questions about his involvement with German call girl Gerda Munsinger, only to have Sevigny chase him away with a cane.

The mere presence of John Drainie's co-host — the volatile, pipe-smoking Laurier LaPierre — was an affront to many. "I was doing a show out of Ottawa called *Inquiry* and was looking for a host, and I thought this is ridiculous, we live in a country with French Canadians and never hear their voices," recalls Watson. "So I went to Montreal to check out two men: Pierre Trudeau and Laurier LaPierre. Now, it became clear that Pierre wanted more control than I was prepared to give him. In any case, we made the right choice in Laurier, who had great natural charm and exhibited the kind of passion and risk I felt made for good television. Lord knows, you couldn't get Laurier to act like a journalist."

That sometimes was a problem. Critics in management and the press felt that LaPierre didn't know his place as an interviewer. Why was he always interjecting his own opinions?

98   news and information

"*Playing around with politics*"

WHAT WAS THE power of television? I remember seeing Dief speak on television in 1957. I was twenty-two and I stood up at the end and applauded.

[Documentary producer] Beryl Fox was my camp counsellor when I was a little Jewish boy in Winnipeg. I would walk through fire and die for Beryl. She thought I was the voice of the people. She got me on *This Hour Has Seven Days*, where Doug Leiterman let me use humour to play around with politics. One time, we were told to back off on Gerda Munsinger. Leiterman asked if I could think of anything to do and I said sure. I went up to Upper Canada College, where all the boys are related to cabinet ministers, and asked a bunch of them, "Would your dad ever date that trollop?" They all said "No way."

A lot of stuff never got to air, you know. During the queen's visit I interviewed two Irish Catholic nuns in Quebec City. "Do you think the queen should be coming here?" I asked them. "No ... no," they said. "She could get her head blown off." Then I went to Laval and asked students what they thought about the queen. They got into a heated shouting match, all in English, and then the screen faded to black. That piece of tape never saw air — it went straight to the president's office.

This Hour led to the supremacy of news and current affairs that the network now has. And that, I think, is *This Hour*'s legacy.

Larry Zolf talks to a cameraman after interviewing striking newspaper workers for This Hour Has Seven Days.

In 1965 This Hour *invited two Ku Klux Klan officers on the show. At first, the Klansmen spoke of their admiration for "Negroes." Then interviewer Robert Hoyt put them on the spot by asking them to shake hands with a black minister who was also in the studio. They refused.*

Watson sometimes wondered if they meant he didn't know his place as a French Canadian.

"We would get the nastiest letters," he says. "You know, 'Get that frog off the air.' I debated showing them to Laurier. Finally, I did. He looked at them, nodded, and said, 'Well, I think we're making real progress here.'"

LaPierre outraged many in the broadcast industry by shedding a tear after an item on convicted teen murderer Steven Truscott. "He can't be crying on television!" CBC-TV president Alphonse Ouimet told Watson the morning after the show.

"What happened there," Watson explains, "was Roy Faibish filmed an interview with Truscott's mother late in the week, and it was still being edited Sunday when we were rehearsing. So that night, Laurier and I were sitting there watching the interview for the first time. The last question was: 'When you go to

see your son, in prison, do you cry?' and the mother's chin started to go, then she said, 'Of-of course I do.'

"So we then cut to Laurier, who was supposed to hand off to the next item," Watson continues. "There was a tear in the eye, but what can I say? It was an honest tear." (In 1965, upon the sudden illness of John Drainie, Watson relinquished his production responsibilities and became co-host with LaPierre.)

But it would be a disservice to *This Hour* to dwell on its greatest controversies, or to suggest the public affairs show was simply feverish stunt journalism. At its finest, Leiterman and Watson's creation was the summation of the best in both CBC public affairs programming — the influence of Ross McLean's *Tabloid* and *Close-Up* was readily apparent — and the NFB documentary tradition. For instance, Beryl Fox's *Summer in Mississippi*, a poignant meditation on

American racism that was aired on a 1964 episode of *This Hour,* remains a landmark in TV documentary filmmaking.

And if *This Hour* sometimes had the feel of a yippie free-for-all, maybe that's because its creators were forced by time and budget constraints to turn every show into a scavenger hunt.

"We did the show for $14,000," Watson laughs. "To do that we stole from everyone. We were constantly raiding CBC archives without permission. Fortunately, industry people liked us. We'd get calls from variety shows. They'd say, 'We're through, but have an hour left if you want to come down and shoot. We can light two chairs for you.' In the end, we counted on that help, because our crews were working seventeen-hour-a-day, seven-day-a-week shifts."

This Hour's ramshackle energy and argumentative wit caught on with the public and most critics. Alan Edmonds, in *Maclean's*, captured the spirit of the show when he wrote, "The methods *Seven Days* has used to attract its mass audience have left [the CBC] in the position of a genteel, bourgeois parent who produced a rambunctious, intellectual vulgarian.... It is impossible to simply watch [the show]; you become involved in it, and even when it's lousy (and it can be as bad as it can be magnificent) it remains, for millions who would otherwise switch channels at the start of a public affairs show, something to talk about come Monday. You watch it to see what it will come up with next."

The show was a hit — which gave Leiterman and Watson a fatal dose of confidence. "We thought because the numbers were good we could get away with anything," Watson remembers. "After a while we effectively told management to screw off, don't bother us."

This Hour's final struggle with the parent network came when Leiterman invited the leaders of all federal parties to participate in a debate prior to the 1965 federal election. CBC vetoed the proposal. A tug-of-war ensued.

"We told them finally, 'Okay, you say we can't do the interviews, fine, we'll pull the show and tell the people why we're off the air,'" Watson

A conversation without words

Percy Saltzman, in his tenth year on *Tabloid*, approached interviews like a snooping neighbour peering over a hedge. What the heck is going on? he wanted to know. In 1962 Marshall McLuhan was a good person to ask. Historian Michael Bliss once said the media theorist could talk "on anything in literature, history, and the whole universe, past, present, and future."

For a documentary that year, Saltzman (right) and McLuhan met to discuss something that at the time fascinated us all: a new dance craze, the twist.

"The twist would not be appealing unless it's an irritant," McLuhan began. "It looks like a cool dance — like a conversation without words. An attempt to imitate some profound inner growth problem. Very unsexy. I think sexiness belongs to other dances. In the twist the whole body is involved."

The response was classic McLuhan, who colleague T.W. Cooper suggested was harder to track than a kangaroo. Why would an irritant be appealing? Is the body not involved in sex? Yet there was something in the "conversation without words" line.

The best way to interview McLuhan was to riff off him — to get the TV expert who seldom watched the medium going with precise questions that were calculated to keep the aphorisms coming.

"Is it like the fertility dance in Africa?" Saltzman asked.

"I'm sure the twist doesn't mean promoting crop growth," McLuhan answered. "But the twist does promote the growth of something. [Dancers] look like vegetables, carrots in slow growth."

"Would you call it a sterility dance?" Saltzman then asked, getting the hang of the game. McLuhan talked at some length, then Percy, whose questions kept getting shorter, asked the professor, "Do you twist?"

"I've been told I'm twisting and didn't know it," McLuhan said. "Twisting is an act of untwisting of the daily tasks. It's a way of unwinding."

There we had it at last. The twist was a form of recreation, a way to relax. Saltzman smiled. The interview was over.

remembers. At the last moment the CBC gave in. As it turned out, the show attracted only Créditiste boss Réal Caouette and NDP leader Tommy Douglas. Still, *This Hour*'s staff celebrated the victory with a post-show party.

"I can still vividly remember one moment in that party," Watson recalls. "Reeves Hagan, who was then head of public affairs programming and a staunch supporter of the show, lifted his glass and said, 'A toast to your success boys, but do not think for a second this affair has ended. The bureaucrats won't rest here, and in the end they will exact their pound of flesh.' Five months later we were off the air."

Thirty-six years later, Watson believes his show was done in both by narrow-thinking management and the conceit of youth.

"The CBC at the time was run by older gentlemen who'd grown up in radio in a different, I would assume more sedate, era," he says. "TV in the '60s, our show in particular, had a visceral appeal that probably scared them. And they were up in Ottawa having cocktails with senior public servants, who wondered why they couldn't keep us in line. Certainly, we could have been more judicious and less provocative and still done what we wanted to do. But in 1965 that never occurred to us."

pop up
Patrick Watson

Patrick Watson began his career in 1943 as a child actor on CBC Radio and went on to become the chair of the CBC Board of Directors from 1989 to 1994. In the intervening years he helped create Close-Up, This Hour Has Seven Days, The Struggle for Democracy, *and other programs.*

Right: Watson interviews '60s supermodel Jean Shrimpton for The Way It Is *in 1968.*
Below: An actor again, he enjoys the company of Donald Sutherland and Kate Nelligan in Bethune *(1977).*
Right: With Peter Ustinov on the special World Challenge *(1986).*

Scenes from the haunted aquarium

GROWING UP IN the '30s, Fletcher Markle cured a stuttering problem by impersonating his hero, Orson Welles, the boy genius of radio. The cure was so complete that Markle was a hyphenated sensation by age twenty, writing, directing, and acting in his own CBC Vancouver radio series.

After the war, he created the acclaimed anthology drama series *Studio One* for CBS in New York. Famous for calling television "the haunted aquarium," Markle himself swam with the most luminous of the industry's creatures. He befriended Welles, gave Lorne Greene his U.S. acting break, and was a friend of James Dean. (Markle and his wife happened upon the actor's crushed Porsche hours after he was killed.)

Returning to Canada in the '60s to make the film *The Incredible Journey*, he skilfully adapted *Pale Horse, Pale Rider* and eventually became head of CBC drama, where he presided over the making of *The Beachcombers*. But his lasting personal contribution to Canadian TV was *Telescope* (1963-73), which he hosted, directed, and later produced.

A thoughtful, smartly produced documentary series that always seemed to be in the right place, the show's 1964 triumphs included producer Ross McLean's hard day's night with the Beatles in New York — "Hey Cam," John yells at the cinéma-vérité lensman in their car, gesturing to screaming fans outside, "You're missing the girls" — and Allan King's two-part study of Christopher Plummer during the making of *The Sound of Music*.

Fletcher Markle receives a cosmetic touch-up on the very "'60s" set of the documentary series Telescope.

The distemper of our time

"Television is the most important medium we've got. It can involve millions of people in an immediate and total way, in a communal national experience. People watch a program, and they get up and talk about it next day over breakfast, at the office, in Parliament, in magazines. Television means people [have] to think, and the national consciousness moves forward because of it."

— Documentary filmmaker
Allan King, 1967, from Paul Rutherford's
Primetime Canada 1952-67

Prime Minister Lester B. Pearson lights the Centennial flame on Parliament Hill in 1967. Immediately behind him stands Liberal cabinet minister Judy LaMarsh.
NATIONAL ARCHIVES OF CANADA, C026964

Y ES, IT WAS possible for someone to suggest that "television means people have to think" in the '60s. Public affairs shows like *Close-Up* (1957-63), *Inquiry* (1960-64), *Sunday* (1966-67), *The Public Eye* (1967-69), and particularly *This Hour Has Seven Days* (1964-66) and *The Way It Is* (1967-69), demanded, and got, a response from viewers.

"The excitement came from a combination of factors," recalls Patrick Watson. "We had these great documentary filmmakers and incredible social upheaval. And a filmmaker like Beryl Fox brought that upheaval right into our living rooms. My God, Beryl almost got killed making *Summer in Mississippi* [for *This Hour*] ...and her Vietnam documentaries [for *Document*]."

Some films got killed and wounded, as well. *Warrendale*, Allan King's CBC-commissioned documentary on an Ontario home for the emotionally disturbed, won two awards at the Cannes film festival. But it was never actually shown by CBC-TV because of its disturbing scenes and obscene language. And it took five years for D.A. Pennebaker and Richard Ballentine's cinéma-vérité portrait of Prime Minister Pearson to come to air. (The film was one of the last documentaries aired on *The Way It Is*.)

Although King was an angry young filmmaker at the time, he now views old adversaries with more generosity: "There was a lot of blame attached to the CBC for the fact they didn't broadcast *Warrendale*. However, it is forgotten that it could only have been made in the environment that was created in the CBC by a number of really talented and imaginative individuals. That came through public affairs people like Doug Leiterman and Patrick Watson. But also their management, people like Bernie Trotter, Hugh Gauntlett, and Peter Campbell. Really, it could have only been made in a public broadcasting system."

The influence of shows like *Close-Up* and *This Hour* would show up in the '70s in the journalistic dramas, or "docudramas," on *For the Record*, which featured work by NFB filmmakers Donald Brittain and Gilles Carle, along with a hugely controversial investigation into organized crime, *Connections*.

"It's easy to get caught up in criticism," King says, "but the CBC is an institution that has provided the expressive lifeblood of this country."

Film director and producer Beryl Fox is one of Canada's great documentary filmmakers. In the '60s, her best-known television documentaries were *Summer in Mississippi* and *The Mills of the Gods*.

"*Bringing it all back home*"

I GREW UP in a Winnipeg slum. Rats inhabited the plumbing and the cockroaches considered themselves joint tenants. Me, I gazed at the moon and dreamed of being significant. Significance, I assumed, was public recognition, awards and honours, and zero cockroaches.

Since then I've achieved a number of my girlhood dreams. For instance, I've been warned by the Pentagon that if I ever returned as a journalist to a battle zone under their control, that I could get accidentally shot by friendly fire. That's public recognition enough for me. But in getting from North Winnipeg to "here," I saw some things and met some people that made me think about what significance really is.

In my films, I often used the particular to illuminate the universal. And in my life, there are two men I have met who illuminated for me aspects of the human condition and taught me something about what matters. One was a handsome young Canadian, a sergeant in the American army, who stood beside me on a hill near Hoi An, watching as an aging Vietnamese couple crawled out of their bunker. The young man picked up his M16 rifle and, smiling at me, said, "Hey, you want to see an old man dance?" Hard to forget him.

The other man was an African American Cat-tractor driver working logs in a sawmill in Neshoba County, Mississippi, where three civil rights workers had just been found murdered, mutilated, and buried deep in a nearby cofferdam. Standing with his white bosses and a local deputy, I asked him what he thought about civil rights. He took a long time to answer. And when he did, he turned to the camera, knowing that his livelihood and possibly his life depended on his answer. He said simply, "I believe I have the right to vote, and that's what I'm gonna do."

These two men have become guideposts of sorts for me. I've learned from them, and from others like them, that significance, truly, is how you live your daily life within the circumstances you are given. It is the day-to-day choices each of us make that compound into the life and health — or lack of health — of the nation.

As Henry James once wrote, "Evil is insolent and strong; beauty enchanting but rare; goodness very apt to be weak; folly very apt to be defiant; wickedness to carry the day; imbeciles to be in great places, people of sense in small, and mankind generally unhappy. Life is, in fact, a battle." Yes, it certainly seems that way at times. But in this country there is no enemy. There is only us. And we, by our silences, can assent to wrongdoing, or work together for change. "We" can be effective.

— From Beryl Fox's October 28, 1983 convocation address to the University of Western Ontario graduating class

Beryl Fox trudged through Vietnam jungles with U.S. Marines while making The Mills of the Gods.

Douglas Leiterman began as a producer on *Close-Up* and went on to create
This Hour Has Seven Days and *Document* with Patrick Watson.

"*Let the story tell itself*"

I STARTED AS a reporter and photographer for Canadian Press. I covered everything: crime, politics, deprivation, tragedy, astrophysics, religion.

With newspaper writing, you dig for the guts of a story, always checking the facts against your own biases. You strive for brevity, and try not to let demands of space and time excuse you from honesty and fairness.

As a photographer you try to capture the raw truth of a story in that 1/500th-of-a-second click of your Graflex shutter, recording on silver nitrate an image you hope will tell it like it was. You develop techniques to distract subjects, to catch them with their guard down.

CBC's Ross McLean dragged me out of the parliamentary press gallery and turned me loose with Bob Crone, Grahame Woods, and other intuitive cameramen. With *Close-Up* I tried to meld film with the solid protein of print journalism. Ross trusted my journalism, though he once threw me out of the studio just before air for disputing a credit. He also taught me to be playful, not to take myself too seriously. He was a programming genius.

I shot a hundred hours to make a one-hour documentary. Editing I learned from the masters. Allan King suggested I screen the classics of [Sergei] Eisenstein and Basil Wright. That's how I learned how to collate sound and picture so you didn't need an omniscient narrator getting in the way. "Get yourself off camera,"

Doug Leiterman directs a cameraman. "I had to learn how to translate events into visual stories. It helped that I read poetry at my mother's knee, and at college brought home the great canvases of Lawren Harris on loan from the art library."

Allan used to say. "Let the story tell itself."

I came to do a CBC documentary on Diefenbaker because he trusted me from my parliamentary days. The best shot in *The Chief* is Dief fishing on Vancouver Island, framed from the waist up. He has a wonderfully contented look, which we captured as he was relieving himself into a snowbank.

Another revealing shot has Dief and his wife singing a hymn in the front pew of the First Baptist Church in Victoria. We had a camera hidden in the baptism tank behind the curtain. In another scene Dief talked about Mackenzie King's belief in spiritualism, how King would seek political guidance from his dead mother in seances in the attic of Laurier House. He thought the cameras were off. We used to tape over the little red light and lock off the tripod head.

We were missionaries on *This Hour*. We wanted to improve society and we thought television could bring about much-needed change. We believed passionately that public affairs TV must reach a mass audience. That TV should not shy away from controversial subjects — indeed, it had an obligation to explore those issues. We knew we'd stir up opposition from vested interests and frighten management. But we thought if we did our job and earned public support we could survive a few years. We got fifty programs on the air before we were shuttered.

Drop anchor

EARL CAMERON LEFT *The National* in 1966. Some say he was replaced because the news presenter on CBC Radio who on D-Day delivered the most famous lead in Canadian history — "The dagger pointed at the heart of Berlin has been driven into the side of Nazi Europe" — was too dispassionate for the '60s.

It was time for a bolder, engaged journalist to anchor the news. Stanley Burke, who had won his spurs as a foreign correspondent in Europe, brought zeal and authority to the anchor position for three years. He chafed at the reins, though, and found he didn't want so much to read the news as to explain it. At decade's end he quit the network to devote himself to African causes. Warren Davis stepped up to the plate — briefly — and then, in 1970, along came Lloyd Robertson.

Left: Earl Cameron was the anchor on The National *from 1959 to 1966.*

Right: Stanley Burke assumed the role for the last half of the '60s.

A mask for
the electronic age

Right: This Hour's *Larry Zolf and Pierre Trudeau listen intently to Quebec Minister of Natural Resources René Lévesque (off camera) in a 1964 debate on separatism.*

Below: Progressive Conservative leader Robert Stanfield and Trudeau in the "Great Debate" held prior to the 1968 federal election.

CP (PETER BREGG)

HARDLY ANYONE remembers Pierre Trudeau's days as a CBC-TV interviewer for a simple reason: he wasn't any good.

"Once Trudeau and I were working together on *This Hour*," remembers Larry Zolf. "The subject was timber policy and he was supposed to ask our expert the tough questions. But it wasn't working. He was flat. Halfway through, the floor director handed me a note from [producer] Patrick Watson that said, 'DUMP TRUDEAU, take over the interview — NOW!'"

That was 1965. But after Jean Marchand, then Roy Faibish (another *This Hour* subversive) convinced him to join and then lead the federal Liberal party, Trudeau was no longer a journalist struggling with a script. He was a born-again performer testing the boundaries of an unsuspected talent.

Canada was looking for performers in 1968. Expo 67 had been a great success, and some feared that we'd slip back to the old ways of doing things; that we'd once again be, in one visitor's words, "an archipelago of envy strung along abandoned canoe routes."

So we married Pierre Trudeau, or voted for him anyway. Trudeau defeated Robert Winters in the Liberal leadership convention in April, then trounced Robert Stanfield's Conservatives in June 1968. In between, there was a televised leadership debate on CBC — this country's first — watched by nine million Canadians.

Trudeau was drab and listless in that debate. Peter Newman said of his performance, "The substance of Trudeau's discourse was solid enough, but he managed to look

Trudeau playing to the camera (and country) seconds after learning that the 1968 Liberal convention had elected him leader of the party.
CP (CHUCK MITCHELL)

disdainful while delivering his lines, like a thinned-down Marlon Brando who's just too bored with the squares to do much more than speed-talk his way through their games. What's worse, he's combed the charisma right out of his hair, in an attempt to do what? look like a bank president?"

But then, Trudeau was never good at television — he was good *on* television. (Marshall McLuhan once suggested that the politician's sculptured face was a mask for the electronic age.) Arguably he'd won our attention and votes with previous, unscripted turns in front of a camera. Maybe he was elected in May 1968 when, during a St. Jean Baptiste Day riot in Montreal, he refused to abandon the reviewing stand and sat, scowling at the crowd (and camera), while Coke bottles flew past his head.

Then there was the backflip off a diving board on a Florida holiday. And the time a reporter asked him, "What about your Mercedes?" and he answered, "Do you mean the car or the girl?"

Trudeau understood that television was about gestures and sound bites. He never made a great speech at the Ottawa leadership convention, but people remembered how, upon receiving news that he'd been named leader, he freed a yellow carnation from his lapel, put it between his teeth, then tossed it to the crowd.

And the justice minister who borrowed the line "The state has no business in the bedrooms of the nation" from a *Globe and Mail* editorial had a knack for capturing our attention in perfect TV sound bites — "reason above passion" ..."fuddle duddle"..."just watch me."

Like all great screen performers, Pierre Trudeau was a man of secrets. And the camera loves hidden truths. "He was," wrote biographer Richard Gwyn, "the elusive jester who dared us to catch him and laughed as we tried."

Once upon a time, not long ago

CUSTOMS OFFICIALS STOPPED the Friendly Giant when he tried to pass from Wisconsin into Canada in the summer of 1958 with a station wagon full of medieval props.

No, Friendly wasn't too tall. Bob Homme, the creator and star of CBC's most popular children's show ever, was actually of medium height and build. Rusty the rooster, purchased for a dime at Kresge's, was okay, too. As was Jerome the giraffe. But what were these vines on a castle wall, some kind of exotic plant that might grow to strangle a wheat field?

Homme snapped off a branch and handed it to the border official. See, plastic? His car was waved through.

At first, Homme was glad to be here. Like many American border residents he'd grown up listening to CBC Radio, so when CBC-TV programmer Fred Rainsberry offered him a national show after seeing *The Friendly Giant* at a regional U.S. TV fair, he was thrilled.

But once Homme began work in Toronto, the Friendly Giant turned a mite, well ... grouchy. The secret to his fifteen-minute show back in Madison was that he could scribble a premise, run through his notes with Rusty-Jerome (friend Ken Oste), then wing it.

Where did you go to find a puppeteer rooster-giraffe in Toronto? A local stand-up comedian, Joe Murphy, had a floating falsetto that was perfect for Rusty, but he couldn't ad lib. Homme had to write and memorize a fifteen-minute script every day.

That ruined everything. For once you got over the premise that a giant, a giraffe, and a bagged rooster were palling around a castle, *The Friendly Giant* was supposed to be realistic. Homme insisted on a gently ambling conversa-

tional flow, which was hard to get down on paper. And memorizing dialogue — there were no teleprompters back then — made the show feel stiff.

Worse news: Jerome was proving impossible to cast. Candidates either didn't have a *giraffey* enough voice, or couldn't coordinate the puppet's flapping mouth to their own delivery.

The news that there was an empty costume waiting to be filled on a kids' show quickly spread through CBC's cafeteria, where performers gathered to eat, bum smokes, and gather job leads.

"I was there one day with Bob Goulet," remembers Rod Coneybeare, a journeyman writer-actor-comedian who hustled to make a comfortable, $10,000-a-year income. "Bob said to me, 'Hey, they're looking for a giraffe on *The Friendly Giant*; good job — five days a week.'"

"I'm not interested in any kids' show," Coneybeare huffed. But after leaving Goulet, he began having second thoughts. Like most freelancers, Coneybeare was looking for a steady job. Although just twenty-seven, he'd been in the business twelve years, and the process of selling yourself hard every day, sometimes catching yourself laughing too loud at producers' jokes, was draining.

"So I showed up for an audition and pretty soon I've got my arm up this giraffe," Coneybeare remembers, "And I'm thinking, 'God this is demeaning, I wish I never came in here.' Then Bob asks me a question, 'I understand you do a lot of radio; how's that?' and I answered him as Jerome, my own voice, only a little deeper. 'Well, it's a lot easier than trying to work this silly puppet,' I said."

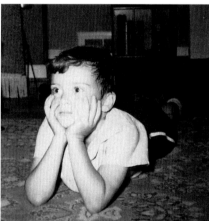

A little boy lost watching his favourite show. Opposite: The friendliest castle on TV.

Homme was impressed that Coneybeare answered as Jerome. But he really perked up when the actor observed that working the giraffe's mouth would be easier if you were looking at a monitor. *This guy understands the process,* Homme must have figured.

Coneybeare was offered and took the job, but *The Friendly Giant* continued to struggle. "I know on TV the castle looked big," Coneybeare recalls, "but it wasn't, and we had two people, Joe Murphy and I, behind the wall. There wasn't much room to tape script pages. After a while, I just started ad libbing my lines."

One day, Homme asked Coneybeare to stick around after work. "I'd like to see if you can do both Rusty and Jerome," he said. "I knew what was up," Coneybeare acknowledges, "and it was hard; nobody likes to push another guy out of a job. But we did [a rehearsal] that night, just the two of us, and it seemed so easy."

Easy was what Homme was going for. The show was supposed to be a toy box sprung to life, with the cast assuming instantly identifiable, reassuring characters: Rusty, his falsetto voice alive with an air of discovery, was the inquisitive little kid. Taller and wiser Jerome, the assured older sibling.

And Friendly was the dad everyone wished they had. Unlike our own fathers, he was at home all the time — *guarding the castle was his job!* — and there was never a question he didn't have time to answer. When winter arrived, Friendly, Rusty, or Jerome might talk about snow. Another show, they'd have a picnic. The stories were as simple and relaxed as an everyday conversation.

And the set-up was always the same: "Once upon a time, not long ago, not far away," Homme would begin, a smile creeping into his voice. After panning the village, the camera introduced us to Friendly, who offered to "hurry over to the castle and go in the back door so I can let the drawbridge down and open the big doors for you."

"Are you ready?" he continued, "Here's my castle." Then as a harp and tin whistle floated into the theme song, "Early One Morning," the drawbridge lowered and we were ushered into a cozy living room, where a giant hand offered "one little chair for one of you, and a bigger chair for two more to curl up in, and for someone who likes to rock, a rocking chair in the middle."

Finally, Friendly asked us to "look up, look waayy up." Soon Rusty stirred from his sack and Jerome would poke his head through the

Puppeteer Rod Coneybeare behind the scenes, working Jerome the giraffe. He and host Bob Homme never made personal appearances, for fear of destroying the illusion of the show.

Tidying up the forest

Shot on a dude ranch outside Toronto, and featuring a Métis guide (Joe Two Rivers) who was in fact a sports car enthusiast from the Ukraine (Michael Zenon), *The Forest Rangers* (1963-65) is as much fun to look back upon as it was to watch.

Any kid who wanted a clubhouse identified with the story of four Junior Forest Rangers (Pete, Mike, Chub, and Kathy) who made cozy an abandoned fort in the mythical town of Indian River.

Mike was always on the ham radio alerting Chief Forest Ranger George Keeley about impending disaster: a fire maybe, or the appearance of shifty strangers. (The kids once caught a Soviet spy in a bear trap.) If all else failed, there was gently authoritative RCMP officer, Sergeant Brian Scott (Gordon Pinsent).

"The show was incredibly linear, yet there were these fantastic things happening to these little kids. I found it very surreal," remembers Pinsent. "And I was astounded later to see the show in colour; it felt like a dream." (The show was shot in colour for foreign sales. Although *The Forest Rangers* played in black and white originally, after 1966 and the advent of colour we saw a picture-postcard Indian River on reruns.)

And hijinks? Virtually every episode had good ol' Uncle Raoul caught up in a lunatic adventure with his pet moose, or the Junior Rangers' best pal, philosopher king Zeke, spouting off in Latin.

The show also promoted sound ecological practices. Chub and Pete got to tidy up the forest while we kids at home were stuck cleaning up our rooms.

The protectors of Indian River from the first season. Bottom row (left to right): Pete (Rex Hagon), Topper, Gaby LaRoche (Syme Jago) who was later replaced by Kathy (Susan Conway), Mike (Peter Tully), and Chub (Ralph Endersby). Top row: Sergeant Scott (Gordon Pinsent), Chief Ranger Keeley (Graydon Gould), and Joe Two Rivers (Michael Zenon). ASP PRODUCTIONS

window — "Hi Friendly!" — and the show was underway.

"The series never changed in twenty-six years, except Bob went from being a father to a grandfather figure," Coneybeare says. "Sometimes a smart young director would come in with a terrific idea. He'd say, 'I got it, let's have a fox.' Bob would just smile, and say, 'No, I think we're all right.'"

Homme believed that young children drew comfort from the familiar. And that to gain a child's friendship, you first had to earn their trust.

"He moved slowly and never raised his voice," Coneybeare recalls. "I like to say he was the Spencer Tracy of children's programming. Very understated. One of the reasons we got along well is we both underplayed. We didn't go for ha-ha jokes. But I like to think there was a droll wit to the show."

Unlike many previous children's shows, the

"Allo mes petits amis"

Hélène Baillargeon's great accomplishment was that she managed to make a cultural directive for preschoolers seem as carefree as a play date with a favourite aunt.

Chez Hélène, which ran from 1959 to 1973, was intended as a French lesson for English children. Hélène spoke French — and Québécois French at that, rolling her r's with evident pleasure — while teenaged friend Louise (Madeleine Kronby) answered in English. As did Susie, a sock mouse (Charlotte Fielder) who always sounded in need of a good shot of 4-in-1 lubricating oil.

A typical 1969 episode offers evidence of the show's slightly surreal, untroubled gaiety. Hélène opens the fridge to discover — "oh-la-la, que-est-ce que ça?" — a pail of snowballs. Louise enters the kitchen in her bathrobe, shivering.

"Guess what's in the bathtub?" she asks.

"Boules de neige?" Hélène offers.

Just then Susie pops up. "Hélène, do you mind if I stick snow in your washing machine?" the mouse asks. Hélène looks at Louise, then the camera, her lips a wide circle of surprise. "There's going to be a snow failure, or if you prefer a snow shortage," a worried Susie explains. "That's what the weather mouse on the mouse hour said ... No more snow this winter."

Hélène's shoulders relax and she breaks into a relieved chuckle. Another small problem easily solved. Then our guardian-host reads Louise and Susie a story about an *homme de neige* while kids at home watch a cheerful, cut-paper animated story of a snowman skiing the gentlest of hills. Later, they all sing a song. Then — *what's that?* — absurdly large snowflakes can be seen dancing in Hélène's window. (Props probably should have cut the paper a little finer.) Susie, of course, is overjoyed. Now everyone is happy.

The hope of *Chez Hélène* was that kids watching at home were building a bilingual nation while the storybook children constructed an *homme de neige* on screen. And if that never happened, you can't blame Baillargeon, whose quest to learn English demonstrated an obvious personal commitment to biculturalism. The last of twelve children, she grew up in a Quebec village, Saint-Martin de la Beauce, where English lessons were a punishment for misbehaviour at school.

After *Chez Hélène* ended, in 1973, Prime Minister Trudeau made the folk singer-actress-performer a judge in the Montreal offices of the Canadian Citizen Court, where she continued to serve the nation until her retirement in 1981.

---

performers didn't fool around much in rehearsal, although the puppeteer remembers convulsing Homme once after a summer hiatus.

"This was a rehearsal, we were getting back in the swing of things, and Bob, as Friendly, asked Rusty what he'd done over the summer. 'Oh, I had a terrible summer,' I told him. 'Why was that?' he asked. 'Well, I got a job I just didn't enjoy at all,' I replied. 'Really, what job was that?' Friendly asked, going along. Then Rusty blurts, '*I was a Judas chicken for Colonel Sanders!*' Well, the idea of Rusty the rooster leading a

flock of chickens into the Colonel's kitchen was just too much for Bob. He kept on laughing and laughing."

With more than three thousand episodes, *The Friendly Giant* was CBC-TV's signature children's program for twenty-six years. The children who first watched the series and identified with Rusty were, a quarter-century later, watching the show with their own kids and marvelling at the gracious ease with which Bob Homme conducted a family discussion.

Still, when the show went off the air in

Opposite: A friendly jam session. Multi-instrumentalist Bob Homme with familiar accompanists Jerome and Rusty.

Above: Hélène Baillargeon and Madeleine Kronby talk to Susie the mouse.

1984, Coneybeare assumed the program would drift from public consciousness. Which is why his sadness at Homme's passing, in 2000, was tempered by a grateful joy. So many people remembered.

"And it wasn't just that people remembered his name," his old colleague and friend says.

"They remembered what Bob Homme stood for. The things that everyone said and wrote — that the show helped children, or that *The Friendly Giant* was an island of calm for children — why, that's what Bob was trying to accomplish all those years. We wanted the show to be a child's friend."

Calling young Canada

If you went to school through the late '50s, '60s, and into the '70s, you were likely in a classroom audience for the National School Broadcasts on CBC. By 1960, there were two half-hour morning National School telecasts a week. Teachers would put a TV in the front of the classroom (the guide suggests "Turn on the set at least two minutes before the program begins, to allow the tubes to warm up") and students would watch, say, William Hutt reciting Shakespeare or Percy Saltzman discussing uranium ore and how to use a Geiger counter. There was Dr. Ivey and Dr. Hume and "The Ideas of Physics," and a teenaged boy carrying out all the steps in making maple sugar using a dummy tree set up in the CBC studios. At the end of the broadcasts, teachers would lead a discussion following the materials prepared by the CBC.

A May 17, 1964 CBC school lesson offered an imaginary look at a computer class in 2064 — five children dressed as medieval bees being taught by a robot instructor standing in front of a mainframe.

Eleven-year-old Michelle Finney hosted the popular after-school show *Razzle Dazzle* (1961-66) in its first years. Later, she co-hosted *Time of Your Life* (1963-65), a program for older kids.

"*Howard was like a father to me*"

MY FATHER CAME from English theatre and worked at the CBC as crew chief for *Open House* and *Tabloid*. One day, *Open House* had a woman from a children's modelling school on and my father thought this would be good for me, because I was so shy. So I went to The Estelle Modelling Agency, at the corner of Eglinton and Yonge. Unbelievably, as soon as I got on stage a completely new persona emerged.

CBC-TV was holding auditions and I went. My father was funny. Going home he told me how this is a "difficult business" and there will be other opportunities. Finally, he asked, "How about getting a budgie?"

But I guess I was noticed. I got called for *The Forest Rangers*, then they changed their minds and put me in *Razzle Dazzle*. It was a different concept: a five-day-a-week variety show for kids. I'd go to school mornings and be at the studio by noon, for rehearsal. We'd go to air at 4, then I was whisked back home and allowed twenty minutes for dinner, then I had three hours tutoring and another half-hour to go over the next day's show.

Coming from English theatre, my parents were strict. I came to work prepared, not like Al Hamel. The joke on set was "Where did Al tape his script?" He never learned his lines. He would tape it on the back of another actor if he could.

Everyone was protective of me. Howard the Turtle — John Keogh — was like a father. Wonderful man. And very professional. When he stepped in the box, cigar and all, he wasn't John anymore, he became the turtle and everyone referred to him as Howard, didn't matter if we were off air.

I was still doing the show when I went to Jarvis Collegiate. It wasn't really a normal high school life; everyone was intimidated by me and I didn't really do the whole prom

thing. I traded a lot for my experience at CBC. But that's okay. The show was live — sets would fall down, magic tricks didn't work. So I learned how to think on my feet. And I loved the people. My father gave me the best advice about the business: "Know the people you work with." And I did. We would all go out afterwards. Looking back, it all seems like *Happy Days*. But really, it was a golden age.

We had 120,000 fan club members! My father made sure I answered every fan letter. Most asked for autographs, but I also got letters from kids who just wanted someone to talk to. I'm glad I answered, because even today I get people going through hope chests and finding one of my letters, and they write me again to say thanks. Isn't that nice?

Above: Our favourite turtle, Howard. Cigar-smoking puppeteer John Keogh once told alarmed young viewers who phoned in that the smoke in the studio was Howard having a campfire under his shell. CANADIAN MUSEUM OF CIVILIZATION

Below (left to right): Al Hamel, hungry Howard, and Michelle Finney.

Cold war

*H*OCKEY NIGHT IN CANADA'S on-air staff were willing captives in the nine-year war (1959-67) that saw the Montreal Canadiens and Toronto Maple Leafs battle seven times in the Stanley Cup playoffs.

Montreal fans called Toronto *HNIC* colour man Brian McFarlane "Brian McMapleleaf," while Leaf enthusiasts spat out the name of Habs' broadcaster Dick Irvin as if they'd bitten into bad fruit.

"Dick and I used to talk about it," McFarlane remembers. "He'd say to me, 'What am I supposed to do if Béliveau has a big night, downplay it just because half the country are Leaf fans?'"

Once, Irvin was in Edmonton attending a party when a friend who worked at *HNIC* sponsor Imperial Oil showed him a letter from a fan. The man was returning his gas credit card to protest Irvin's work in a 7-2 Montreal win over Toronto. Another guest knew the complainant, a Calgary employee of Royalite Oil. Irvin asked for his number and was soon on the phone:

"This is Dick Irvin of *Hockey Night in Canada.*"

"Uh, oh yes."

"I understand you wrote a letter to Imperial Oil because you were upset with my work."

"Yes, that's right.... I'm such a Maple Leaf fan I couldn't stand to listen to you that night. You drove me up the wall."

Just as Irvin suspected. Swallowing a sigh, he continued. "Sir, you know I'm the colour commentator and my job is to describe the replays after each goal."

"Yes, I know."

"Let's see now. Canadiens scored seven goals and each one was replayed probably twice. That means you had to watch the puck go into your team's net about twenty-one times. Was that my fault?"

Below, left: Brian McFarlane and cameraman Al Momford. That's an early Pittsburgh Penguin jersey behind them. The team had a real penguin mascot in 1967.

Below, right: A placid observer in the Montreal-Toronto hockey wars, Dick Irvin.
TOMMY THOMSON & CO.

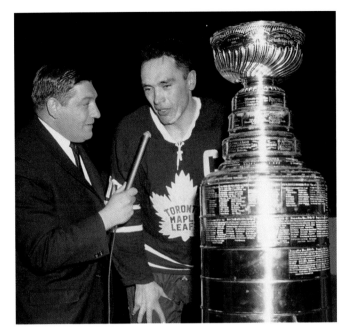

"No."

To hockey fans under the age of forty, the great Leaf-Canadien rivalry must seem as remote as the nineteenth-century competition for beaver tails between the Hudson's Bay and North West companies. Yes, the two teams get together three or four times a year and the affairs are sweetly nostalgic, but other than the respective coaches, no one loses any sleep, let alone changes credit cards when their team loses.

But back in the '60s, the Canadiens' centre, Henri Richard, refused to budge from his house in the summers following a playoff loss to the Leafs. "He was just too embarrassed and ashamed to go outside," former teammate Bryan Watson explains.

One God! Two hockey teams! was how it was in Canada for close to four decades. "The arrival of TV turned Canada into a battleground between Leaf and Canadien fans," Irvin recalls. "Toronto wasn't very good in the '50s, and Montreal, with the Rocket, Béliveau, and Doug Harvey, had maybe the best team ever. Then when the Leafs improved under [coach Punch] Imlach you had this heated rivalry that just got hotter and hotter."

Although no one knew it at the time, the 1967 Stanley Cup final was the rivalry's final chapter. By then, kids following the game knew the players better than the friends with whom they traded hockey cards and yellow-and-orange Beatles 45s. Progressing through school

we recognized Canadiens and Leafs in our own lives. The kid who wore a tie to school photo day and sponsored a foster child in India was Jean Béliveau. An Henri Richard character was quiet, dependable — married his first girlfriend. For the Leafs, Ron Ellis types pitched in to help with props for school plays. The class clown who collapsed an EAT MORE candy wrapper to read EAT ME, then slipped it into Miss Krause's desk? Eddie Shack.

In 1967 the Leafs, who had won everything in 1962, 1963, and 1964, had been through a hard series against Chicago. Montreal, a younger, faster team, had beaten Toronto the two previous seasons (then gone on to take the 1965 and 1966 Stanley Cups). Everything pointed to another Canadien championship, particularly after Montreal's easy opening 5-2 win. But Toronto took the next game 3-0, as forty-two-year-old goalie Johnny Bower was a blur between the pipes for the Leafs.

The series' third game, a see-saw overtime affair in Toronto, was so close, so tense that Leaf owner Stafford Smythe couldn't watch the extra periods and left Maple Leaf Gardens to wander Carlton Street, listening to hear who won. It must have been eerie for Smythe that night, wandering outside a building crammed with fifteen thousand fans, yet unable to hear anything but the echo of his own steps on the sidewalk.

"When people ask what hockey meant back

JOHN
BOCCABELLA
C-1B

EXPOS

"Et maintenant, and now, le receveur, the catcher, Johhhhn Boccccabellllllllaaa!"

They weren't very good, but in the glorious summer of 1969, the Montreal Expos were the best (and only!) Canadian major league baseball team ever.

Maybe mistakes were half the fun. *Hey, it was their first year.* In one double-header, four parachutists were to descend onto the pitcher's mound between games. Three missed Jarry Park. And in one loss, the team made five errors, prompting coach Gene Mauch to say, "We owe Abner Doubleday an apology." After the team dropped twenty in a row, Coco Laboy and Manny Mota asked a priest for a blessing. Mauch's only comment: "I'm just glad they didn't ask for last rites."

Nevertheless, we enjoyed watching Expo games, which were broadcast by Dave Van Horne. (CBC televised the first major league game played outside the U.S., an 8-7 Montreal win over St. Louis, on April 14, 1969.) Expos that first year included John Boccabella (whom the P.A. announcer introduced as "Johhhhn Boccccabellllllllaaa!"), Elroy Face, Mudcat Grant, and Le Grand Orange, Rusty Staub. The pitching coach, as everyone remembers, was Calvin Coolidge Julius Caesar Tuskahoma McLish.

then, I always remember one night," Irvin recalls. "I was working late, and I drove home through a major street in Montreal. The city was empty. No people or cars. Yet it wasn't much past suppertime. What the heck was going on? Then I remembered, ah, Leafs and Canadiens were playing in the finals, in Toronto. Everyone, and I mean everyone, was watching the game on TV."

What everyone but Stafford Smythe saw that third game in Toronto was Leaf Bob Pulford, his skates planted on the edge of the Montreal crease, ending a deliciously tense eighty-eight-

minute struggle by redirecting an errant Jim Pappin backhand past a startled Rogatien Vachon.

Montreal took the next game, with murderous efficiency, 6–2, and Toronto surprised the Canadiens in their home rink, 4–1. The next game was back in Toronto.

The Canadiens were bold — continuously in motion, hurtling themselves at the crowded Leaf blue line. In the face of all that fury, the Leafs were imperturbable, cautious. This supremely coordinated defensive team always felt it was ahead in a tie game. As Dick Beddoes,

Dave Van Horne (left) and Bob McDevitt back when baseball was big in Montreal.

INSIDE BASEBALL

expos

the *Globe and Mail* sportswriter, might have said, "The game was so tense you could've grated carrots on fans' goosebumps."

To go on any further might court disfavour with old Canadiens fans. Suffice to say Toronto won a brilliantly played game, 3-1, to take the Stanley Cup. For those keeping score, that was the last Leaf team to win the Stanley Cup. Montreal, of course, went on to win another eight championships.

"Was I jealous that Montreal won in '68 and '69? Of course I was," says Brian McFarlane, who teamed with play-by-play man Bill Hewitt (Foster's son) on *HNIC*'s Leaf team this decade. "You know why? Because we got paid by the game. And when the Leafs went out of the playoffs, I used to say, son of a gun, if the playoffs go fourteen games, Dick Irvin and Danny Gallivan are going to make an extra $5,000 or whatever. But at the end I always thought, good for Dick and Danny, good for Montreal...."

For his part, Dick Irvin reports that the complaints about his being a homer dried up after expansion and Leaf inefficiency dissolved the Toronto-Montreal rivalry. "Something changed — maybe some fans just weren't as passionate about the sport," he says.

Mind you, he still gets complaints about alleged Montreal bias from back in the '60s.

"It's funny — I was talking to the great Leaf centre, Dave Keon, three years ago," Irvin remembers, "and he said to me, 'Remember that playoff in Montreal in '64? We beat Montreal 3-1, in your rink. I scored all three goals, and I was third star that night. Third star! Geez, what did you have to do in Montreal to get first star?'"

A really Grey Cup

The Winnipeg Blue Bombers and Hamilton Tiger Cats challenged each other for the Grey Cup in 1957-59, 1961-62, and '65, but the game everyone remembers is the one no one really saw — from the stands or in rec rooms across the country.

"The infamous 1962 'Fog Bowl' at the Ex in Toronto was truly bizarre," remembers veteran CFL broadcaster Bill Stephenson. "The game began on Saturday and ended Monday due to fog. In the press box, we would see the ball go up and disappear into the fog.... We couldn't tell if the pass was complete!"

Exhibition Stadium is close to Lake Ontario, which was as cold as December when a warm front moved in that Sunday, creating a sour fog that swallowed the stadium whole. Nevertheless, Bomber quarterback Kenny Ploen flew down the field at peak efficiency, leading the Bombers to a 28-27 advantage with 9:12 left.

That's when the fog became as thick as a sweater, forcing CFL commissioner G. Sydney Halter to postpone the game. Afterwards, Ticat lineman Angelo Mosca invited teammate Bob Minihane to go downtown. "Now there must be ten thousand cabs in Toronto," Mosca remembers. "We flag one down and coach [Jim 'We'll waffle 'em!'] Trimble piles out and says, 'Where the hell do you think you guys are going?' I said, 'We're going for a soda.' Trimble says, 'Soda my ass ... get back in your room.'"

The players returned to their quarters, but it didn't matter; both teams failed to score the following day.

The football game that everybody watched and nobody saw — the 1962 Fog Bowl. CANADA'S SPORTS HALL OF FAME

TV GOES TO THE NORTH

TELEVISION ARRIVED IN the North when Yellowknife received a CBC "frontier package" — a transmitter and a playback machine — in 1967. Four hours of taped coverage was flown up daily. The service attracted a great many viewers, but not many satisfied customers.

Most northern communities soon had their own frontier packages, which meant it took time for tapes to complete the circuit. As one viewer put it, "There's nothing like a week-old hockey game ... to make you feel part of the nation."

That all changed in 1973 when the Anik satellite was launched, bringing full network coverage to Canada's North. Inuit boys in Tuktoyaktuk told a reporter that their favourite sports team was the Edmonton Eskimos, although one fan noted, "They didn't look like the Eskimos in Tuk."

In Frobisher Bay, the entire Hudson's Bay TV inventory was sold the day satellite TV arrived. Villages were alive with talk of "the round thing" (there is no word for "puck" in Inuktitut) and the "talking frog" (Kermit).

Community leaders, however, quickly grew alarmed at the threat TV posed to their culture and languages, and pushed hard for programs that reflected the culture of the North. *Our Ways*, the North's first homegrown program, came to air in 1979. *Focus North*, Marie Wilson's weekly newsmagazine show, provided stories ranging from European seal boycotts to the fire that burned down Slim Semmler's fur trading store in Inuvik. *Focus North* (1982-94) was soon the most popular program in the Mackenzie Valley, frequently beating out *Hockey Night in Canada*. In 1995, CBC North went daily with evening news — in English and Inuktitut — on *Northbeat*.

CBC North serves one-third of Canada, broadcasting in four time zones in Nunavut, the Northwest Territories, and the Yukon and in ten languages — English, French, Inuktitut, North and South Slavey, Dogrib, Chipewyan, Inuvialuktun, Gwich'in, and Cree (where the language used isn't English, there are English subtitles).

Cameraman Doug MacKay shoots a scene near Pelly Bay for the 1960 CBC program High Arctic Hunter. *It would be nearly twenty years before northerners were able to produce their own CBC-TV programs.*
DOUGLAS WILKINSON/ NWT ARCHIVES

Above: Shooting a fuel supply truck on the Lupin winter road in the Northwest Territories, for a Focus North *story.* JIRI HERMANN

Left: Former Focus North *host Marie Wilson stands in front of the satellite dish outside the CBC building in Yellowknife.* JIRI HERMANN

Welcome to the...

CBC

TRANSMISSION CENTRE

SEEING THE COUNTRY

THE DECADE FOLLOWING Expo saw a surge of nationalism, with Canadian content quotas for radio, television, and magazines falling into place. We had warm memories of Expo and a philosopher-king in Ottawa.

Canada wasn't always "in," however. *King of Kensington* star Al Waxman once told Knowlton Nash about his first trip to the CBC building on Jarvis Street in Toronto.

"I sat there in the lobby and heard all these rich sounds coming down the corridor," Waxman remembered. And as the voices of the actors, every one a Gentleman of Verona, it seemed, mingled with the sparkling pure BBC English of staff announcers, young Al was gripped with a sudden fear.

"I wondered if I was going to have a problem with my accent," Waxman said.

"What was your accent?" a puzzled Nash asked.

"Canadian."

By the '70s, however, Al was safe. Where '50s and '60s dramatic specials were frequently studio interpretations of classic and contemporary theatre, the success of location shooting on *Wojeck* and *Quentin Durgens, MP*, meant that almost all '70s dramas were shot outdoors, preferably with a brawling river or snow-topped mountain somewhere in the background. Inevitably, these stories were as big and Canadian as the Rockies — Riel screaming revolution! or Sir John A. whipping a railroad across the nation's spine in *The National Dream*.

And where *Wojeck* and *Quentin Durgens* were urban weekly dramas, featuring actors who migrated to Hollywood, the real star of the series *Adventures in Rainbow Country* (1970-71) and *The Beachcombers* (1972-91) was Canada itself.

Above: The "C" logo, often referred to as the "exploding pizza," was designed in 1974 by Burton Kramer.

Left: Al Waxman was the King of Kensington. Set in the heart of Toronto, his kingdom was a multicultural oasis.

Filmmaker Janet Foster in an episode of This Land. *At one point in 1970, three nature-documentary series —* This Land, This Land of Ours, *and* Audubon Wildlife Theatre *— appeared on the network.* JOHN FOSTER

The picture-postcard scenery certainly found a ready audience. *Rainbow Country* recorded the highest ratings of any Canadian dramatic series, with a following that occasionally topped four-and-a-half million. And *The Beachcombers* was exported to more than forty countries, including Gabon and Nepal.

Significantly, the '70s also saw the CBC draw upon defining characteristics from previous eras, marrying the creative impulse of Mavor Moore and Stuart Griffiths's genre-blurring '50s programming to the social activism of NFB-inspired '60s public affairs shows. The result was journalistic dramas, or docudramas.

The groundbreaking series here was network head of drama John Hirsch's *For the Record*, a weekly anthology showcase that was ripped, as they say, from the day's headlines. Occasionally the series made its own news, as when director Peter Pearson's *Tar Sands*, the story of negotiations over Alberta's oil reserve, led to a lawsuit from the province's then-premier, Peter Lougheed (portrayed in the program by Kenneth Welsh).

"The essence of good television," Hirsch once said in explaining *For the Record*'s mandate to capture real-life drama, "is that viewers recognize themselves in what's on the screen."

Sometimes not all viewers liked what they saw. Director Martyn Burke's *Connections*, a 1977 and 1979 documentary investigation into mob activity in Canada, resulted in eight more lawsuits.

But the form and spirit of risk-taking TV adventures like *For the Record*, *Connections*, and the network's new investigative series, *the fifth estate*, which began in 1975, would prove irreversible. And in subsequent decades, public affairs shows like *The Journal* and *Undercurrents*, along with docudramas and documentaries the calibre of *Love and Hate* and *The Valour and the Horror*, would continue to spark debate and, occasionally, outrage.

Artwork for This Land *created, appropriately enough, by CBC graphic designer Vicki Land.*

High school confidential

TO THIS DAY, Shelagh Rogers can't hear a doorbell ring without cringing.

That's because in 1972 the CBC Radio host attended Lisgar, Ottawa's most prestigious public high school, and was one of five students who volunteered for a *Reach for the Top* contest against Glebe, the city's other big forehead factory.

Only problem was that CBC's high school quiz show required four panellists, not five, and Shelagh drew short straw. It didn't matter that the seventeen-year-old was a Latin whiz and knew Canadian paintings like some kids knew hockey cards. Shelagh was a spare.

Right: Reach for the Top *contestant and future CBC Radio host Shelagh Rogers in a 1972 yearbook photo.*
COURTESY SHELAGH ROGERS

Below: RFTT *instruction booklet mailed to all quiz-show gladiators before their TV appearance.*

"Mr. Weatherspoon, our coach, thought being from Lisgar we were all fit representatives," recalls Rogers, a trace of hysteria edging into her voice. "*He didn't know anything about the show!*"

Rogers couldn't convince her coach that an elite *RFTT* team was as varied and specifically trained as a crew of bank robbers. You needed a generalist who liked sports, music, movies, and knew where all the oceans were. Your captain. Then came specialists — inevitably a squinting math expert, a history buff ("The Treaty of Utrecht!"), and a moody Emily Dickinson loner who lived for poetry and art.

"I sat in the control room the day of the show," Rogers remembers. "And there were all these questions I knew. And my teammates were just so … so quiet. I mean they were way better than me in a lot of things — I would've

been useless in math — but those were my questions they weren't getting. Oh, I should've been out there. I couldn't take it. I was dying."

"Scramble round, teams," Ottawa moderator Brian Smith would begin. "Which Canadian artist painted this famous landscape?"

"*Bzzzzzt.*"

While Lisgar's finest were lost in an old Charlie Farquharson routine — was it Tom Thomson, Jack Jackson, or Jim Jimson? — Glebe answered "Lawren Harris."

"Okay teams, snapper round. How are we in Latin?"

Rogers buried her face in her hands as her friends frowned at the camera. Shelagh knew Latin. Not just the stuff that goes on statues, but tricky past-tense verb conjugations, jokes even (*semper ubi sub ubi* — "always where under where").

"*Bzzzzt.*"

"A Mari usque ad Mare!"

Glebe won. Which to Rogers was worse than Lisgar losing. To think that Glebees were out in the parking lot after the show, chanting "Two bits, four bits, six bits a dollar, everyone from Glebe stand up and holler!" drove her into a silent fury. She couldn't talk to her teammates after the game.

"That loss on public television really stayed with me a long time," Rogers admits. "And I know it was because of the humiliation of that show that I went out next year and campaigned hard for Head Girl and won. Not so much because I needed to win but because I wouldn't allow myself to fail again in public."

Taking things a tad too seriously? Hardly. In fact, Shelagh and Lisgar lost because they failed to understand the degree of fanaticism required to make it to the summit of *Reach for the Top*, a CBC institution that began in Vancouver in 1961, swept across the country in 1966, and lasted for twenty years.

Peter Kenter, author of *TV North*, explains

what kind of commitment was required to succeed on the show:"[At Lord Dorchester High in] London, Ontario, we had twelve intramural *Reach for the Top* teams going all year." When a buzzer came free on the TV team, the school's full-time teacher-coach had close to fifty crack *RFTT* cadets to choose from.

"We tried our best to simulate the *Reach for the Top* set," Kenter says. "We built our own panels, which were wired with buzzers and bells. We got *Reach for the Top* to send us old questions for practice. But even that wasn't enough to satisfy our voracious appetites, so we composed our own questions.... I'd say we spent about thirteen hours a week preparing, studying, and competing."

All that work gave *RFTT*ers the usual after-school club perks: fun, companionship, an opportunity to prove yourself, plus an intoxicating dividend you couldn't get anywhere else. "Today there are so many community cable channels, anyone can get on TV," Kenter

explains. "But growing up in London in the '70s, the only way you were going to make it on television was getting hit by a bus or making *Reach for the Top*.

"And once you got on, it became addictive," he adds. "There were no prizes, really. Just books for your school library. You didn't get dates out of it, no, that's for sure. But there was internal recognition — success offered indisputable proof that you were smart. And the further you went, the more comfortable you became. I really started to enjoy and count on appearing on TV. It was such an adrenalin high."

Kenter's quartet called themselves the Fighting Turtles, a mock tribute to *Razzle Dazzle*'s tortoise, Howard. Peter was the team's pop culture expert. He and the other specialists also had a private arsenal of educated guesses, developed after years of careful *RFTT* study, to help them out in tight jams.

"If you saw snow in a painting, it was Cornelius Krieghoff," Kenter says. "Any British

Queen Elizabeth H.S. won the RFTT *trophy in 1975, overcoming a formal Manitoba assault. "It was an attempt to psych us out," recalls Howard Green (top left), now anchor of ROB-TV. "Didn't work, thanks to my teammates."*

RFTT moderators Alex Trebek (left) and Bill Paul in 1968. Trebek went on to host the short-lived CBC game show Strategy *in 1969, before taking his quiz-show smarts to the U.S., where he updated* Jeopardy.

painter you didn't know was Constable, any Canadian painter you didn't know was Lawren Harris ... and anything in old English was Chaucer."

The Fighting Turtles were a good club league team. Inevitably, however, the Fighting T's came up against a team that was better prepared or more cutthroat than their own.

"One year we played a team where one guy beat us on all the art questions because he buzzed before the painting was shown," Kenter remembers. "Then the painting would come up and he'd guess the right answer. We were stunned ... furious."

And when the siren came on to signal the end of the game, losers.

"That siren was weird," he says. "When you won, it was the sound of triumph. But when you lost it sounded just like an air-raid siren: *here come the bombs, our defences have failed.*"

Some critics thought *Reach for the Top* was

too much like feeding time in a shark tank. "The quiz kids ... scratch and claw for every point, lips smacking and eyes glittering," Heather Robertson commented in *Maclean's.* "The losers swear into the microphones."

Shelagh Rogers thinks the show was another demonstration of a watchful nation's need to celebrate its vigilance. "I don't think it's a coincidence Canadians invented the Trivial Pursuit board game," she says. "Or that shows like *Reach for the Top* were hits. Or that Alex Trebek [former Toronto *RFTT* and current *Jeopardy* host] is a Canadian. We love proving we know what's going on, and are sometimes a little bit smug about it." (A new version of *RFTT* — *SmartAsk* — with quizmaster Justin Landry began on TV in spring 2002.)

In the '70s, our prideful attentiveness was regarded as a civic virtue on *This Is the Law* (1971-76), a game show that asked panellists Larry Solway, Hart Pomerantz, and Bill Charlton to identify arcane Canadian laws. (Paul Soles acted out the crimes like a baggy-pants vaudevillian.)

Unlike the adult panellists on other game shows, though, many of the ten thousand or so young participants on *Reach for the Top* were in some small way haunted by the show.

"One question I got wrong bugged me for years," Kenter remembers. "The question was, 'Which was the first Disney … ' I pressed down my buzzer and answered *Steamboat Willie*, which was Disney's first short. Turned out I was wrong; the question was, 'Which was his first feature film?' *Snow White and the Seven Dwarfs*, of course. Oh, I was mortified afterwards. I don't think I stopped thinking about that one until I was at least thirty."

For her part, Rogers has never let go of the hot shame of her team's 1972 performance. "Even today I can't have doorbells on any place I'm living," she says.

Above: On location at Winnipeg's Westwood Collegiate in 1973 with national quiz master Bill Guest.

Right: The 1967 RFTT champs from Edmonton — (from left to right) John Rasmussen, Janet Mizera, Dianne Hay, and John Day — show off their trophy.

Mini-me's

WHILE BRIGHT YOUNG minds sparred on *Reach for the Top*, many of our most promising young comics traded jokes on *Coming Up Rosie*, *The Hart and Lorne Terrific Hour*, and *Drop In*, or appeared in episodes of sitcoms or children's series.

Above: Michael J. Fox in a 1978 production of T.H. White's The Master, *from The Magic Lie series.*

Below, left: Lorne Michaels and Hart Pomerantz (in Beaver Power suit) on The Hart and Lorne Terrific Hour.

Below, right: Cowpokes Mike Myers and David Ferry on the children's series Range Ryder and the Calgary Kid *in 1977. Mini-me Myers also popped up on* The King of Kensington.

Coming Up Rosie's *Rosemary Radcliffe (seated) lived in an apartment complex populated by oddballs Wally Wypyzypywchuk (John Candy, far right), proprietor of Sleep-Tite Burglar Alarms and contributor to "Almost True Burglar Alarm Stories," and Ding-a-Ling Answering Service rep Myrna Wallbacker (Catherine O'Hara, inset). The building's janitor was Purvis Bickle (Dan Aykroyd, third from right).*

Eveningside

After Angelo Mosca's out-of-bounds attack on Willie Fleming in the 1963 Grey Cup, the worst case of piling-on in our TV history was the critical response to Peter Gzowski's *90 Minutes Live* (1976-78).

No, the late-night show wasn't a success. On radio, Gzowski used the reporter's trick of making guests feel that an on-the-record interview was a kitchen party schmooze. A clapping TV studio audience blew his cover. A silent crowd made him nervous.

Still, *90 Minutes* occasionally got "talk" right, even if "show" remained a problem. The program was best when taped outside Toronto and the strangling clotheslines of invective from local critics. Three nights in St. John's, where tickets were scalped on the street, provided inspired lunacy with Monty Pythoners Graham Chapman and Terry Jones. On another night, Canada and the host were happily lost in space with panellists Kurt Vonnegut, David Suzuki, and Timothy Leary.

Like the more successful docudrama series *For the Record*, Gzowski's show was an adventurous bid to mix program genres, combining interview journalism with showbiz elements. The host gave it the ol' college try, but it turned out that a different kind of education was necessary for a late-night talk show.

The network would try a late-night variety show again in the '90s in the form of *Friday Night! with Ralph Benmergui*, with similar results.

Halifax town crier Peter Cox with Peter Gzowski and John Candy on 90 Minutes Live *in 1976.*

Green alligators, white jumpsuits

MUSIC WAS PRESENTED as a cultural dynamic in the '60s, whether it was the O'Keefe Centre Doors-Jefferson Airplane youth-quake or Catherine McKinnon sharing her Halifax library research for authentic folk material on *Singalong Jubilee*. In the '70s, music was entertainment again, as it was in the '50s. But instead of black and white, shows were shot in alligator green and disco-ball silver. Which is another way of saying that the most popular new CBC music shows were *The Irish Rovers* (1971-75) and *The René Simard Show* (1977-79).

It was hard not to like the Rovers, singing shepherds who escorted "green alligators and long-necked geese, humpty-back camels and chimpanzees" onto Noah's Ark (yet never quite got their mitts on a unicorn). Belfast boyo Jimmy Ferguson met fellow Ulsterman George Millar while working in a Toronto adhesive

tape factory. They sang together, then picked up two more Millars (Will and Joe) along with Wilcil McDowell. After roving across Canada they drove south to San Francisco, where they became stars.

By 1971 they had translated their international hit, "Unicorn," into a CBC series produced in Vancouver. Shows usually began with a fast-bouncing drinking song, and ended with a declaration of working-class solidarity ("May the wind always blow at your back, and may your house be free of rent ...").

In between came an eclectic, tasteful mix of country-music guests — Anne Murray, Lonnie Donnegan, Johnny Cash, Tom T. Hall — plus lots of party jokes, some dreadful, many as good as anything your favourite uncle told before being escorted outside at family mixers.

A typical skit had Jimmy Ferguson attending

Right: The Irish Rovers (from left to right): Wilcil McDowell, Will Millar, Jimmy Ferguson, Joe Millar, and George Millar.

Opposite: René Simard leads with his chin at Disco René in 1977. The Quebec mighty mite had astonished Frank Sinatra at the Tokyo Song Festival five years earlier. "Kid," Sinatra advised, "never grow up."

confession before a priest, who keeps score of the sins committed by drawing lines with chalk on his sleeve:

"Father, I was out with a girl last night."

"Well, that'll do for a start." The priest draws a line below his shoulder.

"Father, I took her for a walk down a long, dark country lane."

"Glory be, it's getting worse." Another mark.

"Father, we went to the graveyard."

"The graveyard! Consecrated ground!"

Now the priest is wearing sergeant's stripes.

"Then Father we ..."

"Oh, I bet ya did." Another bold slash. "Who was the girl now? Out with it!"

"Iris Sprague, Father."

A pause.

"Well, is she not a Protestant?"

"Yes, she is, Father."

The annoyed priest wipes at his sleeve, shouting, "Why the hell didn't you say that before?"

A few afternoon cocktails

At Ease with Elwood Glover was a popular CBC Radio show in the '50s. The title captured the host's implacable calm. Once Glover sampled contaminated ice cream — a stagehand saw bugs around and gave the dessert a blast of fly-tox — but Elwood still delivered the pitch "If it's Borden's, it's got to be good" with a ready smile, before racing to the hospital to have his stomach pumped.

After seventeen years of doing *Luncheon Date* on radio and TV, hosting a live wedding ceremony with a country and western star was another day at the office for Glover. Which was good, because on November 2, 1973, groom Stompin' Tom Connors was as nervous as a cat in a room full of rockers. The pre-wedding fussing at home was bad enough. Then studio "dabbers" (makeup artists) got hold of him.

Ever the pro, Glover held the event together, interviewing celebrities, including New Brunswick premier Richard Hatfield, and telling us about Lena, the bride (judiciously avoiding the story of how Tom's first words to her were, "Where'd you get those, Eaton's or Simpsons?" as the tight-sweatered waitress advanced toward him in a bar).

After a gracious ceremony, and before Tom and Lena cut the P.E.I.-shaped wedding cake, Glover's toil ended as Canada's favourite country artist warmed to the ceremony at last. Why? Minutes earlier a Moosehead truck had arrived off-camera with a wedding present: two hundred two-fours, chilled and ready for stompin'.

Luncheon Date was filmed at the Four Seasons Hotel, where the show's luncheon cocktail-hour vibe was provided by the Sonny Caulfield Trio. Enjoying a noon-hour visit are (from left to right) the show's director-producer Drew Crossan, singer Paul Anka, and Elwood Glover.

Songs in the key of life

Hymn Sing was family to almost one million Canadians every week for more than thirty years.

"The audience attached themselves to certain young singers in the sixteen-member chorus," explains long-time producer David Waters. "They would think of them as a sister or nephew."

"Oh, the fuss people made when a singer left," adds the Winnipeg show's music director, Winnifred Sim. "People sent the most heart-rending letters."

Hymn Sing (1965-95) remained steadfastly the same through the years. Hair and fashion styles barely changed. And Waters confirms that viewers would write in if the show didn't get favourite

songs, like "How Great Thou Art" and "Abide With Me," "right." Despite the odd variation on a popular hymn, the half-hour series frequently registered the highest "enjoyment index rating" on CBC.

The singers were like most kids. There was tomfoolery on the road. "One time the guys were horsing around and sent this kite with pop cans and shower caps out the window," Sim remembers. "Hotel security complained. I told them, I'm only the music director. Well, they were just kids."

"And there were a few romances in the choir," Sim says. "One singer, Craig Johnson, proposed to his wife on set. Bent down on his knee and everything. A cameraman filmed it."

Although *Hymn Sing* went off the air in 1995, its music remains with us. "Many of the singers are music ministers in churches or teaching music in schools," Sim reports.

She believes the power of song is what kept *Hymn Sing* eternal. "When I was four, I sat down at the piano and played 'When I Grow Too Old to Dream.' I'm seventy-one now. Isn't it funny how that was my favourite song?"

Hymn Sing *employed sixteen young choir singers, shown here with musical director Winnifred Sim's predecessor, Eric Wild.*

René Simard's show is primo time-capsule stuff. The twelve-year-old prodigy, who won the 1972 Frank Sinatra Award for Best Performance at the Tokyo Song Festival, was flush with *Saturday Night Fever* by 1977. But where John Travolta was a smouldering disco inferno under the strobe lights, René on the dance floor sometimes seemed like a kid clowning with big sister's girlfriends in a basement platter party. He never looked that way to his fans, though. In the summer of 1978 his Vancouver-produced variety show was the fifth most popular show in Canada.

As well as dance and sing, Simard did scripted interviews with puzzled guest stars like Peter Ustinov, who were clearly there to draw

adult viewers. And at least once a show, he was a good sport while writers gave him an extra-hard pinch on the cheek.

"When Canada asks for a variety show, CBC delivers, with the all-new '79 Simard!" one show joked, presenting Simard as factory display car. "All the cuteness you'd ever want from a host ... the '79 Simard is fun to park with, especially in a drive-in, and just check the upholstered seat ..." (at which point a dancer gives his bottom a tweak).

Musical variety shows were also big this decade. By the end of the '70s, super specials starring Anne Murray, Burton Cummings, Oscar Peterson, and Wayne and Shuster were frequently drawing in excess of two million fans.

One of Canada's most distinguished television talents, Norman Campbell directed many shows for CBC-TV, including Emmy Award-winning productions of the ballets *Cinderella* and *Sleeping Beauty* and productions of opera and Stratford Festival performances.

"*Nureyev was the puck*"

CHOREOGRAPHING *THE BIG REVUE* in 1952 with Alan Lund was my first experience with dance. Eric Till, my assistant on the musical *Anne of Green Gables*, said to me one day, "You'd have a lot of fun with *Swan Lake*."

"Swan what?" I said.

Well, that was the beginning of something wonderful. I did twelve ballets over my CBC career. And the first was *Swan Lake* live in 1956. The first good thing to happen was I met dancer Celia Franca and Kay Ambrose, her design person. Kay would take the curtain off her walls to use on stage. The ballet had no money. We rehearsed in the old Pape Avenue studio, which had rats. The dancers wore hockey stockings to keep warm.

My feeling about ballet is there's a best seat in the house and it's always changing. If you have a leap, you want it from a low angle. If you want to see the ballerinas entering Swan Lake, you want to see the pattern they make from on high.

Lois Smith and David Adams were the lovers in that production. And Barry Morse, wearing a tuxedo, was the host. He explained the plot. We were doing something new, don't forget. No one had ever seen ballet on TV before.

Celia managed miracles of choreography. We did it — full length, ninety minutes — in Studio One. We couldn't have an intermission because it was live, so all the time the dancers had to rest or change was the two-minute commercial break. I'll never forget the dancers running, unzipping each other as they ran, to get through the big change in time.

To show how much TV changed in ten years, I did *Swan Lake* again in colour in 1967. Lois Smith played opposite Erik Bruhn that time. And we used an image enhancer to brighten the colour and Chrome-a-key for effects — like when the prince mistakenly swears his love to the black and not the white swan. As he does, devastation strikes. What we did was shoot a crumbling castle beforehand then insert the image of the prince standing in front, while behind him his world collapsed.

Everyone asks about *Sleeping Beauty*, with Veronica

Tennant and Rudolf Nureyev. Nureyev was impossible and very, very busy. He left me an hour to work with dancers instead of two weeks. When the dancers came on, I instructed the cameras that this was a hockey game and Nureyev was the puck.

After rehearsal, he disappeared before we trimmed what was a two-hour ballet into ninety minutes. Mary McDonald, our rehearsal pianist, and I went to Montreal looking for Nureyev and found him in a restaurant with a film student from California. "Yes, well, the cuts," Nureyev said when we pinned him down. Then he dashed off some edits and said, "These are your cuts."

Still, when we got back and shot the ballet, we were eleven minutes over. So in editing, I took the opening scene of the king and queen's entrance. The king swirls around with this twelve-foot cape and makes a gesture for everyone to dance. As the king made his gesture, I said to the editor, "Stop tape and roll eleven minutes. What's there?" and luckily it was the start of another variation. And that was how we finally got the show down to size.

No one noticed, except Nureyev, who was furious. But I must admit Rudy did one thing that helped [in rehearsal]. He had just done a variation, and had come back to the wings, puffing. Then he heard music and rushed out, but it was Veronica's cue. Suddenly, he became Veronica and did her dance. He charmed everybody and broke the tension on stage.

But I'm afraid that all this talk of editing and cameras doesn't properly describe how you shoot ballet. The most important thing, the thing you have to have as well, is an affection for your material. You have to love dance to make it work on TV.

Above: Norman Campbell with Lois Smith (left) and Celia Franca (right) in Swan Lake, *1967.*

Opposite: Rudolf Nureyev and Veronica Tennant in Sleeping Beauty, *1972. Tennant later produced and hosted programs at CBC, winning a 1999 International Emmy for* Karen Kain: Dancing in the Moment. NATIONAL BALLET OF CANADA

Left: The team responsible for Norman Campbell's 1972 production of Puccini's La Rondine *discusses the model set for Act 2. From left to right: Set director Robert Parker, designer Robert Lawson, Campbell, assistant director Rick Thompson, and head of wardrobe Suzanne Mess.*

Below: The two-level set, part lilac garden and part cabaret, reached almost to the rafters of Studio Seven in Toronto.

Above: The young lovers, as played by Anastasios Brenios and world-renowned soprano Teresa Stratas. The Toronto Star's William Littler called the production a "lavish triumph."

Left: Toronto-born Stratas in a wardrobe fitting with Suzanne Mess.

A pair of kings

THE TWO BEST-LOVED Canadian TV performers in the '70s, Bruno Gerussi and Al Waxman, both came from immigrant families and experienced the sting of prejudice in their formative years. As an Italian Canadian growing up in B.C. during the Second World War Gerussi routinely heard racist taunts, while Waxman was a Jew who grew up in Toronto at a time when "Gentiles Only" signs were posted on the city's beaches.

Both actors used memories of that hurt to manufacture boisterous men of the people for their roles in the '70s hits *The King of Kensington* (1975-80) and *The Beachcombers* (1972-91). Nick Adonidas probably wasn't half as garrulous or enterprising as his off-screen creator, however. Nick may have plucked stray logs from B.C.'s ragged coastline, but Gerussi once defied all laws of geography and finance by importing a fortress of timber three-quarters of the way across Canada.

"That was one of Bruno's deals," laughs *The Beachcombers'* co-creator, Marc Strange. "He did promotion work for a cabin-making outfit in Ontario. In return, a truck hauled enough timber to build that big house he constructed at the top of Gibsons Landing all the way in from Ontario. Bruno must have been the only guy in B.C. with a house made out of Ontario logs."

Strange acknowledges that Gerussi *was The Beachcombers*. And he likens the moment his then-wife and partner, Susan Lynn Strange, happened upon Nick Adonidas to the summoning of a Mediterranean genie from a bottle.

"We had been negotiating with CBC for a series to replace *Adventures in Rainbow Country*," Strange recalls. "We were new to B.C. and fascinated by things locals took for granted. Like how you could get a beachcomber's licence for $25 and make a living retrieving lost logs. Anyway, we were walking the beach one day and Susan shouted, 'Zorba on the beach!' The whole thing just fell together after that."

The couple then composed a quick sketch of beachcomber Zorba: "Nick Adonidas is about forty, wiry and swarthy with a thick mane of black hair turning silver at the temples. There is something about him of the pirate, something of the poet, a raffish charm and style not unlike that of a city tomcat. The key to Nick is that he is passionate, vital, and in love with life."

The description fit Gerussi to a chest hair. A frequent CBC-TV drama star, Gerussi abandoned the scrambling actor's life when his wife, Ida, died in 1965, taking time to look after his two teenaged children while hosting a popular national radio show, *Gerussi!*

But in 1972 when CBC asked if he wanted to return west to gamble on a thirteen-week TV show, Gerussi was more than ready. Probably because in Nick Adonidas, a beachcomber who made more friends than money, the actor finally found a steady role that might contain his restless spirit.

Coming from a minority group, Gerussi also appreciated the show's multicultural shadings. And when one of the characters, Old Moses Charlie (played by Chief Dan George), proved to be a scoundrel, well so much the better. (The actor delighted in repeating George's advice on acting to fellow native actor Pat John: "Always take the money up front.")

Gerussi enjoyed shouting hello to everyone in Gibsons Landing. And he frequently invited

Right: Al Waxman and Fiona Reid sample the fruit in Toronto's Kensington Market. "We shot mostly in a studio," remembers Reid. "I loved it when we went on location."

Opposite (from left to right): The Beachcombers' *Ol' Relic (Robert Clothier), Jesse Jim (Pat John), Hughie (Bob Park), Molly (Rae Brown), and Nick (Bruno Gerussi). Heather Robertson of* Maclean's *said* The Beachcombers *had "a strange and cheerful innocence which is never found in American shows."*

Nick and Jesse Jim log another shift on the Persephone.

the cast and crew to wrap parties in his high-on-the-cliff, Ontario log mansion. Only Robert Clothier, Nick's onscreen nemesis, Relic, escaped Gerussi's charm.

"They had different temperaments," Strange comments. "They were always professional, but very different on screen and off. Bruno, for instance, liked to charge through everything, whereas Robert, who was a fine actor, could occasionally make a meal out of a scene."

The actor who was drawn to playing an independent rogue never got along with head office, either. "No, Bruno didn't like hearing from Toronto," Strange laughs. In fact, Gerussi never liked reporting to anyone. "He never had an agent," Strange says. "He looked after all those deals with McCain's, the records he put out, his cooking show [*Celebrity Cooks*, 1975-79], and a lot of other stuff by himself."

Strange figures that what born-actor Gerussi enjoyed most about his nineteen-year stay on *The Beachcombers* was that it gave him an appreciative audience, on screen and off, for the rest of his life.

"Bruno was always alive," Strange says. "He was either happy or pissed off; that's what got you about him. He was a character people recognized and liked. He loved food and conversation. He liked nice clothes. Even the beat-up leather jackets he wore on the show were tailored. He loved looking good. He just liked being alive. I enjoyed walking with him down a city street because he had a dramatic way of

walking, with his chest pushed out a little.

"Once I remember we were walking down Carlton Street in Toronto," he continues. "Just two blocks, but every twenty yards someone shouted, 'Hey Bruno!' There must have been a hundred people who called out, including Bobby Hull and Jean Chrétien. Their faces just had these big grins when they saw him.... Everyone loved Bruno."

No Canadian actor worked harder at establishing an empathetic screen character than Al Waxman in *The King of Kensington*.

After the early death of his father, Waxman turned to sports for acceptance — and was thrilled to learn that teammates had elected him hockey team captain. Their coach, however, reminded players that they were Christians and that Waxman was the team's only Jew. He wasn't eligible for a leadership position.

"I waited until everyone left, then sitting alone in that locker room ... where Jews were not welcome, I cried," Waxman wrote in his autobiography, *That's What I Am*. "I had been hit by flying pucks, slapped in the face by swinging sticks ... but had never cried before."

Around the same time, the youngster was mesmerized by Al Jolson's jolting performance in the first sound movie, *The Jazz Singer*. Sometime before his twenty-seventh viewing of the film, little Al decided to become an actor — a plan his mother greeted with skepticism.

"You can't sing," she told her son. "You can't dance. What are you going to do? Tell jokes? You're not so funny."

As a young actor, Waxman did what he could to catch on in the business, both in Toronto and Los Angeles, where he was once fired as a short-order cook for over-feeding hungry actors. He managed to make a living, but no lasting impression. By the mid '70s, Waxman had more or less settled behind the camera. That was fine — he loved to direct — but always in the back of his mind there was the nagging regret that he'd never found a part into which he could pour all that he knew about acting and life.

After a 1974 pilot for *King of Kensington*, featuring Paul Hecht and Sandra O'Neill, failed to catch fire, Waxman was asked if he was interested in taking over the foundering series as a director. But the story of a beaming mensch who was elected champion of the little people proved irresistible to the Toronto kid who was once robbed of the captaincy of his hockey team. Direct, nothing, he wanted to act — *he wanted to be the King of Kensington.*

Waxman threw all his energy and hopes into the series. This was his chance to show how the world should be. Polish Jew Larry King had a Protestant wife (Fiona Reid) and a rainbow assortment of friends, yet as the show's memorable theme song announced, "When he walks down the street, he smiles at everyone / All the people that he meets call him King of Kensington ... Wotta guy!"

His crew were less enthusiastic. "Al made people work hard," co-star Reid recalls. "And, yes, he sometimes had a short fuse, but I don't think his behaviour as the star would be questioned at all in Los Angeles, say."

What probably confused the crew was that Waxman's onscreen character was as sentimental as a lace hanky. In the series' best shows, Larry King inevitably played the clown who laughed to keep from crying. In the episode "Fertility for Two," written by Louis Del Grande and Jack Humphrey, the King buys hockey equipment for his boy when he and his wife, Cathy, decide to have a baby. "What if it's a girl?" Cathy asks. So the King covers his bets by buying a pink snowsuit. A trip to the doctor, however, produces disturbing news.

"Your sperm count is 15,000," the doctor tells him. *Wotta guy!* the King smiles. "That's low, you'll need a count of at least 35,000 to succeed in having a child," the doctor says. The show's final scene has Larry back home in Kensington Market, gripping the pink snowsuit, fighting back tears as he advises Cathy that there may not be an heir to the throne.

What the *King of Kensington* crew couldn't understand about Waxman was that his fury and tenderness came from the same place; that the driving ambition was there to protect an everyman clown who represented a democratic ideal. "I always thought he was harder on himself than anyone," says Reid, who confesses she never understood Waxman until long

after she left the show in 1978.

"I didn't understand where the passion was coming from," she says today. "I was a very callow twenty-three. This was my first work in a series. Al believed in me. He tutored me. He tried to teach me that I had to give something back to the community. He was always very active in charities, of course.

"But I didn't understand," she says. "I felt hemmed in, and was desperately afraid I wouldn't be respected as an actress unless I left television. He told me when I left that I was making a mistake, and I realize now that I did. Mind you, he was very supportive of my decision. And after I left he remained loyal. I think he showed up for every play I was in in Toronto."

Fans who identified with the King were less forgiving. "For years afterwards, I had people come up to me on the street and say, 'I'll never forgive you for leaving him,'" Reid says.

Indeed, fans always remembered Larry King and Nick Adonidas. The funerals for both Bruno Gerussi, in 1995, and Al Waxman, in 2001, were emotional, crowded affairs. Waxman would have appreciated that just as many who came to pay their respects travelled by public transit as by jet.

"When I got on the streetcar, the driver said, 'You must be going to the Waxman funeral,'" reported fellow actor Sean McCann. "What does that tell you about Al?"

*Cathy leaves home in 1977. Tina (*Coming Up Rosie*'s Rosemary Radcliffe) would mend the King's heart the following season.*

Heroes and villains

Tory, Tory. John Diefenbaker and his hero, Sir John A. (William Hutt), chat during a break in the 1974 series, The National Dream. *Pierre Berton was host-narrator.*

IT'S NOT SURPRISING that Sir John A. Macdonald was both a hero and villain on Canadian television in the '70s. By 1972, CBC was 70 percent Canadian content and hungry for heroes big enough to fill our swelling sense of self. At the same time, in the decade defined by the October Crisis, good and bad guys were sometimes on opposite sides of an ever-flipping coin.

Front Page Challenge star Pierre Berton's stirring, two-volume account of the building of the Canadian Pacific Railroad, *The National Dream* and *The Last Spike*, provided an ideal setting for hero-watching. Every dad's Christmas present in 1970 and '71, the saga follows wild dreamers from a dozen sides, and contains a central figure, Sir John A., who strides like a colossus through his time.

Theatre great William Hutt was marvellous as Macdonald in the 1974 TV series, capturing the great man's battered nobility and corroding canker of pride as he gargles straight gin through a legendary, five-hour defence of his railroad dream. (A brandy man, Macdonald thought he'd fool the Grits into thinking he was sipping water.)

A more troubled Macdonald (stage and screen star Christopher Plummer) arrived on CBC five years later in Riel.

"I throw myself upon this House," Hutt shouts, in a speech taken from historical records. "I throw myself upon this country; I throw myself upon posterity; and I believe that I know that, notwithstanding the many failings in my life, I shall have the voice of this country, and this House, rallying around me."

Five years after the eight-part *National Dream* went to air, Sir John A. was back on our screens in George Bloomfield's controversial *Riel*. Only this time Macdonald (Christopher Plummer) was portrayed as a grasping schemer gone mad with nation building and toy trains.

The story of a determined prime minister's battle with a fervent Métis nationalist, *Riel* would resonate with a '70s audience, what with a war brewing between two old CBC hands, Pierre Trudeau and René Lévesque, and trouble boiling over on native reserves.

"In one scene, we had a few hundred native extras sitting around on picnic tables waiting to simulate the Battle of Batoche," remembers *Riel* director Bloomfield. "Then these buses pulled up with real RCMP personnel in scarlet tunics. And I just sensed this enormous hostility grip the native extras. You could feel something dangerous in the air. And I thought, my God, what am I doing here, sending these people together into mock battle?"

Art imitated life — but what era? — on another front. A *Globe and Mail* story on the making of the film was headlined "Separatist

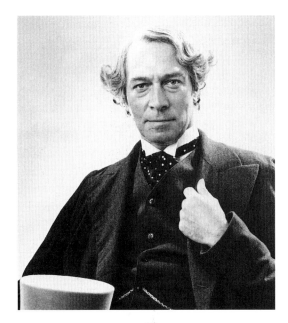

Team Treads History's Path," and chronicled how Roger Blay, who played Riel's devoted military chief, Gabriel Dumont, was a "seething" separatist.

Of the man who played Louis Riel, Bloomfield says, "I've never encountered an actor who invested as much of himself into a screen character as Raymond Cloutier did in the making of *Riel*. He directed himself, really."

While *Riel* included a few epic battles and had a showy cast, including William Shatner, Barry Morse, Leslie Nielsen, and Arthur Hill, Bloomfield remembers one small sequence in particular, a scene that has Plummer's Macdonald lost in play with a toy train.

"That was crucial because I wanted to show that, like Riel, Macdonald ... was also a mad visionary. Here was a powerful man who was visited by a vision of building a great nation and became so obsessed with that vision he was willing to do whatever was necessary. On the other hand you had Riel, a madman certainly, who attempted to preserve his nation, the little guy, the Métis, who stood in the way.... Their real, historic clash is what we were trying to capture in making our film."

Eric Till's *Bethune* (1977), starring Donald Sutherland and Kate Nelligan and co-starring James Hong, brought us another rebel martyr. The Canadian doctor who died at Mao's side in 1939 is a folk hero in China. And certainly Sutherland played Bethune as an epic socialist hero, haranguing against private medicine for

Above: Driving in the last spike on The National Dream.

Below: William Shatner and Roger Blay in Riel.

profit, then engaging in a marathon operating session (sixty-nine hours in real life) where he saves more than a hundred lives.

Another CBC dramatic series, *For the Record* (1977-86), attempted to yoke the NFB documentary tradition to '60s investigative reporting in something new called docudramas.

"People at one end of the country aren't aware of things that have been front-page news for years and years at the other end," executive producer Ralph Thomas once said in explaining the show's purpose. "Somehow the welter of headlines doesn't sink in. In drama, you can personalize it, identify with the central characters, so the whole country can feel involved and care about it."

That Ralph Thomas was a current affairs producer before coming to drama didn't bother department head John Hirsch, who was hoping the series would draw attention to contemporary social conditions in the manner of Dickens's most popular serials. And Hirsch didn't care that many of his filmmakers and writers had never worked in television.

"He took mad chances, appointing me, for example," Thomas said. "And he brought in feature film directors like Claude Jutra and Peter Pearson. Why couldn't they find work here before? We must have assumed they were beyond us."

Eric Nesterenko, a twenty-year NHL veteran, appeared in and helped direct on-ice sequences for *Cementhead*, an exposé of Junior A hockey starring Kenneth Welsh and future *SCTV* comic "Marty" Short. *Ready for Slaughter*, written by Roy MacGregor and starring Gordon Pinsent, was the story of a farmer struggling to hang onto his land. *Goin' Down the Road* filmmaker Don Shebib directed Nicholas Campbell in the legal story *By Reason of Insanity*. And one of the series' best remembered efforts featured Fiona Reid playing an MP (said to be modelled after Tory Flora MacDonald) in Donald Brittain's *An Honourable Member*.

"Donald Brittain had a wonderful ear for truth coming from NFB documentaries," Reid says of the director who went on to make a series of highly regarded films for CBC. "I remember him walking around after a scene, carrying a Styrofoam cup with a little bit of whisky in it. 'Fiona,' he'd say, 'I hear something that's just not right, let's do it again.' And he was always right. Always."

Peeping David

Designed by head of drama John Hirsch as a way to introduce bold young talent to television, *Peep Show* (1975-76) was a wonderful experiment in hit-and-run drama, even if Hirsch was occasionally the one getting run over.

The first episode in the late-evening (10:30 p.m.) series was by the Newfoundland comedy troupe CODCO, and began with Mary Walsh parodying Irish playwright J.M. Synge's *Riders to the Sea:* "That you Herschel, me brawny old fisherperson?" Walsh cries, toiling at the stove. "Sure, it's four score years now since you carried me o'er this threshold, and dropped me by this stove. And since that day there's always been a bun in me oven. And me, never-a-mindin', even when that hungry ol' sea gobbled up eighteen of me twenty-one buns. ..."

In a later episode, *Goldberg Is Waiting*, an understandably nervous Saul Rubinek picks up hyperactive gay cruiser Martin Short. Pick of the series litter, however, are David Cronenberg's three half-hour playlets. One episode has a nervous young woman being hounded by a persistent Peeping Tom. Finally, he makes his move, following the woman into her apartment. As soon as he turns on the lights, the man discovers he's trapped in a cage, and his quarry, wearing a bra and panties, is staring hard at him, whip in hand.

Hirsch saw the film shortly before it went to air and was furious. Nevertheless, the film was shown as Cronenberg intended.

Saul Rubinek (left) and Martin Short (right) in an episode of the experimental dramatic anthology Peep Show.

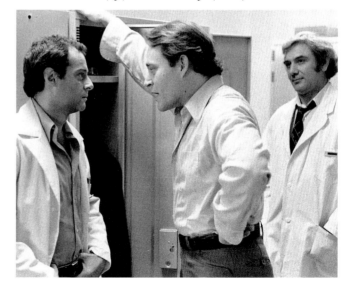

Above: Donald Sutherland and James Hong in Bethune. *The film was shot in CBC's Studio Seven in two weeks. "[In search of extras], the casting people were running down to Toronto's Chinatown, asking people if they'd like to meet James Hong," remembers producer Duncan Lamb. "James was a huge star [in Asia]."*

Left: Fiona Reid was an MP in Donald Brittain's An Honourable Member.

Below: Certain Practices, *a* For the Record *story about a doctor who challenges the practices of a top surgeon, starred Richard Monette (left) and Alan Scarfe (centre).*

A woman's place

LIKE MANY CHILDREN born in the '60s, *Take 30* grew into something unexpected.

The late-afternoon series was launched in the fall of 1962 as a replacement for the food, fabric, and current events show, *Open House*. As its title implied, *Take 30* was meant to give homemakers a thirty-minute break from their chores before they began getting dinner ready. *Maclean's* reported that it would feature "entertainment along with useful hints and chatter."

Nothing resembling a coffee klatch ever went to air, however. Anna Cameron talked to the doctor who invented birth control pills on the very first episode. And while the series was devoted to interviews in its first year, Cameron and co-host Paul Soles fled the studio to discover the world in 1964. For the next twenty-four months, while defiant kid brother

This Hour Has Seven Days fought the parent corporation for authority, *Take 30* (1962-84) quietly went about its business taking on many of the same controversies.

In 1964 the afternoon show interviewed feminist Betty Friedan, recently published author of *The Feminine Mystique*, and presented a three-part instalment on the sexual practices of teenagers, along with a six-part look at the modern family, co-scripted by June Callwood. Later in the decade, roving reporters talked to separatists in Quebec as well as participants in an open marriage in Copenhagen. In 1968, *Take 30* was the first CBC show to do a piece on health conditions in Biafra.

Covering a Hartford race riot later that year, reporter Moses Znaimer (later czar of the CityTV empire) didn't simply ask police to describe the effects of the new crowd deterrent, Mace; he insisted an officer spray him in the face, then tumbled moaning to the sidewalk.

Executive producer Glenn Sarty, who guided *Take 30* through its most influential years (1967-75), felt the show was able to get away with risky subject matter because it was hidden in plain sight.

"We got away with a lot that prime-time shows could never cover," he once observed. "For example, we dramatized a rape case. One of the reasons [we were able to carry it off] was the fixation of CBC executives on [*This Hour Has Seven Days*], which was always in trouble. One day one of those executives told me he'd been home with a cold and finally caught us. It was one of those days when Madame Jehane Benoît was on.

"'You've got a very good cooking show there,' he told me."

Adrienne Clarkson, a Victoria College lecturer and novelist who evolved from *Take 30*'s book reviewer into its star hostess (1965-75) at the age of twenty-six, echoes her one-time executive producer's comments.

Anna Cameron ties down Take 30 *co-host Paul Soles.*

"[Working on *Take 30* at CBC] was kind of like being brought up by an uncle, not even an aunt, but an uncle who doesn't really understand you," our governor general says today. "He's not even the same sex, but is aligned to you because he's your family."

Then again, many women trying to forge a career at the time were treated with a baffled, paternalistic attitude by society. Here's how the *Toronto Telegram*'s venerable Mr. Chips, McKenzie Porter, chronicled a meeting with Clarkson for his paper in 1970:

"From her Chinese ancestors Mrs. Clarkson has inherited enormous, luminous eyes, a skin of tawny satin and the delicate bones and movements of a gazelle. She is an extremely beautiful woman able to bring great taste to her dress in pregnancy and to carry off her condi-

tion before the cameras with insouciance.

"You will understand how relieved I felt when I discovered that Mrs. Clarkson bears no grudge against me for criticizing in strong terms her second novel, *Hunger Trace*. I said that the explicit sex scenes between a young nymphomaniac and a middle-aged Canadian senator in Mrs. Clarkson's novel are incredible.

"'When my friends read what you wrote about my novel,' Mrs. Clarkson said, they said, 'Where has that man been all his life?'"

The passage offers insight into how women were sometimes viewed at the dawn of the woman's liberation movement — defined by their looks and entrusted with "carrying off the condition" of pregnancy.

"[*Take 30*] treated women as people. That was considered radical," is how Sarty once

Take 30 reporter Moses Znaimer (left) and hosts Adrienne Clarkson and Paul Soles visit a Toronto poster shop in 1968.

explained the show's success. Cameron added, "I'd get letters from housewives thanking us for saving their sanity."

For her part, Clarkson says she never felt being the first Asian to host a national show was necessarily a historic accomplishment. "I think I was the first person of Oriental origin to be on television anywhere in the Western world," she says. "But being a woman on air was maybe more important. There were almost no women on camera then." (Jan Tennant was the first woman to read the CBC news, in 1972.)

Although Clarkson guesses she interviewed dozens of women celebrities over her decade-long stint as *Take 30* host, the interview she remembers most vividly from the '70s found her talking with an ordinary soul who had absented herself from the sexual revolution.

"We did a series on women who had not married," she explains. "Because people at the time felt that all women should be married. We asked all kinds of questions — was it by choice? What was an 'old maid' anyway? And I remember this one woman, she had never been

pop up
Paul Soles

CBC-TV's Iron Man award goes to Paul Soles, who has made network appearances for six decades, hosting or starring in Take 30, Flashback, This Is the Law, Canada After Dark, Irish Coffee, Beyond Reason, *and* Riverdale. *Below, left: On* This Is the Law *circa 1974; below, right: with Hana Gartner on* Take 30 *in 1977; centre: on* Riverdale *in 1998.*
EPITOME PICTURES INC.

married and had spent all her life working in a museum. Quite a sheltered life. And she said, 'Well, once I was kissed. It was the most extraordinary thing that ever happened to me and I'll remember it all my life.'"

Bringing that woman's story to life, Clarkson says, was arguably more important than chronicling the life of Rose Kennedy, another *Take 30* guest, because the former's story had never been told. Perhaps more important, her story made good on the show's commitment to help its audience better understand one another and the times in which they lived.

Which is why in her latest incarnation as Canada's governor general Clarkson never tires of hearing about her old show. "All over Canada," she says, "but mostly in the small and medium-sized cities, people come up to me and say 'We remember you from *Take 30*,' and I love that. It makes me feel that, even though it was a long time ago, the show helped them raise their kids or kept them from going nuts, or brought them some ideas. That makes me feel terrific."

pop up
Adrienne Clarkson

Adrienne Clarkson left Take 30 *in 1975 to help establish* the fifth estate. *She also hosted the interview series* Adrienne at Large *and the arts showcases* Adrienne Clarkson's Summer Festival *and* Adrienne Clarkson Presents. *Right: The future governor general on* Adrienne at Large *in 1974; below, left: on* the fifth estate *with Bob McKeown (left) and Eric Malling in the '80s; below, right: interviewing Robertson Davies for* Adrienne Clarkson Presents *in 1992.*

TV gunfighters

"WE'RE MAD AND we're not going to take it anymore," Robert Cooper screamed out a window in a 1976 commercial to promote his series, *Ombudsman*.

The "we're mad" line came from the decade's ultimate social-action movie, *Network*, a film that hoped to empower disgruntled souls who were fed up with "the system."

Ombudsman (1974-80) and *Marketplace*, which began its ongoing thirty-year run in 1972, picked up on '70s grassroots activism. (As, in its own way, did comedy show *SCTV* with a credit sequence that had the cast throwing TVs out the window.)

The son of a Montreal talent agent, Robert Cooper was a boy magician — "The Great Roberto" — and drama student before entering law school. After being admitted to the Quebec bar in 1970, he opened a storefront practice, then shifted from pro bono to Bonanno while serving as special counsel on the Quebec Inquiry into Organized Crime.

But showbiz was obviously in his blood, because in 1974 he took the job as CBC's Sunday Ombudsman and for five years criss-crossed Canada seeking out and defending little-guy plaintiffs. That Cooper himself was such a mild but persistent interrogator gave the show an intriguing dramatic tension. By 1978, *Ombudsman* had received 40,000 grievances, made 12,000 investigations, and resolved 2,137 cases. In 1979 Cooper left to become a film producer, and Kathleen Ruff took over the show for its final two seasons.

In Hollywood, Cooper almost got a movie of his own Ombudsman days off the ground, starring Robert Redford. The film, Cooper suggested, would document how TV consumer advocates were "modern gunfighters."

Marketplace has gone through a posse of gunfighter-hosts in its three-decade run. Where *Ombudsman* went after what was immoral and illegal (the show lobbied to make loan-sharking a criminal offence), *Marketplace*'s top guns specialized in drawing our attention to the unsafe. Thanks to *Marketplace*, our furnaces, cribs, insulation, and pop bottles are risk free. Oh, and the show also documented that lawn darts were unsafe at any speed, resulting in a law banning them.

In addition to hosts George Finstad, Joan Watson, Harry Brown, and Bill Paul, *Marketplace* had one more gunfighter in its stable in the '70s: Stompin' Tom Connors sang the show's theme song, which ended "Yes, we're the people running in the race, buying up bargains in the ol' Marketplace / If there's a sale on something, we'll buy it 'cause it's hot, / We save a lot of money spending money we don't got."

Marketplace *hosts George Finstad and Joan Watson with Tom Connors (centre), who stomped out the show's early theme song.*

Bad connections

PRODUCER BILL MACADAM received a definitive response from Toronto police upon advising them that he planned to interview a mob boss.

"He'll kill you," one officer promised.

How do you know, has a TV reporter ever talked to him? Macadam countered. Not really, the officer admitted. With that slim bit of encouragement, Macadam and director Martyn Burke decided to go ahead with the ambush interview.

Connections, a two-part (1977, '79) investigative report on organized crime, took four years and fifteen journalists to complete. Along the way, the investigative team — code-named "Housing Crisis" — talked to the RCMP, FBI, Interpol, and police forces in Canada, the U.S., and Italy.

But it was the TV filmmakers' conversations with mobsters that made the series compulsive viewing. "We not only talked to scores of mobsters, but with their wives, kids, lawyers, and neighbours," Macadam told the *Toronto Star*.

At one point, Macadam was in Montreal talking to mobster Ziggy Wiseman while Burke was in California visiting syndicate boss Bill Bonanno.

"I just showed up at his door one day," Burke said. "He was so surprised, he talked out of sheer curiosity. The best footage came from such surprise encounters rather than sophisticated technology."

Connections did, however, surreptitiously capture many disturbing incidents, including a scene of mobsters shaking down a Montreal notary by threatening to kill his wife and son.

While the team of Macadam, Burke, and *fifth estate* veteran Jim Dubro were frequently threatened, the only series casualties were mobsters. Three Montreal crime family members profiled on the 1977 series — Paolo Violi, Pietro Sciarra, and Louie Greco — were killed before the 1979 instalment.

The programs resulted in great ratings and critical acclaim, along with enormous controversy and eight lawsuits. Burke later admitted to the *Globe and Mail* that the process of getting the series on air was never easy.

"When deadlines were missed because our wildlife-nature-photography approach of showing mobsters in their natural habitat wasn't working, we ended up attending our share of difficult meetings with CBC brass," he says. "But we never doubted that they wanted what we wanted: an investigative film that would jar the country.... Peter Herrndorf, then-head of CBC current affairs ... believed in its relevance and political importance and was prepared to take his share of the heat from those who disagreed."

Above (left to right): Connections *producers Bill Macadam, Martyn Burke, and former CBC president Laurent Picard at the 1978 Anik awards show.*

Below: A Toronto Sun *cartoon from the period.*

Crisis management

SHORTLY AFTER PIERRE Trudeau's wedding in 1971, the prime minister informed his wife, Margaret, that if she or any of their prospective children were abducted, there would be no bargaining with kidnappers.

"You mean you would let them kill me, rather than agree to terms?" she asked.

"Yes. Yes, I would."

Margaret believed him.

In the fall of 1970, Prime Minister Trudeau stared down two groups of FLQ kidnappers in what became known as the October Crisis. On October 5 and 10, British trade commissioner James Cross, then Quebec labour minister Pierre Laporte were kidnapped in Montreal. Abductors demanded $500,000 in gold bullion and the release of Front de Libération du Québec (FLQ) members in jail for planting bombs.

Canadians were riveted to the nightly news, which showed the unthinkable — troops moving into the streets of Montreal and Ottawa to protect government officials and VIPs. More than three thousand angry students and unionists, shouting *Nous Vaincrons*! ("we will win") rallied in support of the FLQ in Montreal's Paul Sauvé Arena on October 15. How big and determined the "we" were was perhaps unknowable.

The next day the federal cabinet invoked the War Measures Act to "apprehend an insurrection." On the 17th, on instructions from the FLQ, Montreal police raced to the St. Hubert air base and found Laporte's body crammed into the trunk of a Chevrolet, strangled with his own gold neck chain.

A soldier stands guard on Parliament Hill, October 13, 1970.
CP (CHUCK MITCHELL)

According to his wife, Trudeau wept when he received news of his former classmate's death. But in Parliament, and especially in press scrums on TV, Trudeau adopted an unruffled air. Famously, he toyed with CBC-TV reporter Tim Ralfe on the steps of Parliament:

"Sir, what is it with all these men with guns around here?"

"Haven't you noticed?" Trudeau responded, with a hint of amusement.

"Yes, I noticed them. I wondered why you people decided to have them."

"What's your worry?"

"I'm not worried, but you seem to be."

"If you're not worried, I'm not worried."

The two sparred some more, Ralfe counterpunching valiantly until he got his knockout quote: "Well," Trudeau said, "There are a lot of bleeding hearts around who just don't like to see people with helmets and guns. All I can say is, go on and bleed, but it is more important to keep law and order in the society than to be worried about weak-kneed people."

Later, Ralfe asked the prime minister on camera how far he would be willing to go in fighting terrorism. "Just watch me," he snapped.

Political columnist Larry Zolf says "Trudeau shone in what became a television crisis. His defence of the War Measures Act defined him as a political figure."

Both the FLQ — who issued communiqués to one news source at a time, knowing how far journalists would push a scoop — and the government tried to use the media to further their interests. Montreal and Ottawa were alive with rumours. All of this led to what then-head of CBC-TV news and current affairs, Knowlton Nash, acknowledges was a hazardous situation for working reporters.

"George Davidson, the president of the CBC at the time, didn't want any speculative stories," he remembers. "We made a couple of mistakes early on ... not horrendous ones except for the erroneous reporting of the death of Cross — that was a big mistake.

"Initially, the phone call came from the

[federal minister responsible, Gérard Pelletier] to Davidson," Nash explains, "asking to restrain our coverage and not give any publicity to the FLQ. I was told to issue a memo to urge restraint.

"I made a mistake," he says. "I shouldn't have accepted the assertions of the government that there were buildings full of dynamite.... I should have asked for more evidence. The evidence wasn't there. We reversed the memo about an hour and a half later. The extent of the assertions being made by cabinet ministers and even the RCMP ... were alarming."

Close to five hundred people were apprehended during the War Measures Act. Eventually, it was discovered that the terrorists were made up of two disconnected cells, each with a dozen or so members. The War Measures Act, pronounced Tommy Douglas later, was "like using a sledgehammer to crack a peanut."

The mystery of why our most famous civil libertarian came to be the only political leader in Canadian history to revoke civil liberties during peacetime might have been solved by a 1975 CBC documentary, which employed a dozen journalists, including Trudeau biographer Richard Gwyn, in a six-month search for evidence that supported the government's decision to adopt the War Measures Act. No "smoking gun" was found, but when asked why Trudeau and his colleagues took the FLQ terrorists so seriously, Minister of Industry Jean-Luc Pepin offered the following explanation:

"I cannot swear it, but I think we were all thinking about ourselves. We ourselves were a very small group, Trudeau, Pelletier, Marchand, Lalonde, Chrétien, myself, and a few people in the civil service, say fifty all told.... And we were bringing off a revolution. We held the key posts [in Ottawa]. We were making the civil service, kicking and screaming all the way, bilingual. We were a well-organized group of revolutionaries just like them, but working in a quite different way of course."

"The CBC was a great training ground," former CBC anchorman Lloyd Robertson says. "I got a liberal arts education in my [1954] training session. They even taught us how to pronounce Italian opera names."

Desk jockeying

Lloyd Robertson joined the CBC as a staff announcer in 1954 and anchored *The National* from 1970 to 1976. He was followed by former correspondent Peter Kent for two years, then Knowlton Nash.

"I have great memories of the period," Robertson says. "I covered the moon landing in 1969. After the show I remember walking outside and pinching myself."

Robertson says his favourite political interview during his CBC tenure was Prime Minister Lester B. Pearson. "[Secretary of State] Judy LaMarsh, who was responsible for CBC, was always railing about what she called 'rotten CBC management,'" he recalls. So when Pearson came in to see me during an interview at Expo, he said, 'How are you and how's your rotten management?' He completely relaxed me and we had a good interview. He was a bright, capable politician. Very ingratiating."

Robertson didn't always do so well with world leaders, however.

"One night," he laughs, "reading the roll-up to the newscast, I was to say 'Lyndon Johnson's plea for peace,' except I said 'pee for peace.' Then comes the split-second decision: do you correct yourself, drawing attention to your mistake, or plow ahead? I plowed ahead. Then I looked up and saw the camera jiggling, the cameraman was laughing so hard. When I got back to the newsroom, [correspondent] Joe Schlesinger was hoisting a sign that read, 'Robertson's Pee-In for Peace.'"

After Peter Kent's two-year stint in the network's top on-air position, Knowlton Nash, who had been head of news and current affairs, began a ten-year reign as anchorman in 1978, becoming so identified with the position that people began calling the show *The Nashional*.

Like Robertson, Nash had his own awkward moments on air. In his backstage look at the CBC, *Cue the Elephant*, he recalls interviewing U.S. senator Wayne Morse. He advised his guest just before they went to air that he would tap the senator on the knee when the time came to wind down the interview. A few minutes later, as their talk seemed to reach its logical conclusion, Nash reached under the anchor desk for the politician's leg. Morse stopped speaking, mid-sentence, and glared at Nash.

"Why are you grabbing my thigh?" he demanded.

"To tell you, Senator," a reddening Nash responded, "that your time is up."

War stories

"The only given in the job of a foreign correspondent, which is, in reality, a war correspondent, is you will get shot at."

— Knowlton Nash

FROM MORLEY SAFER'S coverage of the Suez Crisis in 1956 to Celine Galipeau, Patrick Brown, and Paul Workman's reporting in Afghanistan and the Middle East, CBC's foreign correspondents and cameramen have been there when hell happened on earth.

While death and destruction remain a constant, the speed with which correspondents cover war and civil unrest has accelerated. "When I was assigned by *Newsmagazine* to cover the Suez Crisis, getting stories back to Canada was a primitive exercise," remembers Safer. "There were no satellites, no expediters to see that bags of film were put on flights. Shipments took days. If film got lost in luggage, your story was gone."

By the 2002 Afghanistan war, however, Paul Workman was able to send visuals instantly, provided no one was looking.

"As I write this, I'm sitting in Kandahar," came his e-mail response to questions for this book. "I'm using a miner's lamp to see the keyboard. There is very little glamour about living in a house with no water, guarded by four men with rifles, and sneaking around military roadblocks to make a satellite feed long after curfew. It always amazes me that outside the front door people are living as they did centuries ago. Yet I can now use my satellite telephone to surf the Internet, file a report that sounds like it was recorded in a studio, and check my e-mail messages."

Above: Morley Safer (left) and Michael Maclear in 1958.

Right and on next three pages: Joe Schlesinger's press passes.
COURTESY JOE SCHLESINGER

Here are reports from eight of the many CBC correspondents whose collective work stretches back five decades:

MICHAEL MACLEAR was a pioneer documentary maker at Newsmagazine, *CBC's first news program. He went on to report from eighty countries, including Vietnam and Cuba.*

"When Batista's dictatorship collapsed in 1958, cameraman Bob Crone and I hired a Cessna in Miami and flew to Havana, where we managed to land despite runway barricades. Then we made our way to an army barracks in Matanzas and waited for Fidel Castro, who'd yet to emerge from his hideout. Nothing was what I expected. This was the story of the decade — a left-wing revolutionary taking over a country on America's doorstep in an age of Cold War paranoia. I expected hordes of news crews, but we were the only ones there.

"I waited for Castro in a room jammed with young soldiers, some no taller than their rifles. When he finally arrived one excited soldier dropped his rifle; it fired, the bullet plowing into the ceiling. Everyone feared an assassination. Castro seemed bewildered. His army hadn't really won in battle; Batista's troops quit in disgust. In our interview, he comes across as a man with no clear agenda. He was then thirty-one, I was twenty-nine — neither of us had a sense of how momentous this moment was. As I'd find so often with history, events were in the saddle, riding man."

KNOWLTON NASH was Washington bureau correspondent from 1961 to 1969, head of news and current affairs in the mid-'70s, and anchor of The National *from 1978 to 1988.*

"There were far fewer foreign correspondents and less security back then. I got to spend time with people you wouldn't dream of now. John Kennedy borrowed five dollars off me. Che Guevara and I spent a day together cutting sugar cane. When I got back to Washington, Bobby and John Kennedy wanted to know all about him. Even though they didn't agree with his politics, they admired his style.

"Getting information was different then, too. In Vietnam there were daily briefings, which we called the Five O'Clock Follies. American military officials would update us on the day's activities. They'd say one thing and we'd go into the fields and see something else entirely. It's called spinning, now. We called it lying.

"Someone once said, 'There is nothing more exhilarating than being shot at and missed.' That's true. And we all got shot at at some point. There was too much shooting back then. I was in Miami on my way back from Latin America when I heard President Kennedy had been assassinated. His casket was placed in the same White House East Room where Abraham Lincoln had lain. Reporters who covered the

As CBC's Washington correspondent, Knowlton Nash (shown here interviewing two American soldiers) watched the Vietnam War unfold from the boardrooms of the Pentagon to the jungles of Vietnam.

CBC Far East correspondent Bill Cunningham (behind taxi) and cameraman Maurice Embra take cover while a South Vietnamese soldier returns sniper fire in Saigon. Cunningham was captured in Cambodia, but managed to convince the Viet Cong that he was a Canadian journalist.

president were allowed to pay their last respects. Nobody spoke. Silent tears streamed down some faces. It was too shocking to be real. For me, his death really didn't sink in until that horrible moment I saw his furniture being moved out of the Oval Office."

DAVID HALTON, over his thirty-five-year career, has reported on everything from the Six Day War to the September 11, 2001 terrorist attacks on the World Trade Center and the Pentagon.

"One of my most rewarding on-air moments was an interview with Egyptian president Anwar Sadat in Cairo in November 1977. Sadat announced he intended to make his historic visit to Jerusalem to make peace with Israel. It was exhilarating to beat Walter Cronkite with this news by six hours! It was extraordinarily moving to see Sadat's arrival two weeks later in Tel Aviv, where Israeli cabinet members and battle-hardened generals wept at the symbolic end of three decades of Egyptian-Israeli hostilities."

TERRY MILEWSKI, The National's Middle Eastern correspondent, has also reported on Central and South America, the Caribbean, and Europe.

"Sometimes a fragment of a story can capture the world's attention. During the Colombian drug war of 1989, the narcotraficantes of Medellin declared a bombing war on the government. The army imposed a curfew, but thousands of homeless people had no way to comply and were herded into a stadium. A ragged ten-year-old girl was among them, clinging to her puppy. As the cameraman zoomed in, a tear fell from the girl's eye and the puppy whimpered. After I returned to Bogota, I was urged by the desk — seriously — to return and find the girl because anguished viewers had been phoning,

begging for a chance to adopt both the girl and dog. What a lesson in the power of a television image."

PAUL WORKMAN has covered wars in the Persian Gulf and Afghanistan.

"The first night of the Gulf War [January 17, 1991] was surreal. The air raid sirens in Israel went off at 4 in the morning as Iraq launched their Scud missile attack. Within a half-hour, a dozen of us were in gas masks and suits crowded into a sealed room with the telephone lines open to Canada. It was the beginning of weeks of interrupted sleep, air raid sirens, and more than forty missiles hitting Israel. The threat of a gas attack was real and frightening.

"My cameraman, Azur Mizrachi, had been at home and came in with pictures of his family donning gas masks and placing their baby in a specially designed crib. The pictures went out on one of the first satellite feeds after all-clear was sounded and were used by every network in the world. I still find it amazing that, under such difficult conditions, his first reaction was to get his camera.

"I also remember sitting in a hotel room in Tel Aviv, with our camera pointed out the window, waiting for missiles. Just after dawn we could see puffs of smoke where three Scuds had landed. I was describing the scene to Peter Mansbridge when the line died and a voice came on saying: 'This is censor seven, you are not allowed to give an exact location where missiles hit. If you do, your press credentials will be revoked.' I have no idea how they found me because we were the only foreign crew in the hotel. Of course, I phoned Peter back and described what happened."

ANNA MARIA TREMONTI, now co-host of the fifth estate, covered the Bosnian war and has filed stories from the Middle East, Europe, and the former Soviet republics.

"Before the Israeli election of 1996, I talked to families who had lost children to Palestinian suicide bombers. I went to a small city outside Tel Aviv to speak to the parents of a fifteen-year-old girl named Batchen. She had begged her parents to let her celebrate Purim in Tel Aviv with girlfriends. They were outside a mall when a young Palestinian carrying a duffel bag full of explosives blew himself up.

"I remember sitting in Batchen's kitchen,

drinking coffee, while her parents showed me her photo albums and diaries. She was a wonderfully creative storyteller. Her mother cried softly as she remembered. Her parents were devastated, but they insisted they wanted their government to pursue peace with the Palestinians. Batchen had been writing to a Palestinian pen pal, and after her death the pen pal and her parents had visited Batchen's family. Her parents told me they'd never had an Arab in their house before.

"I realized, as we sat and talked, that I knew Batchen. I'd gone to the triple funeral of teenaged girls, and had gone back and talked to a shop owner on that street who told me he'd seen three girls burned alive. I realized, sitting across from Batchen's mother a month later, that one of the girls was her daughter. I couldn't tell her that though."

BRIAN STEWART has reported from nine war zones, from El Salvador to Beirut.

"But let's remember, not all our stories are grim. A foreign correspondent witnesses moments that one couldn't put a value on. I was standing at the Berlin Wall the night it was torn down, and watched an old traffic cop trying to direct an ocean of singing and cheering East Germans coming across for the first time. He was having trouble maintaining dignity as tears of happiness streamed down his face."

JOE SCHLESINGER was sent by his family to England when Hitler invaded Czechoslovakia. He later returned to discover that his parents had been killed in the Holocaust. In the years following his first overseas assignment in 1966, he threw cans of film into helicopters during the fall of Saigon, was shot at in El Salvador, and covered the Shah's fall in Iran. Correspondent Patrick Brown calls him "the model for us all."

"The most emotionally rewarding story of my career was going back to Prague to witness the Velvet Revolution that overthrew the Communist regime. It had been fifty years since I had left in 1939 and the Czechs had known nothing but trouble. I'd been back before and had been chased out twice and here I was, and history was on *my* side. It was a vindication — both personally and professionally. It felt like *I* had won."

Dressing up for work

THE PROGRAM THAT comedian Mike Myers listed as one of his five favourite things about Canada would never have happened except for a dust-up in Parliament during Centennial year.

Mr. Dressup (Ernie Coombs) was a regular on *Butternut Square* (1964-67), an ambitious children's show created by a committed group of child educators. The series was a soothing blend of music, instruction, and fantasy. Host Sandy Cohen told stories in a "see-through" house, and Mr. Dressup had two sets — the town square and a toy shop. The show also featured puppet pals Casey and Finnegan.

Butternut Square was cancelled in 1967, to the consternation of moms everywhere. Puppeteer Judith Lawrence, who played Casey and Finnegan, was an emerging feminist with friends in the Voice of Women organization. They took the show's cause to a Member of Parliament, who asked the minister responsible for the CBC, Judy LaMarsh, why her network was plowing under the nation's safest children's

Opposite: Many hands make light work. Mr. Dressup (Ernie Coombs) wears a costume from the bottomless "tickle trunk."

Below: Precocious Casey and the silent, watchful dog Finnegan lived in a treehouse. Judith Lawrence was the puppeteer.

playground. LaMarsh said she didn't know, but made inquiries right about the time Coombs and Lawrence pitched the CBC a more economical and efficient children's entertainment: just Mr. Dressup at home, with Casey, Finnegan, and a "tickle trunk" of costumes.

A short time later, the network announced that *Butternut Square* wasn't being cancelled so much as reformatted. The new show, *Mr. Dressup*, which would last twenty-nine years, probably benefited from the downsizing, Lawrence concedes today.

"I think we were guided by the same good principles as *Butternut Square*," comments the Australian-born puppeteer. "But maybe we were a little less teachy. And maybe children related to a simpler, more recognizable premise."

A graduate of the same Pittsburgh theatre group that produced *Mr. Rogers*, Ernie Coombs was a pleasant everyman with a gift for child's play. Trained as a commercial artist, he drew and constructed props quickly, as if in a hurry to see where his imagination might take him. And there was a childlike, Walter Mitty quality to his ransacking through the tickle trunk for costume characters.

Here was a father figure who loved to play even more than his surrogate puppet children — characters who were in their own way as artful and compelling as Mr. Dressup.

"When little girls asked, 'Is Casey a girl?' I would say, 'That's right,'" Lawrence remembers. "And if little boys wondered if Casey was a boy, I would answer, 'Why of course.'" It was also important that orange-conked Casey had an appetite for mischief, the puppeteer believes.

"If Casey had been passive, just accepting everything Mr. Dressup said, it wouldn't have been very much fun, or good for the children watching, so it was important that Casey was a little bit of an instigator," she says. "We wanted Mr. Dressup and Casey relating to each other, with respect and interest flowing both ways." Finnegan, she adds, was crucial because a silent, secretive dog gave Casey permission to be bold.

"Say Mr. Dressup showed up in a wild costume," Lawrence says. "Finnegan would

Formerly a commercial artist, Coombs shared his love of simple, playful art with three generations of Canadian children.

then whisper into Casey's ear, then Casey would say, 'Finnegan says you look silly.' Something that Casey perhaps thought, but didn't dare say. Finnegan liberated Casey."

An essential factor in the show's success, Lawrence believes, was Coombs's unwavering belief in the puppets as characters. "I don't think he ever saw me sitting underneath the furniture when we were on air," Lawrence says. "He was Mr. Dressup then, and the puppets were real to him. I remember at one period of the show, he would sometimes call Casey 'Chris,' which was the name of his young son."

One memorable show, Coombs found himself frowning at a malfunctioning sink. "What's wrong?" Casey asked, popping up alongside him. "Oh, I just had a leak in the sink," Mr.

Dressup replied, convulsing the set. Lawrence had to fight to keep from laughing, but Coombs had no idea what was going on. After the show he threw his hands in the air.

"How come everyone broke up earlier on?" he asked.

"Because you told everyone you peed in the sink!" he was told. Coombs shook his head. He'd been so immersed in his character, he couldn't recall the inadvertent double entendre.

Mr. Dressup also managed the special trick of encouraging wildly inventive fun while remaining protective of a child's imagination. In one '70s show, Mr. Dressup and Casey are visited by Al the alligator, who asks if they might look after his pet hamsters while he visits his family.

Oh, what are their names? Mr. Dressup

asks. Well, we're all named Al so there's never any confusion, the alligator explains. There's Alice, Alberta, Aloysious, Aloise, Alfredo, Algernon, and Alapatious (who of course drives an Alfa Romeo).

"See you later alligator," Casey calls out when Al leaves. Then he and Mr. Dressup play with the hamsters in a castle constructed out of grocery boxes. When Mr. Dressup breaks into a huge grin and cries, "Wouldn't it be great if the hamsters could carry little flags in their paws!" you realize the performer has slipped completely into the state of childhood.

Both Coombs and Lawrence were also careful never to bruise a child's sense of wonder. Mr. Dressup never adopted a character without tipping off the preschoolers at home first. And he kept the same style of glasses for the duration of the show. Lawrence scoffed at one new director's insistence that Casey needed a make-over and a working mouth to relate to modern children.

Lawrence hoped that she and Coombs would end their professional relationship together. "In 1990, I said, 'Ernie, let's quit now while we're still on top,'" she remembers telling her partner of twenty-six years.

But Coombs, who kept a poster of W.C. Fields in his dressing room and liked to drive a fully restored 1932 Auburn convertible, hung onto the things he liked. And he enjoyed being Mr. Dressup. Lawrence retired to Hornby Island in British Columbia, and Coombs worked his tickle trunk for another five years, retiring in 1995. A few months before "the sweetest guy there ever was," in friend Peter Gzowski's words, passed away in September 2001, he received an honorary doctorate at Trent University. Coombs's last words to the students were, "Keep your crayons sharp, your sticky tape untan-gled, and always put the top back on your markers."

Judith Lawrence says she never really understood what Mr. Dressup meant to Canadians until one winter when a group of Hornby Island friends threw together an amateur talent revue. "I decided to get Casey and Finnegan out again after all those years," she says. "And everyone loved them. And I'll never forget this one woman, she was crying she was so happy. I said, 'Why are you crying? They're just a couple of old puppets.' And she said, 'No, no, they're not, they're my childhood.'"

A '70s poster for the current affairs show for teenagers, What's New? *(1972-90), with hosts Harry Mannis and Sandy Lane.*

From Russia with love

YEAR AFTER the 1972 Canada-Soviet Union hockey series, Ralph Mellanby returned to Luzhniki Arena in Moscow with a film crew. Filing through the Zamboni entrance, he heard scattered applause grow into an appreciative roar.

"What's happening, why are they clapping?" *Hockey Night in Canada*'s executive producer asked his interpreter.

"You," the man said, smiling. "They're clapping for you."

"What do you mean?"

The interpreter pointed at a red flag on a crew member's jacket. "Canada," he said.

No wonder Mellanby was shocked. The twenty-seven-day, eight-game "Summit on Ice" hockey series the year before had been a vicious sporting battle and distrustful cultural exchange. Team Canada's Bobby Clarke maimed Soviet star Valeri Kharlamov, and organizer Alan Eagleson gave the Moscow crowd "the eagle" in a huffing, cross-ice shuffle. On the TV side, the Soviets tried to maintain control of every image that entered or left their country.

"The Russians had a representative, Igor Sharikov, stationed in our studios for all the Canadian games," remembers broadcaster Johnny Esaw. "They were using our feeds and were sure we were going to try and sneak commercials — capitalist propaganda! — back to

Russia." (No wonder Russia censored our commercials. Labatt's ads made us look like playboy Formula One racers, chasing through Montreal during the week, then leaping — *there, made it!* — on board a ferry to an exotic island for a Friday night sunset.) "And when we were in Moscow, using their feed," Esaw continues, "John Spalding, our guy in the truck, tried to get the Russian camera people to film Soviet premier Brezhnev in his box, but they wouldn't do it."

Not that the Canadian TV crew wasn't above the odd attempt at espionage.

"We thought the East German referee, Joseph Kampala, who was clearly for Russia, might be a little friendlier if he got to know us," Esaw recalls. "So we took him out and tried to get him drunk before game eight. Didn't work. He drank a lot, but never got drunk. Or particularly friendly."

Such was the paranoia in Team Canada's camp that left-winger Frank Mahovlich advised teammate Guy Lapointe, "In Moscow, we should camp outside in the hills beyond the city."

"What the hell for?"

"The Russians will start construction in our hotel at 4:00 a.m. just to ruin our sleep," the Big M replied.

"But Frank, most of our guys won't be in bed by then anyway," Lapointe laughed.

So why would a Moscow hockey crowd, a few months after a devastating loss, happily acknowledge a visit from a Canadian hockey delegation?

"Two reasons," Mellanby suggests. "First of all, you have to remember there was a big difference between the totalitarian Russian political regime and the Russian people. And I think the people, who had fought valiantly through two brutal wars in the last century, appreciated the heart and courage of our players. So I think, yeah, they were saluting our players coming from way behind to win that big series in Moscow.

"But I also really believe the '72 series was the beginning of the whole perestroika movement," he says. "Don't forget, five thousand

Opposite: The only foreign army ever to emerge victorious from Moscow was led by Paul Henderson (shown here jumping for joy after scoring the winning goal in the 1972 "Summit on Ice").
TORONTO STAR (FRANK LENNON)

Below: Canadian schoolchildren celebrate what became the most famous goal in Canadian hockey, depicted in the documentary Summit on Ice.

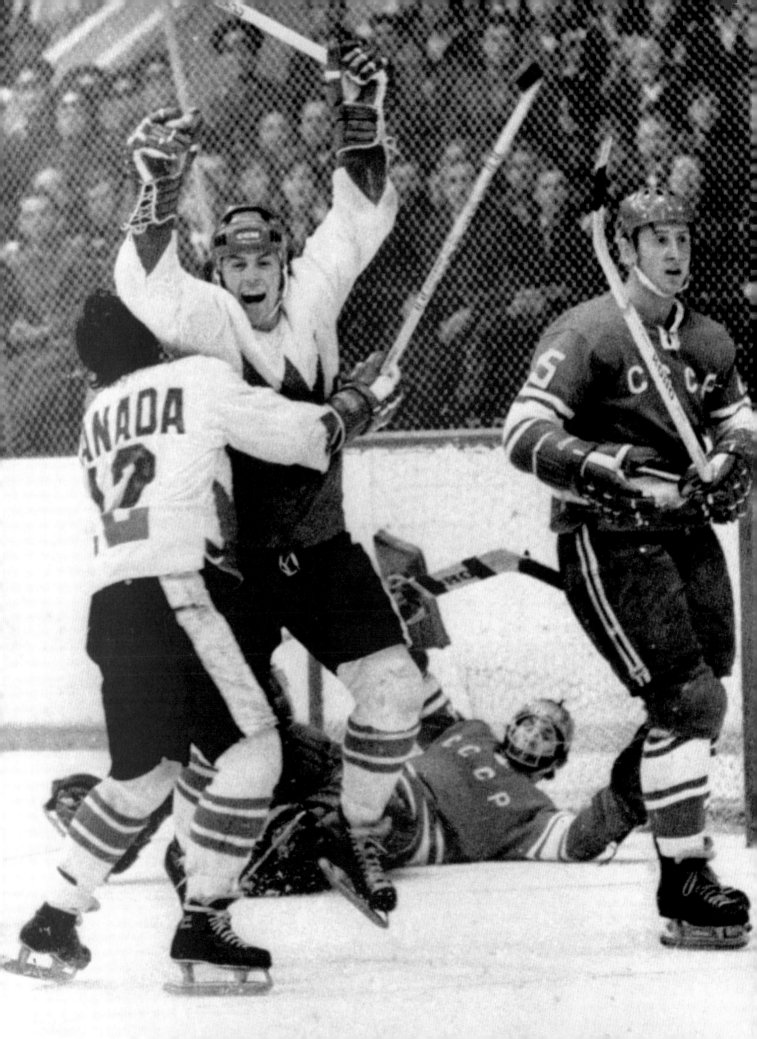

Phil Esposito's pep rally after game four: "People across Canada, we tried, we gave it our best," he told Johnny Esaw. "For the people who boo us. Jesus, all of us guys are really disheartened…. Every one of the thirty-five guys that came out and played for Team Canada did it because we love our country and not for any other reason."

Westerners invaded Moscow that September in 1972. You had cowboys from Calgary and hockey fans from Halifax roaring into hotel lobbies. Then at the games, you had three thousand Canadians singing "O Canada" at the top of their lungs and shouting their heads off for three periods. That made an impression, believe me."

Johnny Esaw agrees. "The Russian crowd changed through the four games we played there," he says. "At the beginning, they sat quietly, like they were at an opera. But they got an enormous kick out of the way Canadian fans behaved, and they loosened up through the course of the series."

The Russians might have lost a hockey series in 1972, but Mellanby suggests they won something more important — a tantalizing first glimpse of a different way of life. "As big and important as that series was to Canada, it was far more important to the Soviet Union," he says.

That would be saying something. For the 1972 Canada-Soviet series left indelible TV images in our collective memories:

Game one, Montreal — payback time for those Christmas tours where the Russian bear mauled Maritime all-star squads 12-1. Or so we thought. The next day's headline in Montreal's *Dimanche-Matin* said it best: *Le Canada humilié 7-3.*

Game two, Toronto. A disciplined Canadian effort produces a 4-1 win, with Pete Mahovlich slaloming the entire Russian team to score a short-handed goal.

Winnipeg next, and a ragged 4-4 tie that ended with a few boos.

"I knew Esposito was upset after Winnipeg, so after we lost 5-3 in Vancouver, game four, I went to the side of the rink to grab Phil for an interview," remembers Esaw. "He was emotionally shot, the sweat pouring off him. And all the frustration and desire came pouring out. He asked for Canada's help. Phil has since told me that that TV interview turned the series around, because after that the whole country was behind them. You know, the funny thing about that interview was that, just as Phil got going, I had an assistant frantically give me the cut-off sign. News was coming on. I waved him off. You get interviews like that once in a lifetime."

The next day more than a thousand fans responded to Esposito's emotional outburst with a show of support at Toronto's airport.
TORONTO STAR

Game five in Moscow started well, with Canada going up 4-1, but after that all we heard were referees and fans whistling. The final score was 5-4 for the Soviet Union and Canada was now three games to one, with three games left.

Canada won the next two games 3-2 and 4-3, with Paul Henderson scoring the winning goal both times (the second borne aloft over a defenceman's hip as he whistled a high one over startled goalie Vladislav Tretiak's shoulder). These superbly played contests were so tense that viewers had to be careful who they sat beside. "Howie Meeker was next to me the whole time over in Moscow," colour man Bill Good remembers. "And every time he got nervous or something happened, he slapped me hard on the thigh. I swear to God by the eighth game I had a big blue bruise on my leg."

On September 28, 1972, two out of every three Canadians — 12.5 million of us in all — watched game eight, which started at noon in St. John's and at 9:30 in the morning in Vancouver. Schoolchildren watched in classrooms or assembly halls. Offices were empty. Streets deserted. In the TV department of Toronto's downtown Simpsons store all two hundred sets were tuned to CBC and surrounded by nervous viewers.

Canada was down 3-2 after one period and 5-3 after two, but jumped back early in the third on a goal by Esposito that we had to take play-by-play man Foster Hewitt's word on because of satellite interference. Yvan Cournoyer scored a little later. Then with time running out in what we were certain would be a tie game and series, Foster had this to say:

"Savard clears to Stapleton.... He cleared to the open wing to Cournoyer. HERE'S A SHOT! Henderson made a wild stab at it and fell.... HERE'S ANOTHER SHOT, RIGHT IN FRONT, THEY SCORE!!! HENDERSON SCORES FOR CANADA, AND THE FANS AND TEAM ARE GOING WILD."

Below: Class is in session at Howie Meeker's hockey school.

Jumpin' Jehoshaphat

Howie Meeker was in Montreal on business in 1968 when he bumped into broadcaster Ted Darling. After an exchange of pleasantries, Darling asked Meeker if he would be guest analyst in an upcoming Montreal-Toronto hockey game.

The 1947 NHL rookie of the year thought hockey fell through the ice in the '50s, and that TV analysts were afraid of their shadows. Here was his chance to speak up about the game he loved. The only thing he had to remember was not to swear if, and when, he got wound up.

No one remembers his first on-air sermon, but it probably went something like this: "Look at Béliveau coming in alone! Jumping Jehoshaphat, what's Walton doing? Looking in the stands for pretty girls. Can't these Leafs finish their checks? Back it up. Stop right there. Nice pass by Rousseau. And hey-hey, the big fellow puts it home, easy as picking strawberries."

"Howie was an immediate sensation," remembers former *HNIC* executive producer Ralph Mellanby. "He changed us into real sports reporters. Howie was from Newfoundland. He didn't owe the league anything. If Béliveau had a bad game, he said it."

"His bravado gave other people courage," Mellanby says. "Suddenly, Dick Irvin and Brian McFarlane felt comfortable saying what was on their minds.... No one broadcaster ever changed TV hockey coverage more than Howie."

The spirit of '76

CBC covered the 1952 Helsinki Olympics by lending a camera to future long-distance runner Bruce Kidd's dad, who just happened to be making a business trip to Scandinavia.

By the 1976 Montreal games, the Olympic coverage team had grown to almost three hundred. And whereas Kidd brought back fifteen hours of footage that was trimmed to a highlight kinescope, in Montreal the network produced 169 hours of mostly live coverage.

These games defined all subsequent network Olympic coverage. While ABC interpreted the games as theatre in 1976, taping all but a few marquee events then editing them into seamless dramatic packages, the CBC covered the Olympics as an all-encompassing, live spectacle.

This revolutionary approach to Olympic coverage — which allowed viewers to attend and not simply follow the games — was at first a hard sell, reports Gordon Craig, who managed the network's TV coverage in Montreal and later became head of sports.

"We started to plan for the event two years in advance, but it was only a year before the games that we managed to convince management how big these Olympics were going to be," he remembers. "I kept saying, 'When the games begin there's going to be an emotional binge in this country the likes of which we haven't seen since Expo. We're inviting the world to Montreal; all of Canada is going to want to watch what happens. If we don't show them, we won't have fulfilled our mandate as a public broadcaster.'

"There was lots of skepticism, believe me," he says. "I remember people in advertising kept saying, 'Man, how are we going to sell a full day of Olympic coverage?' Of course a few months before the event they found that advertisers couldn't get enough of the Olympics."

Neither could viewers. Ninety-two percent of us — more than eighteen million Canadians — watched CBC's 1976 Montreal Olympics, a fifteen-day event that witnessed the emergence of fourteen-year-old Romanian gymnast Nadia Comaneci and Cuban boxer Teofilo Stevenson as international sports celebrities.

"The Montreal model is still in use today," comments 1976 executive producer Bob Moir. "Even if there is a fifteen-hour time difference, as there was in Sydney in 2000, [the CBC] still covers the Olympics as a live, unfolding news event."

In the months subsequent to the games, though, athletic accomplishment was overshadowed by scandal, as the event that Montreal mayor Jean Drapeau had promised could "no more have a deficit than a man have a baby" grew from a $124-million estimate to a $1.5-billion expenditure.

But for two weeks in early September, few of us cared about price tags as a TV team led by Moir, Ted Reynolds, and Lloyd Robertson, all decked out in brand-new, melon-coloured blazers, captured the performances of the world's athletic elite. Canadian silver medal winners at the event included Greg Joy (high jump) — replayed for years on CBC's nightly sign-off — John Wood (canoeing), Michel Vaillancourt (equestrian jumping), and Cheryl Gibson (swimming).

Romanian gymnast Nadia Comaneci was the darling of the Montreal Olympics, winning three gold medals. Today she owns a gymnastics club in Norman, Oklahoma. CP/COA/RW

His résumé lists twenty-one different sports, but Don Chevrier is perhaps best known as the play-by-play announcer for the popular CBC Saturday afternoon *Curling Classic* series from 1972 to 1981.

"*Breakfast with Ali*"

HEAVEN FOR ME growing up in Edmonton was watching boxing on TV with Don Dunphy on Friday night and hockey with Foster Hewitt on Saturday. I loved sports. I even wrote a sports column for the *Edmonton Journal* in high school, then caught on with CJCA radio. Station manager Morris Carter talked me out of college. "Give you $225 a month," he said. "That's money in your pocket and you'll learn more than in journalism school."

I banged around — CFRA in Ottawa, CJAD in Montreal — before CBC hired me in 1966. You know, I covered twenty-one sports at CBC. White water rafting, volleyball, everything. People identify me with curling, though. CBC invented curling coverage. We got the first "top shot" by putting a cameraman up a ladder on top of a raft. I'll never forget one Brier, producer Leo Hebert saying to ladder man Bob Brockhill, "Better go to the bathroom now, you'll be up there a long time." Bob waved him off. Two hours later, we hear Bob saying, "Leo, I gotta go." They argue for a while; Leo finally got mad. "Do your job!" he said. Game's over, Bob climbs down, one boot off, limps over and drops the boot in front of Leo. "Told you I had to go," he said.

The CFL was a great way to see Canada. I went to the Grey Cup anniversary in 2001 and Russ Jackson and I visited old haunts in Montreal, our favourite city. Brought back memories. You went out after games to calm down. Even doing a late sportscast in Toronto, I couldn't sleep until 3. Adrenalin helps though, too. I remember the Muhammad Ali-Zora Folley fight. I did a prelim and was awful. I thought, uh-oh. But when the bell rang, I was fine. The game takes you away.

Ali was the most exciting athlete I ever saw. What people don't understand was how big he was. Like a big football player. And he really could float like a butterfly. He always put on a show. I think he enjoyed what he was doing. In Germany I interviewed him for the Karl Mildenberger fight. Day of the fight, I saw producer Bob Helm. He was ashen. "Tape was blank," he said. "We're screwed." Just then, Angelo Dundee, Ali's manager, came by. We told him what had happened. Minutes later he came back with a scrap of paper. "That's his room number," he said.

So I went up. Sure enough, Ali was there, with Bundini Brown, eating breakfast. "Like something to eat?" Ali asked. "Some juice?" I declined, waited for them to finish, then Ali gave me more time than I needed.

I inherited the play-by-play job at ABC while working with Howard Cosell on the Larry Holmes-Tex Cobb fight. Holmes was beating Cobb easily and Howard said at one point, "This referee is writing boxing's obituary. This exhibition warrants no further comment from me." Then for the first time ever, he shut up. Producer Chet Forte said, "Chevy, take over." Every time I said something, Howard glared at me.

Sports took me around the world and gave me recognition, which was nice. I remember a CFL game in Ottawa when producer Cec Barnes said, "Go to a commercial, Chevy, get a load of this." On the monitor were five kids wearing headsets, white shirts, ties, dark-rimmed glasses, and dark wigs, looking a lot like you know who. Then they threw up a big sign that said "The Don Chevrier Fan Club." Oh yeah, I got a kick out of that.

Left to right: Doug Maxwell, Don Duguid, and Don Chevrier at a championship curling game. Behind them, on the right, a soundman walks the ice with a parabolic microphone reflector.

REGIONAL ACCENTS

REX MURPHY ONCE had a friend, a fellow Newfoundlander, who phoned his wife at seven o'clock every Friday when work took him to the mainland.

"Woman," he'd ask, "Get that goddamn *Land and Sea* on tape for me, will ya please!"

Land and Sea was one of hundreds of CBC regional music, drama, and current affairs shows. Winnipeg produced *Spotlight*, where antic weatherman Ed Russenholt underscored his signature phrase, "weather from the heart of the continent," by doodling a heart around Manitoba. And everyone who lived in Kingston in the '60s and '70s remembers sportscaster Max Jackson's sign-off, "If you don't play a sport, be one."

Edmonton had *The Tommy Banks Show*. Toronto, *Sylvia Tyson's Country in My Soul*. Ottawa's local music show was *Country Report* (with Wayne Rostad), while Regina offered *Prairie Roadhouse*, Halifax, *Country East*, St. John's, *Wonderful Grand Band* and *Newfoundland Country*, and Winnipeg, *Red River Jamboree*.

But in Newfoundland it was the current affairs show *Land and Sea* (1963-present) that, in Murphy's words, "enjoyed an almost magical rapport with the people."

Long-time host Dave Quinton deserves much of the credit for making the series work, Murphy believes. "There was a man," he says, "who could go out and cover any aspect of fishing, an industry that can be as esoteric as university economics, and turn a report into a true story.

"When he travelled to the outport fisheries in the late '60s, and talked to the eloquent, biblical fishermen who spoke in dialects that few today would understand, he did nothing less than record the history of a way of life just before it disappeared."

Quinton's special art, CBC-TV commentator Murphy says, is that he accomplished all this in a seemingly casual, easy manner that charmed both his interview subjects and audience.

"It was all so natural, the way he talked through a script, that even though he was talking about culture, there was no sense of a coddled heritage," Murphy says. "People just watched the f'n show because they liked it. It meant something to them."

Above left: Weatherman Ed Russenholt of CBWT-TV Winnipeg's current affairs show Spotlight *gives sportscaster Jack Wells the grand pooh-bah treatment in the early '60s.*
Above right: Long-time Land and Sea *host (1964-91) Dave Quinton.*

Left (clockwise from bottom left): Host Deborah Lauren, Murray McLauchlan, Diamond Joe White, and k.d. lang on Country West *from Regina in 1987.*

Below: More than five thousand citizens successfully protest the cancellation of CBET-TV Windsor's local newscast in 1990. Because its transmitter is close to the American border, CBET was forbidden to air U.S. shows, which meant that from 1975 to 1984 the station was the first network affiliate to present entirely Canadian programming. Warner Troyer's On the Record *was just one CBET show that went national.*

THE WE NETWORK

PERHAPS THE DEFINING CBC moment this decade came off-camera, after a 1985 investigative report on *the fifth estate* revealed how the federal government approved, then attempted to cover up the sale of one million rancid cans of tuna to supermarkets.

The resulting uproar led to the resignation of federal fisheries minister John Fraser. ("You don't fool around with people's lunches," commented *fifth estate* host Hana Gartner.) Days later, when Prime Minister Brian Mulroney showed up to throw out the first pitch at a base-

ball game, the entire stadium took up the chant, "Tuna! tuna! tuna!"

The '80s were the so-called "me decade." In an era of conspicuous layoffs, trust company failures, corporate bankruptcies, and ecological villainy, the two most popular shows on American TV for the first half of the decade were *Dallas* and *Dynasty*, evening soaps celebrating the filthy rich and famous.

At the CBC, however, the mood was considerably more egalitarian. "Mr. Thatcher, how do you like being compared to J.R. Ewing in *Dallas*?" a female reporter asks rancher-politician Colin

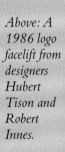

Above: A 1986 logo facelift from designers Hubert Tison and Robert Innes.

Right: Louis Del Grande (right) with guest stars Ross Petty and Karen Kain on Seeing Things.

Barbara Frum appears on a commemorative stamp and is portrayed by Greg Malone of CODCO. *Frum loved Malone's impersonation. (CBC's first president, Alphonse Ouimet, also appears on the stamp.)* CANADA POST; SALTER STREET FILMS LTD.

Thatcher (Kenneth Welsh) as he dances down the steps of the Saskatchewan legislature in the network's 1989 docudrama, *Love and Hate*. Upon being likened to the definitive TV patriarch of the greed-is-good '80s, Welsh's character fixes the reporter with a sulky smile and barks, "I think you better turn off your TV and get back in the kitchen."

The dark pleasure in Welsh's voice reminded us of J.R., but Saskatchewan isn't Texas, and unlike *Dallas*, *Love and Hate* offered no winking approval of its lead villain — Thatcher ended the acclaimed miniseries in prison, convicted of murder.

Jail was also the final stop for most of the scheming fat cats in the comedy-drama *Seeing Things*, which starred former *King of Kensington* writer Louis Del Grande as Louie Ciccone, a clairvoyant police reporter.

"A lot of Louie's apparitions involved rich, greedy people murdering someone for selfish reasons," remembers the show's head writer, David Barlow. "That social commentary came naturally out of the '80s."

Del Grande's forlorn police reporter was a pair of brown shoes in a room full of tuxedos, Barlow says. As it turns out, Louie's weren't the only boots kicking back at the decade. When asked by a Toronto journalist what show best captured the spirit of the times, Del Grande replied, "*SCTV*, although I'm sure its creators don't regard it as social criticism ... the show is a perfectly drawn moral universe ... full of villains and fools."

CBC news, public affairs, and nature programs also ran against the grain of the decade. David Suzuki was brought on to host *The Nature of Things* in 1980 and turned the show into an environmental protection agency. And on *The Journal*, the network's boldest experiment in public affairs programming since *This Hour Has Seven Days*, interviewer-host Barbara Frum read faces instead of teleprompters as she pried the truth out of reluctant potentates.

The classic '80s CBC show, *The Journal* offered further proof that there was a *we* network in the *me* decade. Once, a few days after the Seoul Summer Olympics, *Journal* producers scrapped plans for an entire show an hour before air time when Jamie Astaphan, disgraced Olympic sprinter Ben Johnson's doctor, finally ended his media ban by agreeing to speak to Frum. The resulting cross-examination had the crackling air of a classic courtroom drama. Later, a producer explained the decision to throw out a prepared show in favour of an ad hoc interview: "Ben Johnson was the story of the day. And we were always committed to telling the story Canadians had to know."

Coo-roo-coo-coo!

Rick Moranis and Dave Thomas as Bob and Doug McKenzie. Their "Great White North" segment offered valuable hoser tips, such as how to roll a smoke with snowmobile mitts on.
OLD FIREHALL PRODUCTIONS

ANYONE WHO BELIEVES comedy is misdirected anger would appreciate the genesis of *SCTV*'s most famous characters, Bob and Doug McKenzie.

The toqued tandem came out of a CBC request for more Canadian content on a show that was produced, written, and performed by Canadians. The first performers who heard the directive, Rick Moranis and Dave Thomas, were outraged.

"What do you want us to do?" they asked. "Throw up a map of Canada and sit there wearing toques and parkas?"

Manager Andrew Alexander could only smile and say, "Yeah, and if you could have a Mountie in it, that would be great too."

Which is how, in the fall of 1981, Bob and Doug McKenzie came to welcome us into their rec room with a drunken loon call, "Coo-roo-coo-coo, coo-coo-coo!" A chug of beer later, the boys began riffing on various Canadian topics. Like how come doughnut shops always have more tables than parking spots.

"After we improvised about forty Canadian Corners in one day, we forgot about it," recalls Thomas. "Then Rick and I got a call from the Saskatchewan Roughrider cheerleaders, who invited us to a homecoming party. Now remember, at this point when people asked what we did for a living, we'd be embarrassed because no one seemed to know what *SCTV* was. Anyway, we show up in Regina and there's two thousand kids at the airport, dressed up in parkas and earmuffs, screaming

at us. I turned to Rick and said, 'Holy shit!'"

Eventually, Bob and Doug's self-directed TV bits — "zoom in, beauty!" — resulted in a million-selling record album, the movie *Strange Brew*, and who knows how many attempts at ripping off breweries by ski-jacketed hosers hoping to trade mouse-filled empties for free cases of beer.

While they did almost no TV parodies in their Old Firehall Productions stage show, cast members Moranis, Thomas, John Candy, Eugene Levy, Joe Flaherty, Andrea Martin, Catherine O'Hara, and later Martin Short began to cannibalize the medium the instant they hit the air as *Second City* in 1976.

"We found that the stage stuff just didn't make us laugh on TV," Thomas says. "When we lampooned TV, we started having fun. We didn't have the budget for guest stars so we started fooling around, doing impressions. All that we were doing was trying to make ourselves laugh [with] those weird juxtapositions, like 'The Benny Hill Street Blues' and 'Bowery Boys in the Band.'" (Wayne and Shuster engaged in similar buffoonery with spoofs like "Ben Casey, Auto Mechanic.")

The series remains one of the best Mixmaster blends of movie and TV satire ever accomplished on television. In time, the show became a metaphor for show business itself, with every character, from Flaherty's scheming station manager Guy Caballero to Short's demented fan Ed Grimley ("This anticipation — it's making me mental!"), acting as a symbiotic partner in an intricately corrupt entertainment world.

The success of Bob and Doug changed *SCTV* (1980-83 on CBC). Suddenly, the cast had the impetus and nerve to focus on the parent network. A few *SCTV* Canadian sketches cut so close to the bone that one wonders if anyone had second thoughts about the show going native.

One segment was filled with ads for imitation Yank programming (*Magnum P.E.I.*) and Information Canada blurbs ("Canadian football actually has four downs, but Canadians always punt on the third down to play it safe. That's a Canadian fact"). The show's most biting parody was of *Front Page Challenge* and the Canadian star system.

"A popular Canadian actor," muses panellist Austin McGrath (Short), trying to identify a hidden challenger. "Pass."

"You say you're a *popular* Canadian actor," panellist Phillip Marks (Flaherty) wonders aloud, shaking his head. "I'm afraid I'm going to have to pass on that one, too."

Eventually, the challenger steps forward. Still no one recognizes him, although all concede his voice is familiar. Then an audio clip is played: "Active during the day, the woodchuck hibernates in snowy climbs ..."

"Ahhhhh," the panellists smile and scold themselves. "Why it's Morley Markle of *Hinterlands Who's Who!*"

Ironically, the success of "Can Con" superstars Bob and Doug McKenzie hastened the demise of *SCTV*. In becoming stars, Moranis and Thomas pricked the *Truman Show* membrane that protected the mad fantasy that was *SCTV*. Both left the show at the end of the 1982 season. Candy and O'Hara began making more films. Was it possible to be both a satirist *and* a celebrity? Shaking hands one show, biting them the next?

Probably not. No *SCTV* cast member ever again found the comfort zone they enjoyed playing in relative anonymity, "trying to make each other laugh" on their *SCTV* days. "I think everyone involved agrees *SCTV* was their purest creative time," Rick Moranis has said. Joe Flaherty agreed, adding, "We will never have that chance again."

Catherine O'Hara, however, begs to differ. "I hope one day we all do something together again," she once told Dave Thomas, "even if it's to launch a new line of bathing suits."

SCTV *cast (clockwise from bottom right): Andrea Martin, Joe Flaherty, Catherine O'Hara, Eugene Levy, John Candy, Dave Thomas, and Rick Moranis. Missing in action: Martin Short, who arrived in 1982.*
OLD FIREHALL
PRODUCTIONS

Love and respect of country

CANADA'S COUNTRY GENTLEMAN, Tommy Hunter, was the rare TV star who took off jewellery *before* he went on the air. Which is why he was embarrassed when Eddy Arnold appeared on his show one night and turned a song segment into a gold rush.

"During makeup, Eddy told me all about his fifty-three-foot yacht," Hunter once told Knowlton Nash. "Now Eddy's one of the wealthiest men in Nashville. Owns all the water in Tennessee. Every time somebody flushes, Eddy gets a nickel.

"As we're leaving makeup I look for a tie, but the producer says, 'Don't bother, Eddy's just wearing a sports jacket,'" Hunter recounts. "So Eddy does his number and I come on and say, 'Ladies and gentlemen, the Tennessee Plowboy — Eddy Arnold.' Eddy's supposed to smile and say thanks. Except he sees this gold chain around my neck and says, 'Hmmn, that's nice.'"

Tommy Hunter on guitar with The Rhythm Pals *— Mike Ferbey, Mark Wald, and Jack Jensen — on* The Tommy Hunter Show.

Hunter was mortified. "I don't like flaunting things at all," he explains, "so I said, 'Thanks, Eddy, it's a gift.'"

"Boy, oh boy," Arnold replied. "I wish I had a nice gold chain like that."

"It's from my wife," Hunter answered through a tight smile. Then thought to himself, Gee, Eddy, you're playing the Tennessee Plowboy right to the hilt tonight, aren't you?

"Well, I sure wish I had a wife who bought me nice things like that," Arnold continued, freeing the strand of gold from Hunter's collar to let it play in the studio lights.

"Yeah, I think your wife did," the host finally said, returning serve with a crashing volley. "Didn't she just get you a fifty-three-foot yacht?"

While Hunter was embarrassed by Arnold's playful remarks, he was also being sensitive to fan sensibilities. Being seen wearing a lot of jewellery, he figured, might be considered putting on showbiz airs. "However long I did the show," he says, "I always tried to think of some guy out in Rosewater, Saskatchewan, who just wanted uncomplicated entertainment."

This Hunter did with distinction and a minimum of fuss for thirty-six seasons, serving the TV public well-scrubbed country tunes from the Louis St. Laurent right through to the Brian Mulroney years.

"Grab your toothbrush, laddy, and polish up those pearly whites, because you're going on television," is how fiddler King Ganam informed Tommy he was joining the cast of *Country Hoedown* in 1956.

His earliest fans were scrimping for engagement rings when they first glimpsed Tommy cavorting with Gordie Tapp and Tommy Common on *Hoedown*. Back then Hunter was a raw-boned kid with a lacquered blond pompadour. CBC gave the London, Ontario, artist his own show in 1966. Over the next twenty-six years, as the singer's hair turned Porter Wagoner silver, his fans wrestled down mortgages, raised families, and collapsed in sofas Friday or Saturday nights to wind down with Hunter, ace fiddler Al Cherny, and The Rhythm Pals.

The kid who recited Hank Williams instead of Shakespeare in high school had as much respect for country music as he did for its fans, which is why Hunter imposed a few rules when he finally got his own show. First off, there would be no hay bales or overalls. Rural audiences, Hunter felt, should never be treated like hicks.

"I remember one producer coming up with what he thought was a great idea, saying, 'Let's have a down East segment for our Maritime fans,'" Hunter groans. "'You know, we'll have everybody dress up in fishing gear and sing, "I'se the b'y that builds the boat, And I'se the b'y that sails her."'

"I told him, 'No, that'll be awful. Real country fans in the Maritimes will string us up if we do something like that, and rightly so.'"

Hunter wanted his program to be as familiar and comfortable as an old pair of shoes. Every show featured regulars like Pat Hervey and Debbie Lori Kaye singing recognizable favourites. Fiddler Al Cherny would offer a sprightly solo at some point. The Rhythm Pals would get a workout behind Tommy, who would also offer an inspirational reading, like "What is a boy?" or "Friendship is …." A featured guest, maybe Hank Snow or Tammy Wynette, would then sing a few of their hits.

But they had to sing their hits. Superstar

Tammy Wynette stands by two men here — host Tommy Hunter and guest Ian Tyson in 1990.

Conway Twitty once wanted to play only new stuff to promote his current album.

"I'm afraid we can't do that, Conway," Hunter told him. "Your fans will want to hear a few of your big hits." Twitty refused to do the show.

Each *Tommy Hunter Show* also contained at least one purposefully corny joke that was calculated to make the audience feel they were settling down to an evening of old-time entertainment. Tommy is still telling these jokes on the road today to appreciative audiences.

"Is Father Delay in the house?" he'll shout, starting off a show.

No response.

"I said, Is Father Delay in the house?"

More quiet.

"Well, without Father Delay, here we *gooo!*"

Hunter says he learned his most important show business lesson at the feet of his hero, country and western legend Roy Acuff. "This was at a TV taping of The Grand Ole Opry in Nashville," Hunter recalls. "There was this entertainer and he was good — flashy. Musicians loved him. But Roy saw the audience sitting on their hands. So he grabbed the microphone and said, 'Well that sure was nice, but do you know …?' and he mentioned some standard. The singer did it, and sure enough the crowd really got going.

"Which is as it should be," Hunter argues, "because if there's no audience, there's no show."

Travelling man

Wayne Rostad hasn't left the highway since he began *On the Road Again* in 1987.

Along the way, the genial broadcaster-singer-storyteller has sought out and palled around with thousands of not-so-ordinary Canadians, from the guy who conducts boat tours out of Dildo, Newfoundland, to the entrepreneur in Terrace Bay, B.C., who turned the back end of a '59 Cadillac into a hot dog cart.

"We don't do the rich and the famous as a rule," Rostad has said of his show. "So we're not influenced by anything other than plain, ordinary people who do some of the most incredible and extraordinary things."

Like the New Brunswick buddies who race their belt sanders for charity. Or Sally Milne of La Ronge, Saskatchewan, who imprints delicate patterns of dragonflies and birds on birchbark with her teeth. (The artist is one of the few remaining practitioners of the aboriginal art of birchbark biting.)

The still-running show has proven as popular as it is populist. By its third season, *On the Road Again* was reaching over one million fans. And Rostad's book of the same name became an instant bestseller.

Wayne Rostad's on the water this time — off the coast of Newfoundland — filming an episode with cameraman Keith Whelan and soundman François Pagé.

A strange kettle of fish

BEFORE *This Hour Has 22 Minutes* there was *CODCO*. Or perhaps more accurately, because of *CODCO* we now have *This Hour Has 22 Minutes*.

Right from its 1973 theatrical debut, *Cod on a Stick*, the Newfoundland satirical group brought a welcome savagery to the polite world of Canadian comedy. Religion, sex, the Commonwealth, crotchless underwear — *CODCO* (1988-93) lampooned them all. Sometimes in the same skit. One show ended with the queen commenting on "a French pope who ate a large rubber novelty item," just before an impersonator of then-CBC president Pierre Juneau arrived, dangling women's undies on his finger.

CODCO, a Salter Street Films production, featured the work of four talented female performers and three gifted male comedians. That Greg Malone and Tommy Sexton belonged to both groups only added to the confusion and fun. Malone did a classic Barbara Frum. And who can forget a leather-miniskirted Sexton, as Anne Murray, trilling a fishy version of "Snowbird": "Beneath the frozen water cold and drawn, / The rainbow trout lies waiting for its roe to turn to spawn, / The rainbow sings a song it always sings / And speaks to me of frying pans and boil-ups in the spring."

Other *CODCO* highlights included future *22 Minutes'* stars Cathy Jones and Mary Walsh as the hard-up Friday Night Girls:

"Yer ugly, yer ugly, yer freggin' ugly!"

"Wha?"

"I'm just teasin' me hair."

And Andy Jones starred in a sketch, "I Am Beano Balacator," that defined how far-out and funny *CODCO* could be. Shot in '50s black and white, this classic meditation on Irish Catholic guilt begins with Beano wandering a dark alley, trembling, vulnerable to sin. He's then lured into a speakeasy, where over-excited men loll about tickling each other's feet.

Afterwards, flushed with shame, Beano returns home to his heartbroken wife. "You were ticklin' weren't you, Beano?" she cries. "Sure, I can smell it on yer fingers. Ah, ticklin' — the curse a the Irish."

Wildly original and entirely successful on its own terms, *CODCO* redefined the boundaries of Canadian TV comedy while marking the way for subsequent Maritime-based satires (*This Hour Has 22 Minutes, Made in Canada*).

Right: The Urban Peasant*'s catch of the day. In addition to hosting a TV show, James Barber has written a dozen cookbooks.*
WWW.THEURBANHUB.COM

Below: Bruno Gerussi and Madame Benoît on Take 30. *A few years later, in 1975, Gerussi would have his own cooking show,* Celebrity Cooks.

KITCHEN HELP

FOUR CBC CHEFS have captured our attention and spice racks over the years.

First, in the early '60s, *Take 30* contributor Madame Jehane Benoît taught us how to clean a goose (vinegar) and cook Christmas Eve tourtières. Then came kitchen cad Graham Kerr, the English-born *Galloping Gourmet* (1968-72). A typical 4 p.m. show began with Kerr vaulting a chair with a spilling goblet of wine, ripping off his coat, then slurring, "Throw your breasts in the pans, ladies!" in the manner of a soused prince

stumbling into a favourite bawdy house.

Kerr's Ottawa studio audience was flattered by the attention, and the show was an immediate sensation. Within three years, Kerr was seen by 200 million fans in thirty-eight countries. How big was *The Galloping Gourmet*? In 1969, the *New York Times* carried the headline "Gourmet Sets Fire to Dishcloth" below its main story, "Man Steps on Moon."

The irrepressible Stephen Yan was the network's third highly successful afternoon chef. His show, *Wok with Yan*, lasted twelve years

(1980-92) and a thousand bad puns — "a wok of art," "genius at wok…."

But somehow the jokes that seemed so maddening at first became funny when Yan began cooking, lifting his head for a staccato shout while his knife moved in a flashing blur through vegetables. "I never cook asparagus in my restaurant," he might yell. "People never leave me any tip. Ha, ha, ha." If someone groaned, Yan countered with, "Don't wok the boat!" then threw the veggies into his wok, tossed in oil, and for some reason shouted, "A-right Saw-gent!" when his stove became a hissing curtain of steam.

When the chef was asked how he managed eight shows a day and around-the-calendar tours to promote cookbooks, his response was characteristically absurd yet flavourful: "Old Chinese expression: better to be at foot of chicken than tail of cow."

James Barber also likes to throw a little comic seasoning into his Vancouver-based show. "Cooking is like sex: you do the best with what you've got," is Barber's culinary philosophy. Since 1991, *The Urban Peasant*'s classically simple recipes (most dishes can be prepared in a frying pan) have been popular with fans in more than a hundred countries.

Finger food — Pierre Berton nearly sliced off a pinky demonstrating a food processor on a 1977 episode of Peter Gzowski's 90 Minutes Live.

Stephen Yan (left) and Graham Kerr in action on Wok with Yan *and* The Galloping Gourmet.

A comic visionary

*S*EEING THINGS WAS born the moment drama executive Robert Allen complimented Louis Del Grande on a TV performance.

"That was great," Allen said. "Do you have anything you can play lead in?"

"Sure," Del Grande replied. "How about me playing a reporter-clairvoyant who solves mysteries?" One other thing, he added, my character is separated but trying to patch things up with his wife because she's the centre of his moral universe — that and she knows how to drive and he doesn't.

"I think I could sell that," Allen smiled.

Del Grande made up the pitch on the spot. He and *King of Kensington* co-writer David Barlow had once sketched out a mystery series with a cop and a clairvoyant bookstore owner. But *Seeing Things* (1981-87) was more Del Grande selling himself than a concept. For starters, the show's lead character, Louie Ciccone, was, like Del Grande himself, a writer-clairvoyant.

"He didn't talk about it a lot because he felt people would call him a crackpot," *Seeing Things* co-creator Barlow says. "But, yeah, Louis anticipated events. One time, he had an image of his son in a cast, then went home and found he'd broken his arm."

Also, Del Grande, who was so hyper he didn't dare drive, had recently remarried former wife

Opposite: Louie hears his mummy calling in an episode called "The Eyes of Ra."

Below: Seeing Things' stars Janet-Laine Green (left), Louis Del Grande, and Martha Gibson in a hot tub.

(and frequent chauffeur) actor Martha Gibson. Since she had already memorized the part, Martha would also play Louis's recently reunited onscreen driver-partner. The couple would barely change their names in taking their domestic act to TV — Louis and Martha became Louie and Marge.

Barlow isn't surprised that Del Grande managed to hatch a classic TV series in an instant. "What did Churchill say when asked the secret to extemporaneous speaking?" he asks. "Preparation. And really pitching stories is what TV writers do. You tailor them to whatever comes up. All of us have a subconscious filled with half-baked ideas."

Besides, riffing was Del Grande's stock in trade. "One of the reasons I left *King of Kensington* was because Louis was going," says Fiona Reid. "I wondered how the show could survive without him. He has such a fertile comic mind. He could just take off and go."

Here's a little Louis-Louie from *Seeing Things*-period press clippings:

"When I started *Seeing Things* my major goal was to act without shaking. I went from that to a manic Perry Como. My relaxation started to worry me. I knew if I got more comfortable, I would atrophy and be incapable of using certain muscles. Already, I've had a dream about half my foot going missing and I have to hop on one leg. I think if I stay one year longer, I may never be able to put my foot down again....

"I'm more Canadian than anybody. When you grow up in New Jersey, you keep looking across the river obsessed by the New York skyline, which is perfect training for being a Canadian — they're obsessed with what's across the border....

"I always see at least three sides to every story. Part of me says, What's TV? It's sucking shadows and..."

Finally, Liam Lacey stops Louis mid-segue. "Sucking shadows?" the *Globe and Mail* reporter asks.

"Sorry," Del Grande responds sheepishly, "that was supposed to be a clever reference to Plato's cave."

Janet-Laine Green (left) with guest star Kate Reid. As with most TV mysteries, guest stars invariably played villains on Seeing Things.

The trick to *Seeing Things*, Barlow believes, was harnessing Del Grande's hyperkinetic personality. A deeply moral Roman Catholic allergic to the me decade, Del Grande was drawn to the style and substance of '30s screwball comedies (*Bringing Up Baby*, *The Awful Truth*). There was also the ESP thing. Plus, Louis was wound so tight he required a mini-trampoline on set to work off excess energy.

"The other big thing," Barlow adds, "was getting the mystery right. That's what we worked hardest on, figuring if we worked in the clairvoyant stuff properly, everything else would flow naturally out of ... who Louis [Del Grande] was and the way he approached the world."

The "everything else" included a cracked romantic triangle involving characters Louie and Marge Ciccone along with assistant crown attorney Heather Redfern (Janet-Laine Green). (Marge suspected Redfern was secretly warm for her husband's pear-shaped form.)

The series' brilliant stroke was casting Del Grande as a stalled, mid-career police reporter.

"Being a reporter gave Louie access to crime assignments," Barlow suggests. "Also, being stuck in a job gave him blue-collar empathy."

That Louie Ciccone always seemed to be battling a bossy plutocrat was entirely in keeping with the period and Del Grande's character, Barlow believes. "That was an interesting time," he says. "The film scene in Toronto was really taking off, with studios like Atlantis being created. There was a lot of money in town. But Louis had come out of the underground movement and Factory Theatre. So he was maybe a bit suspicious about some of the things that were happening.

"We got Canadian stars to play bad guys because we thought they'd have fun, as would the audience," Barlow continues. "One season we had Bruno Gerussi, Kate Reid, Barbara Hamilton, Gordy Pinsent, Barry Morse, and John Ireland on the show. We were desperate to get Wayne and Shuster, too, but couldn't figure out the mystery angle."

If Barlow and Del Grande captured the '80s

thematically, they simulated '30s screwball comedies with a bold creative strategy.

"What we did was shoot a lot more pages than necessary," Barlow recalls. "We usually ended up dropping a whole scene. Then tightening everything. More than any other writer-performer I know, Louis had an objective sense of what worked. I can remember him in the editing room, saying, 'Oh, I can't stand seeing so much of myself, let's cut it off there.' Most actors don't do things like that," he laughs. "Believe me."

By abandoning two dizzy, '30s-era romantics in the lean-mean '80s, *Seeing Things* produced a pair of oddball — alternately vulnerable and resilient — heroes whose struggle to stick together resulted in the show's quirky charm. Louie and Marge might have tracked killers every show, but *Seeing Things'* best mystery was always the Ciccones' relationship.

Here they are, stranded with a couple of rich stinkers at a swank cultural exhibit in the episode "The Eyes of Ra." Louie puts a foot in his mouth with his first few words to Mr. Spencer (Austin Willis), the museum president, by assuming the woman whose face he was making a meal out of in the parking lot the previous scene was Mrs. Spencer. "Ciccone, this is not my wife," Spencer hisses, quitting the room.

After Redfern explains that the Spencers have been separated for two months and that Mrs. Spencer is on a yacht with her plastic surgeon, Marge and Louie are left to contemplate the mad world they share.

"Two months and these people are sex maniacs," Louie says. "The world's going bananas. Too many soap operas. Look at us, we were separated for what? three years. No wingdings, right? Not a single wingding."

Marge clears her throat.

"I didn't have a wingding, you didn't have a wingding, right?"

"Well ..."

"DID YOU HAVE A WINGDING?"

"Let's go look at the hieroglyphics."

Seeing Things worked for seven seasons for a simple reason, Barlow suggests. "Louie and Marge were people the audience wanted to invite to their house every week. That's how series television works.... It's easy to say, but really, really hard to do."

Old Never-Let-Go

The Great Detective (1979-82) was based on the true story of a tenacious if somewhat dour detective, John Wilson Murray — "Old Never-Let-Go" — who combed Ontario for murderers during the last quarter of the nineteenth century. On TV, the master crime solver was played with a lot more pep and padding by renowned stage actor Douglas Campbell.

With the aid of devoted Dr. Chisholm (Sandy Webster) and a bird-dog police sergeant (Jim Duggan), Ontario's first detective solved Victorian crimes of the heart. Inspector Alistair Cameron always got his man. And he didn't miss many meals or drinks either. (Murray, by contrast, was a lithe teetotaller.)

Maclean's critic William Casselman captured Campbell's act with the following description: "Acted by Douglas Campbell as a huffing walrus with soup-strainer moustache, a brusque old bachelor given to spewing bad whiskey in an innkeeper's face with the line, 'Stuff would rot the belly of a cast-iron stove,' Campbell waddles engagingly through the stories, almost bursting from his grousing tweeds, bloodhounding the spoor of a felon, filleting each red herring laid in his path, until the criminal unpleasantness is resolved."

That's the spirit. Inspector Alistair Cameron (Douglas Campbell) watches Madame Zorah (Barbara Hamilton) conjure up a ghost (Tony Fletcher).

Two bays, a rooming house, and borders

CBC'S COMMITMENT TO programming from "the regions" resulted in a British Columbia family series that travelled to more than forty countries and a charming comedy-drama from Newfoundland that never properly made it to the mainland.

Long-time tenants of Verna Ball's (Mary Walsh) boarding house regarded the four walls of the St. John's establishment as the ends of the earth. So did the makers of *Up at Ours* (1980-82), who made no effort to market the show to tourists. Sharply written by a collective of Maritime writers, including its creator Gordon Pinsent, Walter Learning, and poet Alden Nowlan, the acclaimed half-hour series rarely got around to translating jokes for the rest of Canada.

Mary Walsh was Verna Ball (seated) in the St. John's boarding house sitcom Up at Ours. *From left to right: Journalist-actor Ray Guy, Janis Spence, and Kevin Noble.*

A 1980 episode entitled "CFA" — local slang for Come From Away — follows a hand-kissing antique dealer, Henri Ouimet, who arrives at the boarding house hoping to separate locals from their prize belongings. Soon one character begins pronouncing his last name Emmett. Probably only Newfoundlanders knew that "emmet" was Old English for "insect."

Elsewhere, beachcombing wasn't the only B.C. profession being documented on TV in the '80s. *Danger Bay* (1984-89) followed the exploits of an aquarium curator, Dr. Grant Roberts (Donnelly Rhodes), and his junior marine ranger kids, Jonah and Nicole (the appropriately named Christopher Crabb and Ocean Hellman). In a typical episode, "Doc" weds long-time girlfriend J.L. Duval (Susan Walden) after saving a family of wounded seals. The series was sold to forty-four countries, including Vietnam and Costa Rica.

Farther up the coast, Karl Ritter (Hans Caninenberg) and grandchildren Robert and Arnie (Dale Walters and Craig Kelly) flew an aquaplane in *Ritter's Cove* (1980-82). And farther inland, four Northwest Mounted Police officers, played by Terence Kelly, Greg Ellwand, C. David Johnson, and David Matheson, battled lawlessness and headstrong girlfriends in the nineteenth-century adventure series *Red Serge* (1986-87).

Above (from top): Lounging on the dock of the Bay *in the show's first season are Donnelly Rhodes, Deborah Wakeham, Christopher Crabb, and Ocean Hellman.*
DANGER BAY PRODUCTIONS

Left (clockwise from bottom left): Red Serge *soldiers C. David Johnson, Greg Ellwand, future Moxy Früvous lead singer David Matheson, and Terence Kelly.*

From left to right: Brenda Robins, Nicola Cavendish, and Hilary Strang in Red Serge.

A death in Saskatchewan

"I must admit it's a strange feeling to blow your wife away."

— attributed to Colin Thatcher,
Love and Hate

KENNETH WELSH WAS in Los Angeles when he heard that CBC was planning to make a miniseries based on Saskatchewan politician Colin Thatcher's murder of former wife JoAnn Wilson.

Welsh knew all about Thatcher's trial. Who didn't? In 1984, *Dallas*, the story of "human oil slick" J.R. Ewing, was the most popular show on television. When Thatcher, a real-life millionaire rancher, was accused of slaughtering his wife in her garage, his trial was front-page news for months.

Kenneth Welsh and Kate Nelligan in a staged photograph of JoAnn and Colin Thatcher's wedding photo.

"I thought it could be an important work," Welsh remembers. "This was a story that had to be told." As the production fell into place, the Edmonton-born actor, who was hoping to move back to Canada, found himself increasingly drawn to the story.

Francis Mankiewicz (*Les Bons Débarras*) was to direct. Kate Nelligan would play JoAnn. And Suzette Couture had written a tense, perceptive script, capturing Colin and JoAnn Thatcher's story with unexpected flourishes. For instance, one of Thatcher's speeches in the provincial legislature, ostensibly about politics, is instead a damning critique of a culture that allowed a powerful man to run roughshod over his wife and the criminal justice system. ("In this house, we have a double standard," Thatcher thunders. "One set of rules for one side of the house. And a completely different set of rules for the other.")

Welsh's agent got him an audition for *Love and Hate: The Story of Colin and JoAnn Thatcher*, but the actor knew he wasn't an obvious fit for the lead. "Thatcher was much taller and heavier and had a whole different hairstyle," he says. The hair was easy to fix, but Welsh didn't have time to bulk up for the audition.

"So I rented high-heel boots and a jacket that was four sizes too big," he recalls. "And before I went in I threw on four sweatshirts under my coat. I believe the apparatus helped, if not me, then [producer Bernie Zukerman and Mankiewicz]."

To his enormous relief, Welsh won the part. Next came the challenge of, in the actor's words, "getting behind the eyes of Colin Thatcher."

"I started with Maggie Siggins's book, *A Canadian Tragedy*," he says. "From there, I watched trial footage. Saw Thatcher make speeches. I tried to get a vocal impression and the way his eyes moved."

Finally, he interviewed Thatcher contacts — people who told him about the politician's charisma, then growing sombre, about how the son of former premier Ross Thatcher could turn furious with the wind. Those closest to the murderer described a tormented only child who desperately needed to be surrounded by children he wasn't equipped to care for.

"So what you do as an actor is gather up all that information and stir it around inside you, then let the person you're playing come out," Welsh says. The character that escaped, he now confesses, occasionally terrorized the set.

"I remember scaring Kate one day in the scene when Colin comes to a barbecue, and JoAnn's with her boyfriend," Welsh recalls. "JoAnn says, 'Colin, you have no rights here.' To which Colin says, 'This is all mine! This is my house!' Then improvising within the character, I shouted, 'This is my father's house! And these are my damn steaks!' and I swept the food off the table.

"Then Kate was supposed to follow me," he says, "but she turned to Francis and said, 'I can't. In his state of mind, he'd kill me.'"

Welsh reports that the staging of the actual murder scene, a vicious, minute-long beating that ended with Thatcher shooting his wife in the head, stayed with him long after he finished the film.

"I was shocked while I was doing it," he once said. "And it was macabre to think that Colin Thatcher himself would be watching the film [from jail], and making a judgment on whether we got it right."

The battles of Brittain

"Get a good subject and crew, then get the hell out of the way," documentary filmmaker Donald Brittain once said.

Wonderful advice, although Brittain was never *out of the way* in his own films. His '60s documentaries on Leonard Cohen and Lord Thomson of Fleet were skeptical, "unofficial" portraits filled with incidental detail that other filmmakers might have edited out. Brittain's genius was knowing that there was often more truth in a nervous cough than a prepared speech. (The filmmaker's goal, a National Film Board colleague once wrote, "was to make the common person great, the famous person common, and both groups human.")

Many of Brittain's '60s and '70s NFB documentaries were co-produced by and appeared on the CBC. (He also contributed two documentary pieces for *This Hour Has Seven Days*.) Brought to the network in the '70s during John Hirsch's drive to rejuvenate drama, Brittain turned his talents to docudramas. One of his most memorable films was the 1985 CBC-NFB co-production *Canada's Sweetheart: The Saga of Hal C. Banks*.

The real-life saga of an American felon recruited in 1949 by the government to clean Communists out of the Canadian Seamen's Union, Banks's story is a sordid tale, which Brittain made all the more alarming by introducing glints of mad humour. As with his early documentaries, the best moments here are the oddly jolting interludes, as when Banks (played by baby-faced hulk Maury Chaykin) bloodies an enemy's face before returning to a greasy meal with the savagery of a hawk picking at carrion.

Other distinguished Brittain CBC-NFB co-productions include *The King Chronicle*, a 1987 docudrama miniseries on William Lyon Mackenzie King, and *The Champions*, a 1986 documentary on Pierre Trudeau and René Lévesque.

Maury Chaykin (left) consults with writer-director Donald Brittain (centre) during a break on the crime docudrama Canada's Sweetheart: The Saga of Hal C. Banks. NFB/CBC

Following Anne

MEGAN FOLLOWS HAS lived with Anne Shirley for half her life now. She first played the girl whom Mark Twain called "the dearest and most lovable character in fiction since the immortal Alice" when she was sixteen, in 1985. And she read *Anne of Green Gables* to her own two girls after making the final instalment in the *Anne of Green Gables* TV trilogy in 2000.

It was only after seeing Anne through her daughters' eyes that she came to fully understand the role she had played to astonishing popular success. (When *Anne of Green Gables: The Sequel* appeared in 1987 it was the highest-rated miniseries ever to air in Canada, attracting 5.4 million viewers.)

"Some people suggest that the TV audience, particularly girls, are drawn by the romance of the period and glorious setting," Follows says.

"But I don't buy that at all. Anne's is a cold, hard world, despite all the lace doilies and strawberry socials."

The magic of Anne's universe, the actress says, is its emotional landscape, not its physical setting. What modern audiences respond to, she believes, is the indomitable spirit of Lucy Maud Montgomery's heroine.

"I think we grow up as girls having to deal with a lot of oppressive beauty myths," Follows says. "And Anne is a girl who fails by all standards of what is acceptable and beautiful. She's not pretty. She's not rich. She has no parents. But through sheer exercise of will she makes the world understand how beautiful she is. It's her specialness, her ability to transform how people perceive her, that audiences, particularly girls, want to believe in."

Megan Follows first took on the role of intrepid adventurer Anne Shirley in 1985.
SULLIVAN ENTERTAINMENT INC.

What made Anne special, however, also made her difficult to play. "She's obviously not a modern character," Follows comments. "Anne has about her a wonderful naiveté, an optimism in the face of insurmountable odds. She sees the irony in things, but it's not modern irony because it's not tainted by cynicism."

In the first part of producer-director Kevin Sullivan's *Anne* trilogy, Follows's orphan is dropped into the Cuthbert household, where she turns the elderly brother's and sister's frowns right-side up. She works similar magic at school, bewitching Gilbert Blythe and new "bosom friend" Diana Barry.

The second time out, in 1987, Anne has to decide whether she should marry Blythe. In the 2000 episode, screenwriters Sullivan and Laurie Pearson ventured beyond Montgomery's novels to construct a feverish storyline. At one point Anne is blown by fate overseas, where she is forced to crawl through the trenches of First World War France in search of her dashing, lost husband.

Follows says that Anne got progressively more difficult to play as she grew older than her onscreen character. "I've never been able to fake emotion very well; I have to feel it, or it doesn't work," she says. "So I found it hard to keep Anne's world alive between takes."

Still, she came back because she wanted another chance to work with Schuyler Grant, who played show-offy Diana Barry, and Jonathan Crombie, who played Gilbert Blythe. "Schuyler has become a close friend," she says. "And I always enjoyed working with Jonathan. He's such a funny man."

Perhaps she also came to understand the wisdom of Montgomery's observation that "youth is not a vanished thing, but something that dwells forever in the heart."

"Anne's a wonderful, inspirational character," Follows says. "I respect the role because I know how hard it is to play.... How can you ever say no to Anne?"

The finest hour

IT WILL NEVER work, industry observers predicted.

Moving the most popular news broadcast in the country, *The National*, from its long-time 11 p.m. slot into prime-time competition with *Dynasty* and *Hill Street Blues* was considered foolhardy.

That the news, at 10, would then be followed by a thirty-eight-minute experiment in current affairs programming co-hosted by yet another radio personality, Barbara Frum, invited further skepticism — hadn't the network learned its lesson with Peter Gzowski's *90 Minutes Live*?

And to outfit *The Journal* with a videotape technology that its staff didn't know how to use seemed the final folly.

Executive producer Mark Starowicz certainly feared that was the case when the Electronic News Gathering (ENG) gear arrived in December 1981. "You expect on a $1-million sale that perhaps the camera manufacturer would send representatives to set up the equipment, but they didn't," he says. "We arrived one morning to find ten large boxes at the receptionist's desk."

Although these video cameras had recently come into use in news, *The Journal*'s staff were unfamiliar with the equipment. "We had to dig through the Styrofoam pebbles, dig out the gear, and start reading manuals," Starowicz says. "I was terrified; at that point we were on air in a month."

When *The Journal* crew finally figured out ENG, which eliminated film processing and produced a cleaner, more "alive" image, Starowicz's dream of making a two-hemisphere conversation seem like a chat across a coffee table suffered another blow: during a dry run, Barbara Frum's interview with a teddy-bear exhibitor a continent away took an inadvertently comic turn when the interviewee began moving a bear's head to answer questions. Frum couldn't see this, of course, as she was looking into a blank screen to simulate an actual conversation. (Footage of the interview subject was later projected onto the screen to complete the illusion of a natural conversation.)

Adrienne Clarkson once doubted that a woman would be allowed to host an evening news program, but in 1982 The Journal *went to air with two: co-hosts Barbara Frum (left) and Mary Lou Finlay, who is currently host of CBC Radio's* As It Happens.

Starowicz decreed that from then on someone had to take notes on location interviews. But the premiere was now days away, and so much of *The Journal* seemed out of synch with contemporary TV news. The portrait of NFB founder John Grierson in *The Journal* offices was more than window dressing. Ten documentary units had been dispatched throughout the world. Then there was the idea of two female hosts. The show's second anchor, Mary Lou Finlay, formerly of *Take 30*, still chuckles over the image of "a herd of guys gathered in Mark's office, whispering, 'Hey, can we do it, can we really put two broads on the air?'"

Before *The Journal* was launched on January 11, 1982, CBC executives held a pool on what the numbers for *The National* and *The Journal* would be once the novelty wore off. Only one executive had the hour pulling in more than a million viewers. As it turned out, *The National-Journal* (1982-92) package wildly exceeded everyone's expectations, settling into a 1.7-million audience. "The hour-long ten o'clock package was much more geared to the rhythms of people's lives," says former CBC vice president and general manager Peter Herrndorf. "We knew we'd got it right by the end of the first week, when the audience for the news from 10 to 10:22 doubled to 2.5 million. It was an instant success."

Former executive producer of *The National* Tony Burman says the country was more than ready for prime-time news in 1982. His news team certainly was.

"In the late '70s, early '80s, it was becoming a scary world," Burman says. "The separatist movement in Quebec was gaining momentum. The Cold War seemed to be getting out of control. There was a strong feeling here that we had an obligation to help Canadians navigate their way through all this. But this could hardly happen if you ghettoized your newscast at the very late hour of eleven o'clock. [Before the change] I remember once we went off air at 11:30 and I threw open our office windows, overlooking a very dark and sleeping Toronto, and to the shock of my colleagues, shouted out, 'Canadians, get out of bed and turn your bloody televisions back on. You just missed a damn good newscast!'"

Starowicz gives Herrndorf and Barbara Frum credit for creating what news analysts consider to be CBC's finest hour. "Peter Herrndorf," he says, "had the idea of presenting a definitive hour where the news of the country would take place. First the news, *The National*, then the debate, *The Journal....* And the great thing was that by putting those shows together we were fulfilling our mandate as a public broadcaster and defining our own programming [niche]."

He explains the show's success by adding: "At last we were asking the questions. That's what I kept hearing over and over again. You see, before then, people had grown up watching American correspondents ask the questions. Now we had Ann Medina on the front lines in the Middle East, Peter Kent in Cambodia ... and Barbara Frum talking to newsmakers all over the world."

Frum, Starowicz says, was "our safety net. On the radio show *As It Happens* she interviewed sixteen people a day, fifteen thousand

Frum interviews Ben Johnson's doctor, Jamie Astaphan, in 1988. "Did you ever give him any anabolic steroids? Ever? Ever?"

Peter Herrndorf, then-head of CBC English Radio and TV, came up with the idea of presenting The National *at 10 p.m. followed by* The Journal.

In her own way, Frum personified the risk and commitment it took to put *The Journal* on air. She had been diagnosed with leukemia in the late '70s, and close friends tried to dissuade her from hosting the new program.

"Barbara, why do you want to do this?" Knowlton Nash asked.

"Because I might think myself a coward if I didn't do it," Frum answered.

Daniel Gelfant, a former *Journal* producer, suggests that one quality that defined Frum as a human being also made her an ideal interviewer. "She lived in the moment better than anyone," he says. "She once told me she and her husband, Murray, would go to an airport without tickets and decide where in the world they wanted to go at the last second. She was always hungry for experience and truth.

"And she looked for authenticity in people. 'There is so much fudge out there,' she used to say. 'So many people on TV trying to be nice to each other.' It's true. So often, you watch interviews and see the interviewer stop trying. They'll switch into a professional mode and let the process take over. She never did that. With Barbara, there was a moral imperative to get the truth."

While some interviewers scanned teleprompters or crib notes, during her in-studio one-on-ones Frum read her interview subjects' eyes.

"Has the government of Canada sold its vision under the Meech Lake Accord?" she asked Prime Minister Brian Mulroney in 1991.

"How frustrating is it," she wondered aloud in Jimmy Carter's presence, "to be president of the greatest and most powerful nation on earth and see fifty-two of your people captured by a fifth-rate power [in the Iran hostage crisis], and you were helpless to do anything about it?"

Gelfant says the interview that defined *The Journal* for him was the show devoted to Jamie Astaphan, Ben Johnson's doctor, which was broadcast after the sprinter was stripped of a gold medal for steroid use in the 1988 Olympics.

"Everyone in the country wanted to know what happened," he remembers, "but Astaphan wasn't talking. Then he showed up at the studio at 5 to 9 one night and said, 'Okay, I'm ready to talk.' We threw everything we were going to do out because Ben Johnson was the story of the day.

interviews in all. No one had her interview skills, her background. Who else, with five minutes' notice, could do Henry Kissinger, then, with a three-minute warning, do a segment with a scientist on the left-right hemispheres of the brain?

"No one. Only Barbara."

Crucially, Frum was asked to perform the same job she did on *As It Happens*. "Given some of the lessons Mark and I learned on [*90 Minutes Live*], we realized *The Journal* had to be built around the host's strengths," Herrndorf says. "So Barbara was not asked to do things she wasn't comfortable with. From the beginning, she was at ease and so was the audience, and the show just steamrolled — there was such a symbiotic relationship between Barbara and the audience.... She had great instincts about Canada and, for ten years, was a transcending figure."

"The atmosphere was electric in the studio. And Barbara kept asking the question everyone wanted to know: 'Did you ever give him any anabolic steroids? Ever? Ever?' Astaphan kept denying it, but eventually you could see that while he said one thing, his body language said something else.... Maybe you couldn't hear the truth, but you could [see it]. That was great television."

Starowicz suggests that Frum's commitment to getting the news was best demonstrated during a week she never appeared on air.

"On the eve of the Gulf War she was sick — laryngitis — and sounded awful," he recalls. "I had to take her off the air. So I went up to her and said, 'Barbara, you know in baseball when the manager walks out to the mound when the pitcher's arm is getting tired?'

"'No,' she said. Barbara didn't follow baseball. Finally, she said, 'You can't take me off, there's going to be a war.'"

"Barbara, the switchboard is lit up," Starowicz replied. "People are telling us to let you go home. Barbara, go home."

Still hoarse, Frum showed up two days later. "She logged feeds, brought coffee to the desk," Starowicz recalls. "You looked up, it was late, and she had some fast food on a plate for you. 'Ketchup?' she'd ask. If Barbara wasn't going to be the host of *The Journal*, she'd be the copy clerk."

Frum's passion for interview reporting and Starowicz's curiosity and zeal for the possibilities of television would carry on at the CBC long after *The Journal*. Starowicz himself went on to produce *Canada: A People's History*, while the show's documentary chief, Bernie Zukerman, refined the art of docudramas (*Love and Hate, Net Worth*). *The Journal*'s documentary unit also

produced Terence McKenna (*The Valour and the Horror*) and *fifth estate* host Linden MacIntyre.

At the time, the show changed how television covered news. "From then on, networks gradually started introducing information programs into their prime-time schedule," Burman says. And Frum's double-enders revolutionized TV reporting.

"The double-enders gave us an enormous advantage," Starowicz suggests. "We could show up on someone's doorstep in Paris, set up a camera unit, connect to the phone where Barbara was waiting, tape the interview, then, while the unit was still packing equipment, toss the tape to a bicycle courier, who would whip through traffic to a satellite delivery point. We'd have the interview within an hour.

"We could do this in war zones. Once we did an interview with Ann Medina when the Israelis were shelling Beirut. The city was surrounded. But Ann made three copies of the tape — one driver took it to Damascus, one took it through Israeli lines to Herzolia, and the third flew to a British Armed Forces satellite in Cyprus. We knew one of the tapes would make it back to Canada."

Nooners

Instantly dubbed the "Baby Journal," *Midday* (1985-2000) proved itself an impetuous child in its first show when host Valerie Pringle asked Patrick Watson, guesting to promote his new series, *Venture*, if he was going to shill for corporate Canada. At its best, the noon-hour current affairs show was like a productive, two-drink business lunch. First, there was the topic of the day, then bubbly conversation. A typical *Midday* from the '80s segued from a free trade debate to an item suggesting that Easter eggs were produced by chocolate hens. One show featured a rabbit hypnotist who performed her magic with long, careful strokes of the bunny's back. After the demonstration, co-host Peter Downie lifted a brow, advising us, "For the first year, Valerie hypnotized me like that."

After a fifteen-year run, Midday *held a reunion of hosts on its last day in June 2000. From left to right: Ralph Benmergui, Bill Cameron, Tina Srebotnjak, Brent Bambury, Valerie Pringle, and Peter Downie.*

Fifth business

Hana Gartner's 1977 interview with Jane Stafford, the Nova Scotia woman who killed her abusive husband, Billy, was interrupted by news that *the fifth estate*'s sound-man had picked up a rhythmic hammering. Upon investigation it was discovered that the noise was the beat of Stafford's pounding heart coming through on a lapel microphone.

Gartner's segment on Jane Stafford was a classic *fifth estate* piece. Stafford had been tortured by her husband and abandoned by her town and police force. But in registering the woman's palpable fear, in letting Jane tell her own story, television, Gartner feels, turned her tragic tale into an important cause.

"In the end," Gartner says, "Jane's story became a rallying point for abused women everywhere, and I quickly understood the power of the program and the degree to which it can reach people."

Designed by then-head of current affairs Peter Herrndorf and former *Take 30* producer Glenn Sarty, *the fifth estate* was dedicated to a brand of investigative journalism that was, to quote the show's 1975 mission statement, "aggressive, candid and iconoclastic."

At its best, *the fifth estate* has always allowed us to feel tragedy and understand bureaucratic malfeasance in a deeply personal way. The Academy Award-winning 1981 documentary *Just Another Missing Kid*, produced by Ron Haggart and John Zaritsky, showed how a nineteen-year-old Ottawa adventurer, Eric Wilson, met his tragic end on a Colorado back road. (Wilson was killed and his murderer allowed to go free for years, the documentary showed, because one state was unwilling to spend $400 to extradite a vicious criminal and another failed to spell his name correctly on a warrant.)

Over the past twenty-five years, the series has prompted the firing of a federal fisheries minister who approved the sale of bad tuna to supermarkets, and helped free a man, Guy Paul Morin, falsely convicted of murder. (In doing so, the latter program risked judicial penalty by presenting new evidence to jurors who had sentenced Morin.)

Early on, *the fifth estate* broke television news taboos by abandoning front-page developments to other media and putting reporters and crew members on camera. The show did, however, develop its own rules for telling stories.

The program's longevity, says current co-host Linden MacIntyre, can be explained by its ability to present succinct moral dramas that audiences have a rooting stake in. "And there's a bit of a formula to it," he adds. "The stories we tell are what went wrong and what can be done about it, or something happens to somebody and it shouldn't have. There's an element of Storytelling 101 to television: make the viewer interested in the first sixty seconds, then use the rest of the time to make them understand the story. Part of the story has to be accountability."

Fifth estate hosts in 1989 (from left to right): Bob McKeown, Hana Gartner, Sheila MacVicar, and Eric Malling. Hosts over the years have included Stevie Cameron, Victor Malarek, and Warner Troyer.

That *fifth estate*'s formula is simple doesn't make it easy to execute, particularly in a world that is increasingly dominated by what MacIntyre calls "the sixth estate." (The first three estates were the clergy, nobility, and commoners; the press became the fourth estate in the nineteenth century, with radio and TV becoming the fifth estate in the twentieth century.) "The sixth estate," MacIntyre explains, "is the phalanx of communicators, lawyers, and psychologists that are hired by corporations and institutions to ... set up a wall while creating the illusion of transparency.

"The most absurd conversation I ever heard," he continues, "took place between a producer here and the government of Saskatchewan. The communications person actually said, 'Your mission statement requires your stories to be fair and balanced. That means you have to tell both sides of the story. We cannot or will not give you our side of the story, therefore you have to go away.'"

The fifth estate did the story anyway.

The investigative series doesn't always require a villain. Hana Gartner says her most memorable piece was the story of a tragic hero who turned a country into a small street of concerned neighbours.

"I remember doing the story of Bryce Davidson, a six-year-old boy from Whitehorse who had a terrible kind of cancer," she says. "It was a difficult assignment. I mean here I was, a stranger, coming into this family's house and asking profoundly personal, straight-ahead questions about their child who may not survive. They were very generous and thoughtful. But I phoned them the next day and apologized for the intrusion."

She didn't have to. The Davidsons, it turned

out, had been greatly moved and comforted by the response to the show.

"What happened," Gartner says, "is that as soon as the show went on air, starting in Newfoundland, people began phoning the Davidsons' home. Apparently there weren't too many Davidsons in Whitehorse, and everybody got their number from the operator and just phoned up to wish them well."

Linden MacIntyre (left) interviews Guy Paul Morin in 1992. A fifth estate *story helped free Morin, falsely convicted of murder.*

A change in trench coats

A change of command on *The National* occurred on May 2, 1988. That's when Peter Mansbridge, host of network specials as well as weekend anchor, took over the helm from Knowlton Nash. Mansbridge had been weighing a lucrative offer from CBS when Nash, chief correspondent of *The National* since 1978, convinced Mansbridge to stay by suggesting he would step down from the anchor chair and do more documentary work. The two men shook hands on the deal, Nash said, "over a post-midnight cup of cocoa." As it turns out, Mansbridge had to wait a little longer than expected to take over the anchorman position. His first night on the job, the news was delayed fifty-nine minutes when a playoff hockey game went into overtime.

The National's chief correspondents for a quarter century: Peter Mansbridge (left) and Knowlton Nash.

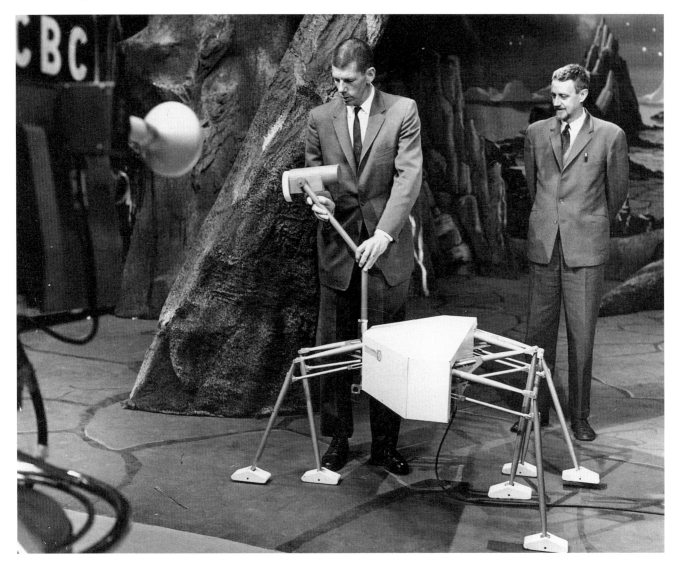

The nature of David Suzuki

Host Lister Sinclair (right) looks on in 1962 as Ewan Whitaker of the University of Arizona demonstrates a TV camera-carrying apparatus designed for lunar exploration.

LAUNCHED IN 1960, *The Nature of Things* was for twenty years the quietly thoughtful centrepiece of CBC's science department.

With hosts Patterson Hume, Donald Ivey, and Donald Crowdis — all modest, bookish types — then the more animated Lister Sinclair, the show won an international reputation for science and nature coverage. In 1979 renowned geneticist David Suzuki was named host, and the show was expanded to an hour.

Suzuki became a passionate environmental-ist after reading Rachel Carson's 1962 book, *Silent Spring*. That he was also a social activist was hardly surprising, given that his family was interned during the Second World War and his maternal grandmother poisoned at Hiroshima. He saw TV as an opportunity to educate. And was impatient to get at the task at hand.

"I came out of science," Suzuki says. "If you wanted to experiment, you'd go into a lab and do it. Early on I found TV frustrating. I remember we were in New Orleans once.

The cameraman, Rudy Kovanic, lined up the camera, checked the meter reading, then lined up the camera again. He did this about six times. Finally, I couldn't take it, so I said, 'Rudy, for God's sake, shoot the damn thing.'

"Jim Murray, the producer, dragged me into the next room and said, 'Listen, everyone is busting his ass to make you look good.' I slunk back saying to myself, Who did I think I was?" (Murray was a central figure in CBC science programming. In addition to *The Nature of Things*, he produced *The Naked Mind* [1973-74] and *Man at the Centre* [1968-74], which examined topics as wide-ranging as puberty rites and computers. Lister Sinclair was a frequent host.)

Eventually, Suzuki found the rhythm of television. And *The Nature of Things* found its purpose, which was nothing less than trying to save the world. Humanity and nature were on a collision course! was the show's constant refrain.

When critics called him a doomsayer, Suzuki suggested he was being a realist. Occasionally, he'd also explain that his love of science was rooted in an abiding passion for the natural world that saved him during the Second World War, a time when his self-image was so low he refused to be seen in public with his family. ("The most definitive event of my life was Pearl Harbor," he once said.)

Still, as a boy, there was always an Eden where he could lose himself. "As a child in British Columbia," he wrote in *Maclean's*, "I hiked virgin forests, drank from creeks and ate raw food pulled from the soil or off a tree. My family moved to London, Ontario, in 1949 where … I spent a lot of time fishing in the Thames River to feed the family.

"Walking the banks of the Thames, I had some of my most memorable experiences with nature. My grandparents owned a farm just outside the city where I spent happy days hunting freshwater clams or turtles in their creek or watching foxes and pheasants in the fields. Often, I would stop off at a nearby swamp where I would find salamander eggs, catch frogs, or collect insects. Those were magical times, imprinting an indelible love of nature that led to a career in biology."

Occasionally, Suzuki has been able to use *The Nature of Things*, now in its fifth decade, to protect that Eden.

"The best response we ever had was to a show called *Windy Bay*. [Windy Bay] was in the Queen Charlotte Islands," Suzuki remembers. "MP Jim Fulton called and said, 'You'd better get down here.' The Haida were standing up to loggers. We had interviews with loggers, natives, politicians. I tried to establish that this

David Suzuki has been The Nature of Things' *host for more than twenty years.*

location was a jewel of the planet. We ended up doing three shows and getting great ratings. Later, Mulroney paid $40 million to make it into a national park."

Suzuki once believed that victories like Windy Bay would be commonplace. Over the years, however, he's come to a more practical understanding of the nature of television.

"When I began in 1962," he once said, "I had the conceit which comes from youth. I thought I was going to give information and people were going to take it and use it. I now see that my career from that standpoint is a failure. What I have recognized is there is a small subsection of the viewing audience that is entertained ... and empowered by what I do. They see it and go, 'I never knew that,' or 'I needed that bit of information,' and [that] gives them the ability to do something. That's why I continue to do it."

Fair place to speak your mind

When host Roy Bonisteel began *Man Alive* in 1967, *Toronto Star* critic Nathan Cohen commented, "Finally CBC has a face the camera can get a grip on."

Bonisteel's square-jawed integrity and untroubled manner probably helped a religious show launched in an era consumed by moon and acid trips. But *Man Alive* was never a safe haven for the timid. On the contrary, the show won a devoted following by responding to as opposed to railing against the times.

First on Sunday afternoons, before *Hymn Sing*, then weeknights on prime time, *Man Alive* (1967-present) explored the moral concerns of the day with searching honesty and care. Bonisteel's program was the first national show in North America to interview the Dalai Lama or report on homosexual priests. In 1982 the series featured a controversial report on a scandal at the Vatican Bank. (Two billion dollars had disappeared.)

More interested in gathering perspectives than venturing opinion, *Man Alive* sought out leading spiritual thinkers, including Malcolm Muggeridge, Mother Teresa, Archbishop Desmond Tutu, and Elie Weisel. Eventually, the show won a reputation for being a fair place to speak your mind. When acquitted nurse Susan Nelles tried to put the Sick Kids' murder investigation behind her, she chose *Man Alive* for her first public forum.

Hosts Peter Downie (1989-96) and R.H. Thomson (1996-present) would later put their imprint on the show, but it was Bonisteel who defined the program's character and purpose.

The series occasionally attracted two million viewers in the '80s. Some fans were a few beads short of a rosary, according to Bonisteel. "Because our subject is religion, the programs elicit their share of 'kook' mail," he once wrote. "My favourite came from a Saskatoon man who wrote: 'Dear Mr. Bonisteel. This may come as a surprise to you, but I am the Son of God. And my father and I don't like your show.'"

Roy Bonisteel interviews Desmond Tutu for Man Alive *in 1985. The show's title comes from St. Irenaeus, Bishop of Lyons: "The glory of God is man fully alive."*

David Suzuki is an award-winning scientist, environmentalist, and broadcaster. Host of *The Nature of Things*, he has been explaining the natural sciences to viewers for more than thirty years.

"*Turning people around*"

I FIRST DID TV in 1962. I was a young professor at the University of Alberta and did televised lectures. Nothing big, but I did begin to understand TV as an educational tool.

I guess the CBC saw me as a hot young scientist. And I was trying to persuade people they had to pay attention to science. So when Knowlton Nash asked me to do something, I said yes. But my first show was pathetic. We had a budget of $1,500 a week, which barely covered film. Know how we got the name? Once Knowlton called checking about that "Suzuki on Science thing," so the show was called *Suzuki on Science*.

Then the story gets complicated. At the time, *Whiteoaks of Jalna* bombed, and CBC was looking for a hit. Jim Murray, who had been doing *The Nature of Things*, produced Pierre Berton's *The National Dream*, which was a hit. And they wanted to kick Jim upstairs — that's how it works in TV — except he wanted back doing science. I wasn't happy where I was, so they threw us together with *Science Magazine*.

Jim wanted something fast paced. We did two to five items a show. I did a feature called *How Things Work*, which explained everyday objects. We did that show for five years, then Knowlton made me host of *The Nature of Things* in 1979.

The show has allowed me to continue my education, for which I'm grateful. I went to places I might not have gone. Visiting the Amazon was a big event in my life. I became involved with stopping a dam near the village of Altamira. Pico, the village leader, gave me a feathered headdress his mother made. It's one of my most treasured mementos.

Our greatest accomplishment was the documentary series *A Planet for the Taking*, which I did with Jim. We were

David Suzuki on location in 1984, filming what he calls his greatest accomplishment, A Planet for the Taking.

given millions of dollars and three years to travel the world and reflect — something you're seldom allowed to do on TV — on man's relationship with the environment. It was a great challenge. I worked with John Livingston, for instance, who was a "deep ecologist."

There were problems between John and people on set, because he took an anti-human line. He loved birds and hated humans because they ruined the environment. Well, you can't go to viewers and tell them they're all bad. So we had to use John judiciously. But he gave the series an edge. The 150,000 miles we travelled making that series, working with John and going to Africa and meeting anthropologist Richard Leakey, whose father got Jane Goodall started with gorillas, that was the high spot of my career.

We haven't turned any industries around. You can't. All you can do is turn people around. After he retired, Adam Zimmerman, former CEO of Noranda, which once owned MacMillan Bloedel, became a supporter. When we shot *Voices in the Forest*, MacMillan Bloedel went nuts. Adam wrote to employees telling them to cool it, saying, "You know, this guy could make this a lot worse."

Our challenge is to touch people. Especially after the terrorist attacks of September 11, 2001, which pushed environmentalism off the agenda. But that's always been the challenge. *The Nature of Things* was born during the space age. We've gone through the computer revolution, the genetic revolution. The challenge has always been to capture the layman and provide him with clear, usable information. My father was my biggest fan and critic. He would call and say, "Look, I support you, but if you can't make it clear to me...."

School of life

WHILE YOUNG BETH MORRIS and Michelle Finney sometimes had trouble with the real world after performing on their pre-sweetened, after-school kids' shows, *Maggie Muggins* and *Razzle Dazzle*, *Degrassi* star Pat Mastroianni gladly took the role of Joey Jeremiah with him everywhere he went.

After a while, in fact, it was hard determining where actor Mastroianni stopped and character Joey Jeremiah began.

"One day everybody in the cast was waiting for the bus driver to go somewhere," Mastroianni remembers. "We were getting restless, then the other guys start saying, 'C'mon Pat, drive the bus!' 'Sure, why not?' I said, 'I can drive.' So I did, even though I was only fifteen. Well, I got about four feet and one of the line producers came running up, screaming. I ended up getting suspended from the shuttle bus for three weeks."

By then, Mastroianni says, "I'd turned into Joey in real life. I was always in [creator] Linda Schuyler's office getting reprimanded."

Ordinarily, actors who tumble into their onscreen roles are headed for trouble. But that wasn't necessarily the case on the *Degrassi*

series, which revolutionized young people's TV programming by allowing kids to be themselves, or better yet, encouraging them to be who they really wanted to be.

"When I auditioned for the show I was four-ten, in the ninth grade, maybe ninety-five pounds, and picked on because of my size," Mastroianni remembers. "I was shy and a D-minus student. But I put all that aside and portrayed someone I hoped to be. During the interview, I told them I was a B-plus student, and acted confident and cocky."

Linda Schuyler sensed a credible tension between the young actor's stutter and strut. Mastroianni was every sharp, nervous kid shopping for an act to get him through adolescence.

"That's our Joey," she cried after Mastroianni's audition. Soon the young actor had his break-out act. Joey wore a fedora, frequently with a Hawaiian shirt. Midway through *The Kids of Degrassi*'s first season he'd become the show's most identifiable character — a little bantam rooster who seemed to be on a nickname basis with the world.

Occasionally, Pat's real-life infractions made it on screen. "A month after the bus thing," the actor recalls, "the producer wrote an episode in which both Snake and Wheels [Stefan Brogren and Neil Hope] go for a joyride. I jokingly demanded a writing credit."

Mastroianni would be first to suggest, however, that being a writer on *The Kids of Degrassi* (1979-86), *Degrassi Junior High* (1987-89), or *Degrassi High* (1989-91) was anything but a joyride. The trilogy won universal critical praise and countless awards, including an International Emmy, not to mention huge international and domestic audiences. (Seven million of us watched *Degrassi Junior High*'s 1987 Canadian premiere.) Still, series writers faced the gruelling task of satisfying thirteen teenaged actor-critics every week.

"There were extensive workshop sessions," Mastroianni explains. "The first

Joey (Pat Mastroianni) pledges his support for Stephanie (Nicole Stoffman) during a school election as Voula (Niki Kemeny) looks on in an early episode of Degrassi Junior High.

PLAYING WITH TIME INC.

From left to right: Kids in the hall — Lucy (Anais Granofsky), Arthur (Duncan Waugh), Yick Yi (Siluck Saysanasy), Spike (Amanda Stepto), Stephanie (Nicole Stoffman), and Joey (Pat Mastroianni) — on Degrassi Junior High, *1988.*

PLAYING WITH TIME INC.

Voula (Niki Kemeny) looks on in astonishment as Stephanie (Nicole Stoffman) transforms herself from a "nice girl" into a bombshell.

PLAYING WITH TIME INC.

three weeks of shooting, we'd go after school, every day, doing acting exercises and reading sessions. In the reading sessions, we tore head writer Jan Moore's scripts to shreds. You know, at sixteen you don't have the ability to be subtle. We hated anything that sounded phony. Stuff like once he had a girl asking her father for permission to go to the dance. We said, 'C'mon, no one would ask permission. They'd just go.'"

Schuyler and co-creator Kit Hood of Playing With Time trusted the teenagers' instincts. And why not? After all, they'd hired consultants instead of performers. The cast were amateurs chosen from Toronto high schools — kids who learned how to be actors, in contrast to series like *Beverly Hills 90210*, where overaged actors were instructed to play kids.

"We'd never say 'He's a square,'" Stefan Brogren (Snake) once told a writer. "We'd say 'He's a narbo.'" While the show's audience appreciated hearing themselves on screen, *Degrassi* was always more than just period verisimilitude — knowing for instance that "broom" meant "good," whereas "broom-head" was Spike's (Amanda Stepto) Billy Idol haircut.

The show literally got down with kids by placing cameras at the characters' eye level, even way back on *Kids of Degrassi*. And the later series captured the Orwellian world of high school by having the school principal, Mr. Lawrence, referred to but never seen.

Crucially, unlike many prime-time TV dramas, the series was never squeamish about life. When Dwayne (Darrin Brown) went to a doctor for an AIDS test, the camera remained tight on his arm as the needle punctured his skin. And here's how Snake learned the truth about his basketball-star brother:

"I'm moving in with this guy."

"Yuh, so what?"

"Well, he's gay."

"Why would you want to move in with one of those guys?"

"Because I'm gay."

Degrassi always looked to its own cast for stories, no matter how difficult the subject matter. "Neil Hope, who played Wheels, his father passed away from cancer during the second season," Mastroianni remembers. "And the producers asked him if he would be comfortable playing the role where his parents on the show were killed in a car accident. He was the only one on the show who had this experience. Well, he embraced the challenge."

Because they always worked so close to the bone, the producers and cast of *Degrassi* developed a sometimes tempestuous relationship. "At the beginning they protected us by telling

Sharon Hampson, Lois Lilienstein, and Bram Morrison on the musical variety program The Elephant Show *(1984-88).*
CAMBIUM FILM & VIDEO PRODUCTIONS LTD. (BRUCE MACAULEY)

us not to worry about acting," he says. "They used to tell us, 'Don't worry, it's all in the editing,' because they wanted us to relax on screen. Then after we found a comfort level, they started playing games with us. Hood would get angry sometimes. Once he threatened to fire me. Afterwards, he said, 'I'm not really firing you. I just did it to get you upset.' He was just trying to draw me out. Later, I appreciated what he was trying to do."

In the series' final years, "the shows were who we were," Mastroianni says. "We helped create those characters. They were an extension of our real-life personalities and experiences. The producers were like second parents to us.

"We took vacations together," he continues. "We spent New Year's Eve together. It was very, very close. There was always someone to talk to. You knew you were not alone."

Millions of fans felt the same way — and not just here at home. Close to five million kids watched *The Kids of Degrassi* every week in Britain. The show was also shown in China, Yemen, and of course the United States (PBS). Today, there are thousands of *Degrassi* Web sites around the world.

Five o'clock rock

The Jim Henson-CBC co-production, *Fraggle Rock*, was a playground slide into a world held together by magic.

In theory, the show's location was Doc's (Gerard Parkes) workshop, but the inventor's dog, Sprocket, and the show's one-and-a-half-million viewers knew better. For every Sunday at 5:30, Sprocket and the kids would peer into a little hole in a workshop baseboard down a tunnel to find ...

Fraggles Gobo, Red, Wembley, Mokey, and the always-quaking Boober. (We won't bother with the Fraggle Fire Department.) Fraggles were singing, joke-telling mops who lived in harmony with their industrious cave mates, the Doozers. Frequently, Fraggles dashed above ground to snatch a bit to eat from the Gorgs — huge Creole furballs — or to collect wisdom from Marjory, a heap of trash who read tea leaves, coffee grounds, and banana peels.

Smartly written by a group that included Canadian poets bp Nichol and Dennis Lee, the show's playful, pro-kid spirit is captured in the following lyric: "Only one thing can save us / Only one thing will do / Stand up nice and straight. Don't capitulate / Courage lives and it's you."

The five Fraggles at the end of another Fraggling work week. HENSON ASSOCIATES

For twelve years children's entertainer **Fred Penner** captivated kids around the world on *Fred Penner's Place*; the show is still in reruns.

"*The camera was a real true eye*"

I MADE MY first record, *The Cat Came Back*, in 1979 and had been touring cross-country for years when Dodie Robb, head of children's television in 1985, called me out of the blue and said, We think you're the guy to do our new kids' series.

I picked up my jaw and thought, What's the process? I had appeared on *Sesame Street* and *The Elephant Show*, but had to come up with something unique. We decided on a natural setting — someplace secluded where the child could come and feel safe. That's how we came to a wandering, marked path that led to a hollow log.

The log was my idea. Once you made the journey, well there you were, in this warm, secret place with a guy and his puppet friends. I wanted a real person for the kids to relate to, not an inanimate object. It seemed to work. I'm still getting e-mails from young adults all over North America.

Mostly they thank me for being part of their childhood. Or say they're taking music or going into teaching because of the show. That's nice.

Other than the log maybe, the Word Bird is what most kids remember. We wanted to have some easy tool that taught the alphabet, words, and counting without intimidating children, and Pat Patterson, who along with Peg McKelvey were the original driving forces of the show, came up with the Word Bird, a colourful, parrot-like creature that introduced educational concepts and show themes.

The main puppet characters were Giorgio, Penelope, and Nikki, the youngest, who was very self-confident. That was important because the preschool audience identified with her, and we always wanted to validate children's feelings.

The secret to *Fred Penner's Place* was I never thought of myself as a preschool entertainer. Talking to puppets, even that was person to person. There was never condescension. My first job in this world is being a father to my own four children, and I would never talk in a cutesy voice to them. So I wouldn't talk that way to the puppets or kids at home.

Even the music was not three-chord "row, row, row your boat." And lyrics were important. I like to end shows today with the song "Take Good Care of Each Other, That's What Friends Like to Do." And I always tell the audience to pay attention to the words. In a way, that's what I did on TV. I always considered the camera as a real true eye that would carry my words and image to the hearts and vulnerable souls of these children, and I always thought it was possible to make a difference in the life of a child.

The singer-host of Fred Penner's Place *in a characteristically sunny pose.*

Of ice and men

DON DUGUID WAS introduced to curling in 1944 when his father, an icemaker for the CPR rink in Winnipeg, would take time off to attend to his other curling responsibility — bootlegging — leaving Don, then nine years old, to groom and water the ice.

"I used to throw rocks, too, but of course being so small I had to use both hands," recalls the 1965-70-71 Brier champ, who went on to provide curling commentary on CBC for twenty-nine years.

"A few sociable drinks was part of curling back then," Duguid says of his dad's amateur distillery work. Indeed, a flask was as crucial to the sport as a rock or broom was in the nineteenth century, when prairie curlers required an occasional nip of antifreeze to protect them from cutting winds. (One historian suggests the sport was introduced to Canada by General Wolfe's troops, who melted cannonballs into rocks in the mid-eighteenth century.)

By the 1980s curling had become a weekend TV staple, with two million fans tuning in for championship matches. Technical innovations added to our enjoyment of the spectacle. Overhead cameras were introduced in the '70s, allowing an unimpeded view of the game. And in 1983 CBC convinced reluctant curlers to wear body mikes, giving us access to strategy sessions.

But Duguid thinks it was how fans related to curlers that made the sport work on TV. Gizmos like lapel mikes just brought out the colour in competitors.

"Okay guys," Ed "The Wrench" Werenich told his crew and Canada during the 1983 Brier in Sudbury, "I'll just throw this and you'll sweep the piss out of it."

Duguid roared when he heard Werenich's comment, but says no one was upset by the remark. "C'mon, Ed was a fireman!" he says. "After the weekend, he went back to his job just like everyone else. Anyone in a pressure situation could have said that, which just brought home ... what a working man's game curling really is."

Curling writer Bob Weeks suggests that men's curling has always had a boys'-night-out flavour. "When the sport took off after the war, women curled during the day and men at night," he says. "Matt Baldwin, the great Alberta curler, told me that when the McDonald Train took curlers across Canada for the Brier in the '60s, picking teams up in Vancouver with a stop in every city along the way, sometimes the boys would climb out in Moncton after six days of hard drinking."

Predictably, horseplay became part of the Brier. Once, during a power failure, Baldwin's team tiptoed down the darkened sheet with their rocks, depositing them in a tight circle inside the rings, then threw their hands in the air when the lights returned. Viewers enjoyed watching athletes who remembered they were playing a game. And several Brier winners became instant national celebrities. Newfoundlander Jack MacDuff's boyos so captured Canada in winning the 1976 Brier that they were able to tape telegrams from well-wishers across every inch of their Regina hotel room.

The sense that curling championships were festivities as well as sporting challenges continued right through the '80s. "Joan Mead, who produced CBC curling for years, told me about how in Chicoutimi in 1989 Ed Werenich and Paul Savage were having an awful tournament," Weeks remembers. "They were sure they were out of it and began partying pretty hard. Then they got hot. On the final day they came back to win, with Paul skipping and Ed playing third. But Paul looked awful. At the fifth end break CBC's Colleen Jones interviewed him. Paul was sweating bullets. He got through the interview, then bolted to the washroom in time, but didn't turn his mike off. Fortunately, they were able to turn the sound down in the booth so that Canada wouldn't have to share his misery."

Even though international exposure at the Salt Lake City Winter Olympics brought the World Curling Federation an estimated $15-million (U.S.) windfall from TV revenues, Duguid doubts the sport will ever transcend its small town, curling club origins to become a big money game, like golf.

"No, the game is a community sport, regardless of how big the stars get," he says. "That's where the allegiance is. When I grew up in Manitoba we had 600,000 people and twenty-five big curling clubs. When we had a bonspiel we might have a thousand teams enter. The sport is big in Canada because every community has a club and their club goes off to compete for the provincial championship. Which is where it gets big. Then you get province against province and country against country. I could name you the last ten Brier winners; so could a lot of fans. But who can remember who won the most money last year, or the year before? Nobody probably."

Don Chevrier, who covered curling on CBC in the '70s and '80s, says the sport's best-kept secret is that most of its TV fans have never

Ontario skip Ed "The Wrench" Werenich shouts to his sweeps during the Labatt Brier in 1997.
CP (MIKE RIDEWOOD)

curled. "Look at the numbers," he says. "Three million people in Canada watch curling, but only three-quarters of a million curl. What does that tell you?"

The majority of viewers, Chevrier believes, are TV passersby who get hooked on the sport's subtle strategies and startling resolutions.

"You know, I've covered a great many sports," he says, "but for surprises and last-second twists to contests, curling might have everything else beat. For proof, I'll take you back to the Silver Broom Curling Championship at Garmisch-Partenkirchen in 1972. The Canadian skip, Orest Meleschuk, played a takeout in the final and rolled too far. The Americans, seemingly, had won. Bob Labonte of the American team jumped for joy, slipped coming down and kicked the Meleschuk rock closer to the

Curling fans identified with players who understood that the sport was a game. Here a spectator demonstrates his support for "The Wrench."
BRANDON SUN
(COLIN CORNEAU)

button. They measured and the Canadian team was awarded last rock to tie the match. In the extra end, Labonte missed his shot and Canada won the championship."

Duguid says that curling is better than ever now, and credits TV, which exposes everyone to the top competitors on a weekly basis, for improved standards of play. Still, he occasionally misses the old days when the Richardsons — brothers Ernie and Garnet and cousins Wes and Arnold — could storm out of nowhere in the late '50s and stun everyone with an idiosyncratic style of attack. (The Richardsons perfected a wide-open, takeout style of game popular in Saskatchewan.)

"There once was a time before television made the sport so popular that every city developed its own style of play," he remembers. "Back then I could look out on a rink full of curlers I'd never seen before and tell you where a player was from just by the way he held his broom."

Kings of the hill

The Crazy Canucks were ski kings with frequently broken crowns. Their spectacular wins and calamitous spills made Saturday afternoon skiing jittery, compelling viewing.

Canadian downhillers earned their reputation with reckless flights down the unforgiving Streif course in Kitzbuehel, Austria. Ken Read won there in 1980. Steve Podborski conquered the cliff in 1981 and '82, while Todd Brooker raced to victory in 1983.

After every win Canadians would repair to the local Londoner pub, where parties were as dangerous as the race being celebrated. (A skier once shattered his knee slaloming off the bar.) Eventually, the myth of the Crazy Canucks became a burden. "They expected us to walk into the bar with a ... chainsaw slung over our shoulder and a bottle of rye coming out of our pockets," Brooker once said.

The furiously aggressive Canadian style of skiing made for great television, but short careers. In 1986, taking the Streif at 120 kilometres per hour, Brooker lost a ski and cartwheeled down the slope, breaking a piece of himself with every hard bounce.

"The '80s were banner years for Canadian skiing," Podborski said, "driven by ... TV and the success of racers Laurie Graham, Gerry Sorensen, Liisa Savijarvi, Karen Percy. The Crazy Canucks — Dave Irwin, Dave Murray, Ken Read, and myself — thrilled fans. Add wins by Todd Brooker, Rob Boyd, and Felix Belczyk, and you have more than thirty victories, a World Cup title, Olympic medals, and dozens of records."

From left to right: Dave Murray, Ken Read, and Dave Irwin celebrate a win. CP

The dean of Canadian sports commentators, Brian Williams has covered a wide variety of events, from the Olympics and Pan Am Games to golf, baseball, and skiing.

"Bad news from Korea"

HAVE YOU EVER seen the *Air Farce* sketch where Roger Abbott does me with ten watches on my arm, asking, "What time is it in Korea?" Well, I wear watches at the Olympics because we do everything live, so it's important I know the times across Canada so I can tell viewers in each time zone when events are taking place.

I've done ten Olympics now. The 1988 games in Seoul, Korea, were the most memorable, though not my favourite.

Those were the Ben Johnson games. The hundred-metre race is the glamour event of the summer games. No Canadian had won since Percy Williams in 1928. Ben won a bronze in '84 in L.A., and he and Carl Lewis were favourites.

Our studio was an underground bunker. The Olympics reflect the world and there was nervousness about attacks from North Korea. Before the race, [producer] Dave Toms predicted Ben Johnson would run it in 9:79. I said nobody can run that fast. Ben did it in 9:79 and the studio erupted. We had to remind everybody to calm down, we weren't there as fans. We went to air with "No Canadian since Percy Williams ..." then, after putting the story in perspective, went to commercial.

When we came back I hear, "You're talking to the prime minister" and there's Brian Mulroney in my ear. [Commentator] Geoff Gowan and Don Wittman were down with Ben so we connected the prime minister through to them and Ben.

Sportscaster Brian Williams (left) with his Royal Canadian Air Farce impersonator Roger Abbott and cyclist Curt Harnett. AIR FARCE PRODUCTIONS INC.

Fast-forward to the next Tuesday in Korea. It's the middle of the night, and I get a call saying, "Ben's tested positive, come to the studio." I was stunned.

I got there in the middle of a huge discussion. What are we now? a sports or a news team? [Head of sports] Arthur Smith said, "We can't cover sports. This is a breaking story and we're going to stick with it."

That decision set new standards for sports journalism in Canada. It was 7 p.m. EST in Canada when we went on the air. We dropped the usual intro and I came straight out of black. "Good morning from Korea. Ben Johnson has tested positive...." Sports was out the window. This was journalism. We dropped commercials to stay with the story.

The question I kept asking was, "If Ben's people knew he was going to be tested, and he was the favourite, how could they be so stupid?" That's what I thought the woman sitting in Dartmouth watching the story was wondering.

When the announcement was made, we went to it live. It was in French and I heard a voice saying, "Translate!" I said, "You've got to be kidding." Camille Dubey from Radio Canada sat with me and translated. We were live on that story for seven hours, all that time interviewing people, chasing the story, and listening to cues in my ears. When we went off the air the tension in my shoulders was so great I could barely lift my arms.

SPECIAL DAYS

THE MEMBERS OF CBC's news specials unit are like volunteer firefighters. They have other network jobs but take on extra work when duty calls.

The unit's first major assignments were the 1954 British Empire Games in Vancouver, the Queen Mother's 1954 visit, and the 1956 International Boy Scout Jamboree. Since then, it has provided live coverage of everything from Queen Elizabeth and President Eisenhower's opening of the St. Lawrence Seaway in 1959 to royal weddings, parades, elections, state funerals, millennium celebrations, and sporting events such as the Pan Am and Commonwealth games.

Above (from left to right): Barbara Frum, Peter Mansbridge, and David Halton cover the 1983 Progressive Conservative leadership convention.

Left: A crew from CHCT-TV Calgary shoots the July 1960 Calgary Stampede opening day parade.

Opposite: Pierre Elliott Trudeau's casket is carried down the stairs of Montreal City Hall on October 3, 2000. Following behind (from left to right): Trudeau's sister Suzette Rouleau, former wife Margaret Trudeau, son Justin Trudeau, daughter Sarah accompanied by mother Deborah Coyne, and son Sacha Trudeau.
CP (FRANK GUNN)

David Knapp has been in charge of special events coverage at CBC-TV for twenty years.

"*Talking with the queen*"

I WAS NORMAN DEPOE'S producer when Charles de Gaulle visited during Expo 67. I had never met Norman before. We met at a Montreal airport and the first thing he said was "Let's go for a beer." It was ten o'clock in the morning!

We met the president's entourage at the airport and were along for the drive to Quebec City. In every town and hamlet, villagers sang "La Marseillaise." I still hear it in my head. The trip ended abruptly with the famous "Vive le Québec libre!" shouted from the balcony.

I've covered countless royal events. They're less formal today. I think the palace appreciates our sensitivity and professionalism. A dividend of all this is we get better access. Once, every conversation between Her Majesty and a civilian was private. Then, in the '90s, we were in Yellowknife and Her Majesty was doing a walkabout with then-territorial leader Nellie Cournoyea at an aboriginal art exhibit. I asked the palace if we could mike Nellie. They knew that meant we would be able to hear the queen responding. But they said okay. That was a breakthrough.

The papal tour in 1984 was the biggest thing we ever did. CBC was host broadcaster. Eight provinces, 10 days, 60 events, 120 hours of live TV. We did 46 drafts of the scenario — a minute-by-minute rundown — before the tour. We visited every single site a dozen times each. We used 50 mobile units, 300 cameras, 16,000 microphones, and 30,000 metres of cable. We used boats, helicopters, airplanes.

The "popemobile" travelled on a Hercules with all the equipment and a cameraman on board. In Ottawa, we had a "popeboat" so the pontiff could travel the canal. We knew when we left Vancouver that coverage had been phenomenally well received. We got telexes from all over the world and fifteen thousand letters of thanks from viewers.

In 1994 we did the D-Day anniversary. We landed at Courseulles-sur-Mer first, and I walked into a hotel right on the beach the Allied forces had landed on fifty years before and said: "Hello, I'm from the Canadian Broadcasting Corporation and I'd like to use your terrace to broadcast the anniversary celebrations." The woman said, "You're from Canada. You helped to liberate us, you can have anything you want."

David Knapp greets Queen Elizabeth, Prime Minister Brian Mulroney, and Commonwealth Secretary General Shridath Ramphal of Guyana outside the broadcast control room at the Commonwealth Heads of Government meeting in Vancouver. The network was host broadcaster of the 1987 event.

Left: Pope John Paul II arrives at Downsview Airport in Toronto.

Below: Get me to the church on time. Police escort His Holiness's "popemobile" past Parliament Hill on the way to Mass on September 20, 1984.

CP (PETER BREGG)

THE RIVER

50 years

KEN FINKLEMAN LEFT Hollywood to return to Canada and the CBC after scrapping with an L.A. studio executive who complained that his characters lacked "arc."

Finkleman blew up. "When was the last time you met anyone whose character went through an arc?" he fumed. "Freud said you are who you are by the time you're four — *that's it!*"

Is that true of the CBC as well? Is the infant network that Mavor Moore and Stuart Griffiths brought into the world in 1952 the father of today's programming? A careful comparison of the network's earliest and most recent work suggests as much. An impulse to blur genre distinctions and a determination to interpret the Canadian cultural experience were traits that defined CBC's first decade.

Fast-forward fifty years, and what do we have? A Friday night full of satire — *The Royal Canadian Air Farce, This Hour Has 22 Minutes,* and *Made in Canada* — and a tradition of historical dramas and documentaries that feed off one another, with *Canada: A People's History* and *The Valour and the Horror* containing historical re-enactments and the made-for-TV docudramas *Net Worth, Million Dollar Babies,* and *Trudeau* based on real-life events.

Mavor Moore suggests that these programming motifs were in place *before* he helped give birth to CBC's English-language television service. Which is, he says, as it should be.

"CBC satire today is wonderful and that is heartening," the network's first executive producer says, "because satire is an ongoing Canadian

Top: The fiftieth-anniversary logo was designed by Daniel Plaisance. Above: Military re-enactors during the filming of a battle scene in Canada: A People's History.

Reacting to the re-enactors (from left to right): Don Ferguson, special guest Graham Greene, and John Morgan in the Royal Canadian Air Farce *spoof, "Canada: A Mildly Informative, Not Overly Long People's History."* AIR FARCE PRODUCTIONS INC.

tradition. We provide for Americans what the Irish, with Oscar Wilde and George Bernard Shaw, provided for the British — an outside perspective they're otherwise lacking.

"And writers like Stephen Leacock, who we put on air our very first year, then later Robertson Davies, whose work we adapted, they taught us to laugh and understand ourselves. No one can carve you up like family. That's what Dave Broadfoot brought to *Air Farce* and what *22 Minutes* tries to do. This kind of comic discourse is necessary, surely, if we are to remain a family."

Docudramas and shows that welcome audience participation, like Peter Mansbridge's frequently boisterous town hall meetings, also represent a crucial link to our broadcasting past, Moore says.

"You know, the first CBC show I did, this was on radio in the '40s, was *The National Farm Forum*. Every show had a dramatic playlet. So this *flexibility*, if you will, is a Canadian tradition. And I'm happy to see the network's recent town forums and invitations for viewer feedback on shows like *counterSpin*. That too was something done on radio to foster a sense of community."

He singles out the documentary series *A People's History* for particular praise.

"It was very good indeed," Moore says, "and something the CBC had to do. This is our cul-ture. Who else can do it properly but a public network free of the pressures of modern advertising? Nobody."

Moore argues that while nostalgia for its own sake is "empty, useless stuff," knowledge of where we come from is necessary for us to determine where it is we're going.

"With satire, for instance, it's important we take from the river that has come to us," he says, "but we also have to change the river, contributing to it, so that it continues to flow, and continues to be relevant to future needs."

The CBC's chief news correspondent, Peter Mansbridge, endorses Moore's suggestion that the public network's greatest challenge and obligation is to ensure that the traditions of the past are carried forward.

"The most rewarding part of our 1994 D-Day and 1995 VE-Day fiftieth anniversary coverage was coming home and reading the mail," he says. "A lot of it was from young Canadians who told me they had no idea we were even in D-Day. And they watched us go into little towns in France where streets are named after Canadian pilots. And little villages in Holland where every student's duty is to light candles on a Canadian soldier's grave on Christmas Eve. We're telling our history here. If we don't tell it, who will?"

The joke's on us

Political four-play (from left to right): Mary Walsh, Greg Thomey, Cathy Jones, and Rick Mercer of This Hour Has 22 Minutes.

SALTER STREET FILMS LTD. (MARVIN MOORE)

IN THE EARLY '90s Canada finally caught up to Newfoundland.

Well, maybe *up* isn't the right word.

"We were hearing nothing but bad news at the time," recalls *This Hour Has 22 Minutes* co-creator and former star Rick Mercer. "There was a recession. People were mad at the government. Everyone was in a bad mood. But in Newfoundland, we'd never heard *any* good news. The economy was always bad."

At last, Canada and the Maritimes were on the same comedy wavelength and ready for a show that, in Mercer's words, "completely took the piss out of politicians."

The first notable extraction came when Newfoundland satirists and co-creators Mercer, Mary Walsh, Cathy Jones, and Greg Thomey contributed to CBC's 1993 election-night coverage. Soon after Peter Mansbridge announced that Jean Chrétien's Liberals had won, reducing Kim Campbell and former prime minister Brian Mulroney's Conservatives to two seats, CBC switched to the *22 Minutes* team in a Halifax studio doing a conga line around a desk, singing: "Mulroney is no

more — hey! Mulroney is no more — hey!"

"That show made us," Mercer says. "Until then we'd been a late-night show. Afterwards, we went to prime time and the show kept building."

In a perverse twist on the Canadian notion of fair play, *22 Minutes* figured they couldn't get away with lambasting one party; they'd have to savage them all. Mercer took Chrétien to lunch at Harvey's. ("My first book was *Straight from the Heart*, my next one will be *Straight through the Heart*," the PM growled over French fries.) And Thomey ambushed Preston Manning in a tunnel under the Parliament buildings and accused the giggling Reform leader of reefer madness. "God," Thomey said, turning away, "you smell like Bryan Adams. Look at the eyes on ya."

But the show's most recognized political assassin has always been Mary Walsh's barging snoop, Marg Delahunty. Here's Marg yammering away as she enters the Quebec Assembly:

"I gotta go in now and face Mr. Lucien Bouchard — Mr. French himself. Oh, I'm half afraid of him to tell ya the truth. Who isn't? I mean the face of him on the news — *it'd stop a clock!* Contrary? He's always in a bad mood. But ... well, we're here now. Come on, we goes in."

Dressed in her Warrior Princess scarlet breastplate and skirt, and wielding a broadsword, Marg merges with a Bouchard press scrum.

"*Oh, Mr. Bouchard!* You're so much more *handsome* in person than you are on English TV," she yells. "I could hardly recognize ya."

"Ha, ha."

"I know what you're thinking ..."

"It is ..."

"Who is she and what on earth is she wearing?"

"Please, let me say something ..."

"I'm Marg Delahunty, sir ..."

"I know who you are. Please, I want to say it is very hard for me to look handsome on English TV."

"You look *extremely* handsome," Marg swoons, as the chuckling Parti Québécois leader is swept away by the crowd. Just before he disappears, though, Marg shouts, "I KNEW NOBODY FROM THE BEE-YOU-TI-FUL PROVINCE A QUEBEC COULD BE THAT MUCH OF A CROOKED ARSE!"

Of course, it's the attackers rather than the attacked that make *22 Minutes* a weekly habit for one million viewers. No series has produced more sharply drawn Canadian caricatures: Walsh as Marg Delahunty is the town busybody who has to shove her way to the front of every line. Thomey specializes in over-refreshed party boys. (His Newfoundland Separatist leader, Jerry Boyle, faces the same question every New Year's Eve — will he end the evening semi-formal, wearing a black tie, or semi-conscious, with a black eye?) And Cathy Jones can play everything from native pathfinder Joe Crow ("Until next time, Ski-Doo careful, eh?") to sashaying sexual affairs correspondent Babe Bennett ("I'm just goofin' around"). Mercer successor and sketch-comedy veteran Colin Mochrie is just beginning to make his mark on the Salter Street Films series, but already does a superb Rex Murphy.

Central Canadian TV humorists, like Wayne and Shuster and *SCTV*, stared at American culture in comic wonder, and certainly *22 Minutes* had a classic Yankee comedy bit, with Rick Mercer's recurring Talking-to-Americans-about-Canada feature. (Sample howlers: presidential candidate George W. Bush blandly accepting greetings from Mercer on behalf of "Prime Minister Poutine," stateside tourists being talked into crossing the Peter Mans Bridge, and a Columbia University professor signing a petition to halt the barbaric Canadian tradition of packing senior citizens off on retirement ice floes.)

More often, however, *22 Minutes* has turned Canada into a comic spectator sport. "Well, Newfoundland was the last in the door, we're also the poorest province, and we're not attached. I guess that gives us a unique, outsider perspective," Mercer says in explaining the Newfoundland comedy group's propensity for Canuck jokes.

22 Minutes' best Canadian joke travelled a thousand times around the world in less than a week.

"I was reading campaign literature the Reform party were putting out before the 2000 election, suggesting they would hold direct referenda on issues that 3 percent of the electorate agreed upon," Mercer recalls. "This is insane, I thought.

Far left: Mary Walsh as Marg Delahunty. "Don't make me smite ya."
EDMONTON SUN
(PERRY MAH)

Left: The smitten — Quebec premier Lucien Bouchard with Marg in the background in 1997.
CP (JACQUES BOISSINOT)

219

Possum night in Canada

Possum Lodge is a mythical male refuge set 168 beer stores north of Toronto.

That's where he of the red and green suspenders, Red Green (Steve Smith), gormless nephew Harold (Patrick McKenna), and various regulars gather weekly, bound by a favourite colour — plaid — and a collective enthusiasm for pointless male endeavour. Ranger Gord (Peter Keleghan) has been studying the horizon for fires now for twenty years. So far nothing. But you never know.

The Red Green Show, produced by S&S Productions, began as a periodic TV spoof of Red Fisher's syndicated fishing show. By 1991, however, it had evolved into an all-out deliberation on men without women (but with a whole lot of duct tape).

What sets Smith's sitcom apart from other shows and movies that have evolved from sketch humour is that the former high school teacher and folk musician has a sure sense of comedy and pacing. *The Red Green Show* is about a funny world, not funny jokes.

Not that Red doesn't get off the occasional howler. Here is one of his poems, a delicious, deadpan parody of one of Scuttlebutt Lodger Red Fisher's attempts at free verse:

The Groundhog

It's spring.
The groundhog comes out of
his hole
and sees a shadow.
It is the shadow of my right
front tire.
That means winter will last
another six weeks.
But not for him.

Steve Smith as Red Green. S&S PRODUCTIONS INC.

The numbers were so low and the cost of a referendum was $150 million. The country could go broke. We had to do something."

Twenty minutes later Mercer chuckled over an idea. The sketch was written in another thirty minutes. But it would require a Web site that allowed for maybe 350,000 hits. He explained what he needed to the show's staff. It took a week's preparation to get the site ready.

Finally, *22 Minutes* went to air with Mercer at a blackboard asking us to sign an Internet petition: "We demand that the government of Canada force Stockwell Day to change his first name to Doris." Before the show was over, the *22 Minutes* Web site began drawing hits. "The next day we were getting forty-three names a second," Mercer says. "It was incredible. Within a few days the petition left Canada and began to

spin around the world. When we closed it a week later we had a million signatures."

And *22 Minutes* had fulfilled Mercer's secret dream. "I'd always hoped that instead of making fun of the news we could make news someday," he says. "Now we had. Doris Day was reported everywhere. Stockwell even went along with the joke and announced his campaign song was the Doris Day hit 'Que Sera, Sera.'"

And how did Mercer feel about *22 Minutes'* leap from the entertainment section to the front page?

"It was a great public joke," he says. "The people had spoken. Or at least had a good laugh."

The jest society

"The Department of Defence has closed our armed forces bases in Germany and converted them into resorts for backbenchers, cabinet ministers, and senators. The resorts will be called Club Fed, Club Well Fed, and Club Dead."
— Royal Canadian Air Farce, 1992

EVEN THE SHOW'S title is a response to a news item.

Roger Abbott and John Morgan were driving into CBC in 1972 with the script for a radio satire called *Beaver Follies* when they heard John Diefenbaker thundering away on the radio about the Liberal government changing the name of the Department of Health and Welfare to Health Canada.

"I said, 'Boy, if Dief had his way, he'd put Royal on everything,'" Abbott remembers.

"The CBC would be 'The Royal Canadian Air Farce.'"

"Hey, that's good!" Morgan commented. Minutes later, they crossed out *Beaver Follies* and scribbled *Royal Canadian Air Farce* on their script.

And *Royal Canadian Air Farce* it has been ever since. For more than thirty years Abbott, Morgan, Don Ferguson, Luba Goy, and frequent guest Dave Broadfoot have won an ever-swelling audience by riffing on all things Canadian. (Morgan retired in 2001.)

The show was a cult favourite on radio. ("I used to think that half our audience were university professors who drove Volvos, but only when they had to," Abbott says.) But *RCAF* really took off upon arriving on TV in 1992, attracting more than two million viewers to its

Reform partiers (from left to right): Reform leader Preston Manning with RCAF's Luba Goy, Don Ferguson, John Morgan, and Roger Abbott.

AIR FARCE
PRODUCTIONS INC./
RODNEY DAW

Kids in the Hall (1989-95) pushed the envelope right off the table onto the floor. "I crush your head" was their famous comedy tag line. From left to right: Mark McKinney, Bruce McCulloch, Scott Thompson, Kevin McDonald, and Dave Foley.
BROADWAY VIDEO INTERNATIONAL

annual New Year's Eve specials. (Coincidentally, the show began its regular-season run on television on October 8, 1993, three days before its partner in political satire, *This Hour Has 22 Minutes*, made its debut.)

On TV the group has enjoyed the challenge of physical comedy, whether it's imitating heads of state or network (Abbott does a mean Jean Chrétien and Peter Mansbridge) or firing Canuck-muck via the Chicken Cannon at deserving politicos. (A Lucien Bouchard dummy took a mix of B.C. salmon and P.E.I. superfries to the kisser on one show.)

"We keep on going and going because the government just keeps giving and giving," is how Goy explains the show's popularity.

Ah, Rita

Rita MacNeil's success story is as beautiful and sentimental as any tale out of Dickens. The product of a broken home who endured seven operations and years of subsistence living before becoming a singing star at age forty, MacNeil was given her own show, *Rita & Friends*, in 1994. And how many friends there were! Her debut drew 1.7 million fans. Canadians immediately felt at home with the performer who was too shy to do much talking, but too full of hope and music not to sing.

Rita and guitar-bearing friends Jeff Healey and Michelle Wright.
BALMUR LTD.

Another openin', another show

The range and interest of CBC's current arts and entertainment showcase, *Opening Night*, is evident in two recent works: The Royal Winnipeg Ballet's production of *Dracula: Pages from a Virgin's Diary*, as imagined through the camera eye of cult Winnipeg filmmaker Guy Maddin, and Diana Krall hosting a Montreal International Jazz Festival special.

Proof that the weekly, commercial-free series is part of an ongoing network tradition could be found in a 2002 episode, *Buried Treasures*, that featured '50s and '60s performances by American jazz greats Duke Ellington, Ella Fitzgerald, Nat King Cole, and Sarah Vaughan.

Other memorable *Opening Nights* include a production of Verdi's *Rigoletto*, featuring Marcelo Alvarez, Christine Schäfer, and Paolo Gavanelli, and Morris Panych's Vancouver Playhouse Theatre production of *The Overcoat*, "a play without dialogue" inspired by a Gogol story and set to the music of Shostakovich.

From left to right: Cyndi Mason, Alan Morgan, and Peter Anderson in a production of the Vancouver Playhouse Theatre's The Overcoat.
PRINCIPIA PRODUCTIONS

Grave expression: Zhang Wei-Qiang (centre) stars in the Opening Night *production of the Royal Winnipeg Ballet's* Dracula: Pages from a Virgin's Diary.
ROYAL WINNIPEG BALLET

Dead beat

DOES IT COME as any surprise that Nicholas Campbell used to sneak into the *Da Vinci's Inquest* offices to read early drafts of the scripts, then complain to creator-producer Chris Haddock if he thought the screenwriters didn't get it perfect first time out? That's just the kind of thing his character, TV coroner Dominic Da Vinci, might do. (Afterwards, of course, Da Vinci would throw up his hands in astonishment when a higher-up questioned his circumventing procedure.)

Haddock probably appreciated Campbell's zealousness. He wanted *Da Vinci's Inquest* (co-produced by Barna-Alper Productions) to throw a floodlight on Vancouver's dark underside, and to do that he knew he needed a performer who could map out a city in shortcuts.

"I wanted an actor who had some experience out on the streets," Haddock once said. "And Nick has that. He lives life large."

Campbell's graduate paper on nightlife was the 1996 film *Booze Can*, his affectionate, shoe-string documentary on after-hours carousing in Toronto. (In a Da Vinci-like move, Campbell surreptitiously filmed one club scene by advising the owner that he was a Hollywood scout who needed some "test footage," thereby saving himself a location fee.)

Well known for his off-screen love of playing the ponies, Campbell says, "An Oscar couldn't come close to winning a $3,200 claimer at Fort Erie." Still, the actor concedes that his greatest career payoff to date has been the part of Dominic Da Vinci, a hard-living civil servant who battles through a chaotic personal life — alcoholism and a recently collapsed marriage — to perform his daily rounds. In bringing Da Vinci alive, Campbell more than pays back the gift that is any great role by delivering a lived-in performance that captures the wobbly charm and panicky conviction of the show's entirely fallible hero.

"As soon as I read a few scripts, I liked Da Vinci because he felt real; he had failings," Campbell says. "The drinking problem didn't seem tacked on. The characters are all stuck in the real world. I knew I wasn't going to do a lot of lobbying to make my character credible because — and this is what I really appreciate about the show — there is absolutely nothing self-righteous about Da Vinci, which sets him apart from just about every other lead character in TV drama."

Campbell adds that as soon as he got inside Da Vinci's skin, tagging along with coroners on late-night rides into Vancouver's Gastown, he began to understand the show's rich potential for human and social drama.

"The first few deaths and autopsies you see are obviously quite disturbing," he says. "But really for me the biggest shock wasn't the blood, it was seeing just how much attention and care these investigators pay to society's cast-offs, like a junkie in an alley whose family gave up on him long ago. They see the humanity there where maybe no one else ever did."

Campbell appreciated how coroners are the guardian angels of lost souls. Beyond that, he also came to understand how in protecting the spirits of ruined lives, Da Vinci might engineer his own salvation.

A key factor in the show's success is that while the Toronto-born, Montreal-raised Campbell understands characters who populate late-night urban landscapes, creator Chris Haddock knows Vancouver itself. Even the parts of the city that don't show up in tourist brochures.

"Chris is so dedicated to Vancouver and loves it so much that he can get into some pretty heavy things," Campbell says. "It's like I could insult my mother but you better not. He loves the city, but man he sure can pick up all the smells on the streets. And it helps that Vancouver actors have such balls. When we go downtown, you're *all the way* downtown. One show we had a gorgeous actress who really made herself unattractive to play a street character. There was no vanity, just a complete commitment to a part. You see her on the show and you could really feel what it was like to be on the street, needing drugs and suffering from a horrible toothache. When do you ever see that on a U.S. network show?"

Campbell thinks the series works best

Opposite: Dominic Da Vinci (Nicholas Campbell) is curator of the boneyard of broken dreams. Campbell is seen here with Gwynyth Walsh (left) and Suleka Mathew (right).

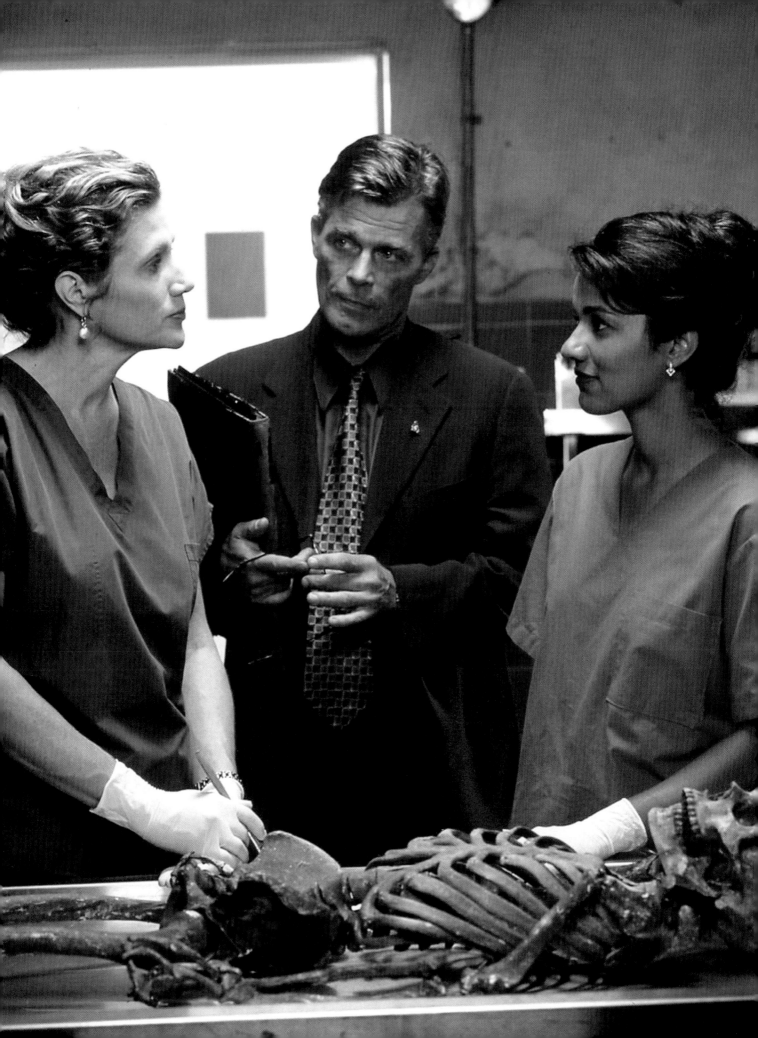

when Da Vinci falls into the rhythm of the city, taking us on twisting crawls through a nightmare cast of law enforcement loud-mouths and squalling drunks.

"My favourite shot in the series was a long walk and talk involving about sixteen characters all the way down the most intense part of Vancouver's lower downtown East Side," Campbell recalls. "This was the day they call Mardi Gras, when the welfare cheques come out. And as it happened there was a torrential downpour, it was freezing cold, and the streets were teeming with people starting to get very high."

The location scout managed to keep "the most unpredictable" people away from the actors as they stole through the razor-sharp sleet, yelling their lines out into the wind. For a few minutes, Campbell felt the show captured the hell and heroism that is the lost-soul salvation business.

"It was unbelievable — seventeen pages in one take," he says. "And I can remember thinking, How could you get something better than this?"

Sarah Strange (Helen) and Nicholas Campbell. Da Vinci's Inquest *won the Gemini Award for best dramatic series in 1999, 2000, and 2001.*
HADDOCK ENTERTAINMENT/ BARNA-ALPER PRODUCTIONS

Northwest passage

WHEN ASKED if *North of 60*'s unique storyline — the RCMP and a band leader keep peace on a native reserve — was a factor in the show's success, star Tom Jackson grows slightly agitated.

"What was unique about the series was that there were no *unique* storylines," he says with some emphasis. "People think First Nations communities are different from their communities, but really, they have the same problems everybody else does. And they have the same celebrations. I think that's part of the enlightenment the show brought about — that you can relate to these characters because they're not so different."

Jackson, who played Chief Peter Kenidi on *North of 60* (1992-98), is living proof that what are sometimes considered the problems of native reserves are in fact universal conditions. The musician-actor, raised on the One Arrow reserve in Saskatchewan, fell into trouble himself only while living in Toronto as a successful entertainer in the '80s. Caught up in a destructive lifestyle, salvation came, Jackson has often said, when he found a man lying on the sidewalk in obvious distress. The six-foot-five performer picked the stranger up and took him to the hospital.

"I didn't save his life," is how Jackson puts it. "He saved mine."

Tina Keeper, who portrayed a native RCMP officer on *North of 60*, endorses her co-star's perspective on the series. "My father said it best," she once observed. "It's Indians as people, not people as Indians."

"We developed a friendship not unlike a brother and a sister, which was appropriate, because that's what we were supposed to be in the show," Jackson says of working with Keeper. "And I think we developed a lifelong friendship, working in extreme conditions, having the responsibility of being lead characters on the series."

By "extreme conditions," Jackson is referring to Bragg Creek, Alberta, location for the fictional setting of Lynx River in the Northwest Territories.

"Bragg Creek is actually forty-five minutes from downtown Calgary," he says. "It was like working in paradise. I was amazed every day I went to work, it was so beautiful. But we shot a lot of the series in the dead of winter at a high elevation in the mountains. I think that added something to the show. We were working, all of us, the actors and crew, at temperatures twenty or thirty below zero. What you got out of people under those conditions was something beyond professionalism."

Above: Eric Olssen (John Oliver) and Michelle Kenidi (Tina Keeper) patrol Lynx River.

Below: A pensive Chief Peter Kenidi (Tom Jackson).
WESTVENTURES II PRODUCTIONS

Your desk or mine?

THE DAY AFTER her lawyer character was killed off by a drunk judge on *Street Legal*, Sonja Smits was confronted by a grief-stricken flight attendant on a plane heading out of the country.

"I almost didn't make it into work today, my daughter was so upset by your death," the woman informed Smits. "Could you please write her a letter and tell her you're okay?"

The actress complied, explaining in her letter that while the character of Carrington "Carrie" Barr had passed away, she was doing fine, thanks for asking. The exchange is an apt metaphor for *Street Legal* (1987-94), a big, teasing continuing drama that, for all its melodrama, was always considerate of audience sensibilities.

Street Legal started out as an issue-oriented law series, with the partners of Barr, Robinovitch (Eric Peterson), and Tchobanian (C. David Johnson) engaged in battles on behalf of society's underdogs. In its third season, however, the emphasis changed from torts to tarts with the arrival of lawyer-on-the-make Olivia Novak (Cynthia Dale).

One of Dale's first scenes with Johnson had them making out in Chuck's office. Except the script never specified where. Well, where do lawyers do most of their work, Dale figured — *their desks!* The actress's impulse brought shooting to a halt.

"The first time I lay on the desk they went crazy," Dale reports. "That was certainly me. I mean there never was a stage direction that said get up on the desk....They didn't know whether they could shoot it. They had to call upstairs."

Upstairs was okay with the scene. So too, eventually, was the cast.

"I was a snob. I said, no, television should be there to illuminate the law," Peterson once said. "But when I saw the ratings go up dramati-

The partners of Barr, Robinovitch, Tchobanian and Associates hit the Street *in 1987. From left to right: C. David Johnson, Sonja Smits, and Eric Peterson.*

cally, I swallowed some pride and admitted I was wrong."

By its third season the show was running a winking ad campaign featuring horizontal images of the cast, with the shout line, "Each week they embrace the law." Carrie had an affair with an undercover cop and married a new partner, Dillon Beck (Anthony Sherwood). Chuck was off and on with Olivia more times than a faulty Christmas tree light. Eventually the madness led to his being charged with murder. Olivia consoled herself with Tom Morgan (Nicholas Campbell). And Leon's (Peterson) bid to become mayor of Toronto was scuttled by sexual harassment charges.

But Dale refutes the suggestion that *Street Legal*'s characters were ever that naughty: "Olivia was only with other guys when she wasn't with Chuck. And there were only three men in eight years and you never saw her in bed with anyone but Chuck.... And Olivia wasn't a bimbo. We didn't do cat fights between women — all those classic clichés. I got as many fan letters from little girls as I did from guys in prison."

Maybe we as an audience simply wouldn't let the show's characters get away with any more mischief. Johnson remembers buying groceries and having a stranger yell at him, "Stay the hell away from that awful woman!"

"Eric used to say that our audience had a very proprietary view of the characters," he says.

Perhaps that's why the series was a hit. The *associates* in Barr, Robinovitch, Tchobanian and Associates were the million-plus who showed up to watch every week. By assembling an attractive cast of civil litigators who weren't so much bad as morally accident-prone, *Street Legal* was a distinctly Canadian-style continuing drama.

Scarlet lawyer
Olivia Novak
(Cynthia Dale)
joins Leon (Eric
Peterson), Chuck
(C. David
Johnson), and
Carrie (Sonja
Smits).

Lawyers in love
(from left to right):
Eric Peterson, Julie
Khaner, Anthony
Sherwood, Sonja
Smits, David
Elliott, Cynthia
Dale, and C.
David Johnson.

**Self-styled TV "auteur" Ken Finkleman created and starred in
The Newsroom, More Tears, Foolish Hearts, and *Foreign Objects.***

"*Staying away from Apaches*"

I WAS AT the University of Manitoba law school when I met a guy who told me he was directing a TV show. That sounded more interesting than law school. I vaguely remember getting on a plane with material I'd written for the school paper. Soon I was writing the Norm Crosby show with Hart Pomerantz and Danny Aykroyd in Toronto.

That was terrible, but fun. My God, Norm Crosby was deaf and hosting a talk show. He had to lip-read. But writers always have fun on sinking ships.

Then I wrote a *King of Kensington*, which got nominated for something. After that I went to L.A. I bounced back and forth a lot. I did a pilot with Rick Moranis for CBC in 1980. A fake current affairs show. Everyone thought it was fantastic, but it wasn't picked up. Mostly I was a hack writer in L.A. I was one of those middle-rung writers who got paid every time I made a pitch. Didn't matter whether they made the movie or not. I still get residuals from some things — *Airplane II: The Sequel, Grease 2.*

Ken Finkleman on the set of The Newsroom *in 1997. He played George Findlay, a self-absorbed character in constant need of muffins.*

But at one point I had had it. I was in Toronto talking to six people in L.A. on speakerphones. They sent me notes on a comedy I'd written. Twenty pages, single-spaced. A perfect document about what's wrong with American movies. Full of stuff about architecture of character and dramatic arcs. And I realized I couldn't do that anymore.

After that I went smaller with something for Atlantis Films and Comedy Central called *Married Life,* a fake documentary. I got up one Friday and was shocked to see my picture in the *Globe and Mail.* John Haslett Cuff had reviewed it and said it was the best thing since sliced bread.

So I took that and my Hollywood reputation and went into CBC and said I wanted to do a show based in a newsroom. Because, I don't know, I hated news at that point. Later I came back with a script. They said it was eight pages too long. So I ripped the first eight pages out and threw them on the floor. I think I do things like that because when I was a kid I saw this western where some settler said if you act crazy the Apaches will stay away.

We did two seasons of *The Newsroom* [1996-97], but frankly I started getting bored the second run, so I flipped out and had George, my character, have a meltdown in a nuclear plant that was itself melting down. The reviews said it was Fellini-like, which was fair. Fellini's $8^1/_2$ hit me right between the eyes. His take on the corruption of media inspired me at many levels.

More Tears [1998] was my response to shows like *Dateline* that used real events and people and twisted them into black-and-white morality tales. I think three episodes of *More Tears* are the best thing I've ever done.

In *Foolish Heart* [1999] there's one line in the last episode that means a lot to me. It's a show called "The Critic." It's in black and white, with me playing kind of a Cary Grant character. And this reporter, played by Sarah Strange, says, "You don't do satire any more." And I respond that there was a time when satire was a thorn in the side of the established order, when it caused an uproar and brought issues to people's attention. But now it's irrelevant, and I realized, my God, that's true. Finally my character admits, "Well, there is nothing more pathetic than a naive satirist."

Daniel Kash (left) and J.W. Carroll portray Leaf Brian "Spinner" Spencer and Hockey Night in Canada *host Ward Cornell in* Gross Misconduct.

On thin ice

Two TV hockey movies were aired on CBC this decade. And while Atom Egoyan's *Gross Misconduct*, a psychological autopsy of a hockey player turned criminal, and producer Bernie Zukerman's *Net Worth*, the story of how NHL bosses quashed the first NHL players' union, tell us something about professional hockey, they perhaps say more about the Canadian psyche.

In American hockey movies like *The Mighty Ducks* and *Mystery, Alaska*, outcasts become team players and go on to beat the odds by becoming heroes; in Canadian hockey movies, the odds and team end up beating outcasts to a bloody pulp. (Two previous CBC hockey movies, Allan King's *The Last Season* [1987] and *Cementhead* [1979], and the '70s features *Paperback Hero* [1973] and *Face-Off* [1971] offered more broken hockey sticks and players.)

"I'm dealing here with doom," Egoyan said of *Gross Misconduct* (1993), which was scripted by actor-writer Paul Gross. The film is the story of Brian Spencer, a ten-year NHL veteran who followed his father to a violent death. "Brian is something of a myth, a golden boy who had no idea how to control the forces that created him, then turned against him.... [Brian] was the creation and victim of other people's projections."

Net Worth (1995) benefited from the presence of Al Waxman, who played counterfeit nice guy Jack Adams, general manager of the Detroit Red Wings. One memorable scene, a one-take, five-minute soliloquy that saw Waxman's character explode into an on-ice fury, left actor-players quaking in their skates.

"You see Al this morning?" one actor was overheard hours later. "I don't think I've seen anything like it — such cold-blooded malice."

Director Atom Egoyan shooting Gross Misconduct *at Maple Leaf Gardens in 1993.*

Dilbert and Sullivan

*T*HIS HOUR HAS 22 MINUTES invented the comic sport of hauling political exhibitionists in front of a camera, where they were filleted as clean as breakfast trout. Salter Street's *Made in Canada* is more of the same, except here *22 Minutes* alumnus and *MIC* creator Rick

Mercer harvests Canadian showbiz types.

Mercer's character, Richard Strong, badgers his way to the top of Pyramid Productions, where he presides over a number of not-so-good but very popular television programs. Part of the show's fun is trying to figure out just who is being tickled and teased. For instance, Pyramid joined with Prodigy Films at about the time the Canadian entertainment studios Atlantis and Alliance merged. Only instead of "A-A," the *MIC* industry powerhouse goes by the kids' bathroom term "P-P."

Beaver Creek, one of Pyramid's big shows, is the story of a plucky frontier waif named Adele, who in *MIC* reality is bitter child star Anne Shirley. Of course, Anne Shirley is also the lead character in *Anne of Green Gables*. Which makes perfect sense because both Annes are played by Megan Follows. (Kevin Sullivan, the producer of *Anne of Green Gables*, is widely held to be the model for Prodigy president Dennis Weston.)

Top (from left to right): Veronica (Leah Pinsent), Alan (Peter Keleghan), Victor (Dan Lett), and Richard (Rick Mercer) on the set of Beaver Creek. *Above: Guest R.H. Thomson and Leah Pinsent toasting something other than each other's health.*

CASTING COUCH PRODUCTIONS / SALTER STREET FILMS LTD. (DAN CALLIS)

Other celebrities who have appeared on the show include Margot Kidder, who guested as a movie star suffering from a spectacular bipolar breakdown, and C. David Johnson and Cynthia Dale, who did a takeoff on their unstable *Street Legal* relationship by playing husband and wife producers.

Of course, maybe only a few hundred people outside of ACTRA (Alliance of Canadian Cinema, Television and Radio Artists) are going to be slapping their knees over Kevin Sullivan jokes, which is why Mercer prefers to think of the series he created as a *Dilbert*-like satire of the workplace.

"You know, this is a series set in the entertainment industry, but it could be set anywhere," he has said. "In every office, there'll always be people who back-stab. That's the field we're mining. It's just human nature."

A visiting Hollywood guest star (Margot Kidder) had a diva breakdown on a 1999 Made in Canada *episode.*
CASTING COUCH PRODUCTIONS / SALTER STREET FILMS LTD. (DAN CALLIS)

pop up
Gordon Pinsent

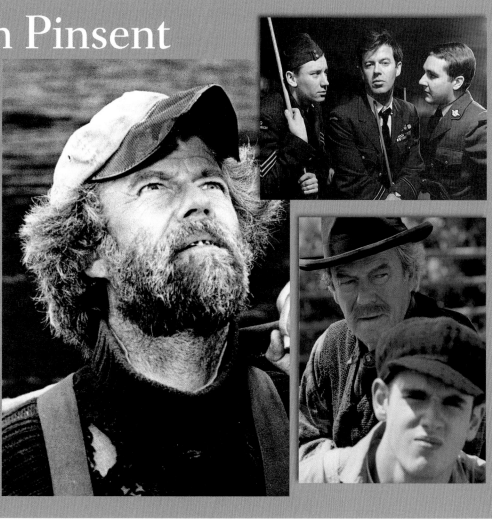

Gordon Pinsent appeared in our first TV soap opera, Scarlett Hill *(1962-64), even while he was looking out for brush fires on* The Forest Rangers *(1963-65). Later, he served as* Quentin Durgens *(1966-69) and starred in* A Gift to Last *(1978-79). Pinsent has recently shown up on* The Red Green Show *and appeared with daughter Leah on* Made in Canada. *Right: Pinsent on* The Beachcombers; *above right: with Terence Kelly (left) and Heath Lamberts in* 15 Miles of Broken Glass, *a 1966 Festival production; below right: on* Made in Canada.
SALTER STREET FILMS LTD. (DAN CALLIS)

Girl guides

THE TELEVISION *Road to Avonlea* began in the '50s when Don Harron recommended Lucy Maud Montgomery's *Anne of Green Gables* to director and composer Norman Campbell, who, with wife Elaine, turned the book into a musical for CBC-TV.

By the '90s, Montgomery's books had become a TV industry. In its seven-year, ninety-one-episode run, *Road to Avonlea* (1990-96) required the services of 462 actors, a crew of 200, and 5,000 extras, not to mention a python, a black bear, countless trained farm animals, and hundreds of unschooled, swarming bats.

Producer Kevin Sullivan's series, which was set in P.E.I. but shot in Uxbridge, Ontario, also made the faces of its principal cast familiar to viewers in 140 countries. Sarah Polley, who played little boarder Sara Stanley, became a star.

"It was wonderful watching the kids grow," remembers Lally Cadeau, who played Aunt Janet. "Sarah Polley was just this little sparrow who they put in a dress with a little bow on and said, 'Okay, honey, you're Sara.' As she grew older you could see how her perception of the character and world changed, and she just took off where she needed to go. Gema Zamprogna as Felicity astonished me. And Zach Bennett grew into a stunning young man. I have nothing but admiration for all those kids."

The series worked, Cadeau says, because it was a celebration of family and the land — the great irony being that her farm family, the Kings, had no idea what they were doing with their land.

"A lot of work went into making *Avonlea* credible, and I loved being around carpenters and sets," she says. "Yet it was such make-believe. I mean, what kind of farmers were we? My character, Janet, was a scatterbrain. I think once in the whole series we talked about weather, and we were awful at haying. Cedric Smith, who played Alec King, and I used to laugh about how we were always in the barn having intimate chats with the children, which real farmers wouldn't have time for. Really, we were the worst farmers in the world. But it was enormous fun."

Cadeau suggests that the emotional core of

the series family was Jackie Burroughs, who played Hetty King, the bustling schoolteacher who took Sara in after her father sent her packing from Montreal.

"Jackie was a real trip," Cadeau says. "At first I annoyed her. When you're playing with a powerful actor like Jackie, you can either fight to get attention or cut way back. As the years went on, I cut back, but there was a steep learning curve. Jackie taught me a lot."

The genesis of the Maritime Gothic *Emily of New Moon* began when producer Michael Donovan of Halifax's Salter Street Films went on a tropical vacation with his daughter. There he met an American woman, a Montgomery fan, who asked why the author's best book, *Emily of New Moon*, had never been made into a film. Donovan, who had read his mother's signed, first-edition copy of the book, couldn't tell her.

Opposite: Felicity (Gema Zamprogna) on Road to Avonlea. *Behind her (from left to right): Sara (Sarah Polley), Felix (Zach Bennett), Hetty (Jackie Burroughs), and Cecily (Harmony Cramp).*
SULLIVAN ENTERTAINMENT LTD.

Martha MacIsaac (right), the star of Emily of New Moon, *and Jessica Pellerin.* SALTER STREET FILMS LTD./CINAR FILMS (BARRETT & MCKAY)

Wind at My Back (1996-present) is another period piece produced by Sullivan Entertainment. The Bailey family survives the Great Depression in the Ontario mining town of New Bedford. Surrounding May Bailey (Shirley Douglas) as the commanding matriarch are (from left to right): Fat (Tyrone Savage), Grace (Kathryn Greenwood), Bob (Dan Lett), and Hub (Dylan Provencher).

SULLIVAN ENTERTAINMENT INC.

A few days later he picked up the three *Emily* books at an airport bookstore. He reread the first and committed to an *Emily* series before his plane touched down in Halifax. "I just wanted to confirm my memory had served me right — that the books were as good as I remembered," he said.

Shot entirely on Prince Edward Island, *Emily of New Moon* (1998-2001) was coloured a darker shade than *Anne of Green Gables* and *Road to Avonlea*. Montgomery once wrote that it was only later in her career, after she had become successful, that she "had the courage to write about rural P.E.I. in Victorian times, the way it really was."

Newcomer Martha MacIsaac, who was discovered on the cover of a P.E.I. tour guide, plays Emily Starr, a clairvoyant orphan who is the unwelcome guest in a series of foster homes. Just as in previous Montgomery books, it's the land that sustains the story's female ingenue. Producer Marlene Matthews, who had worked for six years on *Avonlea* in Ontario, was determined to bring Montgomery home with the new series.

"I thought the time had come for me to see where Lucy Maud lived," she said. "And when I got [to Prince Edward Island] it just stunned me. It's that love and passion for the land that kept those early settlers going, and fueled Emily."

The series also benefits from the participation of MacIsaac, who is every bit as industrious as her onscreen character. (In one season, Martha supplemented her allowance by fining adult actors every time they cursed.) The young actress also proved she had an instinctive grasp of acting in the show's very first season. When asked by a reporter how she approached the series' title role, she said simply, "I just pretend to be Emily."

Trudeau redux

IN ADDITION TO being a thoughtful entertainment, the vigorously playful *Trudeau* demonstrated the versatility of our docudrama tradition.

Talk about multi-purposing: the 2002 miniseries had more uses than a Swiss Army knife. The two-part film used Pierre and Margaret Trudeau's broken love affair as a prism to examine the enduring romance between Canada and its fifteenth prime minister, while offering valuable history lessons on a variety of subjects, including the October Crisis and the constitutional agreement.

Writer-executive producer Wayne Grigsby's (*North of 60, Black Harbour*) and director Jerry Ciccoritti's (*Net Worth*) miniseries was also very much a pop-culture odyssey. The film frequently employed a split-screen technique pioneered in the Canadian pavilion at Expo 67, and at one point compared Trudeau's political arrival to Beatlemania with a dizzy montage reference to *A Hard Day's Night*. There was also a joking allusion to Quentin Tarantino's *Reservoir Dogs* and a K-Tel Canada soundtrack featuring everyone from Robbie Lane and The Disciples ("It's Happening") to Leonard Cohen, Glenn Gould, and Teenage Head.

And while the spectator state of Canada has produced a rich tradition in mimicry, as evidenced by the work of Rich Little, *SCTV*, *CODCO*, *Air Farce*, and Mike Myers, Colm Feore's impersonation and psychological reading of Pierre Trudeau remains a singular achievement.

"A couple of days before we started to shoot, I phoned both the director and producer and said, 'Listen, I'm in a panic here,' Feore remembers. "'It seems pretty clear that I'm not going to be able to get to the London School of Economics, Harvard, and the Sorbonne by Monday, and I'm certainly not going to run the country. I'm simply going to have to pretend. Are you both all right with that?'"

They were. And Feore rewarded his employers with a performance that came tantalizingly close to solving the eternal mystery that was Pierre Elliott Trudeau.

Feore was particularly good at capturing the amused confidence in Trudeau's voice, and revealing how the prime minister's appetite for intellectual gamesmanship — whether teasing Margaret (Polly Shannon) over her infatuation with the poet Keats or baiting Quebec nationalists on the subject of separation — amounted to a defining character trait.

As is the case with the best docudramas, *Trudeau* delighted us with unexpected dramatic flourishes that illuminated documented events. Although the miniseries used a great deal of CBC archival news material, perhaps the most telling journalistic moment in *Trudeau* came in re-enacting the prime minister's famous War Measures Act press scrum on the steps of Parliament.

In that scene, Aidan Devine, the actor playing the prime minister's interrogator, CBC reporter Tim Ralfe, looks almost as often at his tape recorder as his subject, just to make sure he's really capturing what became Trudeau's most memorable (and obeyed) command: "Just watch me."

Polly Shannon and Colm Feore as Margaret and Pierre Trudeau on their wedding day, from the docudrama Trudeau.
BIG MOTION PICTURES (DAN CALLIS)

Zuckerman unbound

THERE'S A REASON why so many made-for-CBC-TV dramas — from *Love and Hate* (1989) through to *Conspiracy of Silence* (1991), *Dieppe* (1993), *Million Dollar Babies* (1994), *Net Worth* (1995), and *Revenge of the Land* (1999) — have the commanding air of a practised trial lawyer's final address to a jury. All were produced by Bernie Zukerman, a former lawyer who refined the art of public argument while heading *The Journal*'s documentary division. (Before that, Zukerman was senior producer at *the fifth estate* and a researcher on *For the Record*.)

Good stories and talented storytellers are what make docudramas work, Zukerman maintains. But you still need an entry into even the most compelling drama in order to capture an audience.

"Whiny victims are a turnoff and crazy people make other people nervous," he says, explaining why he never went ahead with a planned film on mass murderer Clifford Olson, although he had a terrific script.

Below left: Poster for the 1993 docudrama Dieppe, *starring Victor Garber as Vice-Admiral Lord Louis Mountbatten. Below right: Writer Suzette Couture and producer Bernie Zukerman.*

Even *Conspiracy of Silence*, the powerful, tragic story of Helen Betty Osborne, a nineteen-year-old Manitoba native woman who was murdered by four joyriding white men in 1971, didn't proceed until Zukerman and writer Suzette Couture had the right hook.

Couture, screenwriter for *Love and Hate*, wasn't initially interested in the project. The victim, who had hoped to be a lawyer someday, was a wonderful character but wouldn't be on screen long. And the crime itself was brutally straightforward. It took weeks of research, including a careful reading of journalist Lisa Priest's book on the killing of Helen Betty, for Zukerman to find a character and story to build his film around.

"It was the story of the town," he says. "The cover-up. It took sixteen years for the story to be fully told. Everybody knew, but nothing was done. That was the story we had to tell. Once it clicked with me, Suzette got excited and jumped in full bore."

With *Million Dollar Babies: The Dionne Quintuplets*, the challenge was to make what had been the ultimate feel-good story of the Depression (but was in fact the tale of children raised in captivity as a provincial tourist attraction) into a credible TV movie that worked for a more skeptical '90s audience.

Finding and working with babies was difficult in itself. The same team who engineered the Muppets designed the eerily lifelike latex infants. Zukerman also hired two sets of triplets

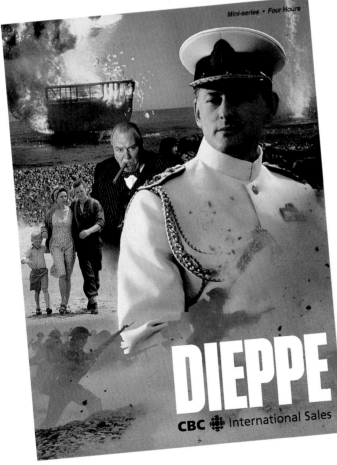

Mini-series • Four Hours

DIEPPE

CBC International Sales

and several pairs of twins — some twenty-two babies in all through the course of shooting.

To update the Dionne story for a contemporary audience, the producer (and writer Couture again) deliberately played it out in a social context that today's viewers would understand. "This was a family that was destroyed by many of the same issues we face today," Zukerman says. "Media hype, commercial greed, government manipulation, rich against poor."

Zukerman's docudramas went to great lengths to achieve period verisimilitude. For *Net Worth*, the story of how the NHL crushed the first players' union in the '50s, the production recruited actors who actually knew how to play hockey, dressed them up in authentically recreated woollen jerseys, and brought in Ted Lindsay, the former Red Wing star and union leader, as a consultant.

With one docudrama, Zukerman got lucky when scouting for an appropriate location. "Incredibly, with *Love and Hate* we were able to rent the real house and garage where Colin Thatcher lived," he says. "We recreated the murder of his wife JoAnn exactly where it happened — kitty-corner to the Saskatchewan legislature."

Beau Bridges (left) and Roy Dupuis were Dr. Allan Roy Dafoe and Oliva Dionne in Million Dollar Babies, *the TV drama based on the early years of the Dionne quintuplets.*
CINAR FILMS

Holy terror

John N. Smith's two-part TV film *The Boys of St. Vincent* (1992), the story of sexual abuse in a St. John's Catholic orphanage, represents a high-water mark in the Canadian journalistic storytelling tradition.

Suggested by contemporary events, the film follows the story of a fictional Catholic priest, Brother Peter Lavin (Henry Czerny). Once a battered orphan himself, he visits the hell of his own childhood upon a series of young boys — children who were, in Orwell's words, "flung into a world of force and fraud and secrecy ... like a goldfish into a tank full of pike."

Despite a court order keeping it off Montreal and Ontario stations by a Toronto judge, who ruled that airing the film would compromise the rights to a fair trial of four Christian brothers facing charges in connection with training schools in Newfoundland and Ontario, Smith's film attracted more than 1.2 million viewers outside Ontario and Quebec when it first aired in December 1992, and an audience of 2.5 million when it was broadcast to the whole country the following year. (The director's subsequent work for the CBC includes *Dieppe* [1993] and *Revenge of the Land* [1999].)

The CBC displayed a helpline phone number several times during the 1993 airings, which resulted in more than a thousand calls. The film would later receive theatrical release throughout the world. The *Irish Times* said of the film, "It burned with barely controlled rage, a rage that left no room for flinching or evasion. It raised all sorts of questions, but answered them with profound moral clarity."

Below: "[The Boys of St. Vincent] *was the pinnacle so far for me,"* Henry Czerny *(middle) said in 1997.* "I didn't realize until later how much it took out of me." LES PRODUCTIONS TELE-ACTION (ROGER DUFRESNE)

Where we're coming from

Canada: A People's History *executive producer Mark Starowicz prior to filming the Plains of Abraham battle. The Plains are now well groomed, so war scenes were shot in a farmer's field outside Ottawa over the course of six days.*

IN MAKING *Canada: A People's History*, the CBC proved it had learned the lessons of its own past.

The network has always prospered when it placed people Canadians identified with and trusted, from the cast of *Don Messer's Jubilee* to Barbara Frum on *The Journal*, in front of the camera. Much has been made of the thirty-two-hour millennial series as a filmmaking achievement. And yes, the bilingual documentary series took almost four years, 400 historical consultants, a legion of researchers and writers, 15 directors, 7 camera crews, 240 actors, and hundreds more military re-enactors to make. But the premise was always as simple and democratic as its title — a narrative history of Canada as told through the writings and stories of the *people* who were there.

All portrayals of historical events inevitably reflect the times in which they are made, and *History*'s executive producer, Mark Starowicz, accepts that his fifteen-part series says a great deal about Canada and Canadians in the mid-'90s.

"The world was changing so rapidly," he says. "Globalization and open borders meant that the Canada we knew seemed to be slipping away before our eyes. Railways were shutting down. Airlines failing. The Quebec referendum made us wonder if there was going to be a Canada. At the same time the millennium was approaching, and there was an idea we were packing for a long, uncertain voyage. When that

happens you begin by packing the essentials. Who were we? Where did we come from?"

When Gene Allen, the series' senior director of research, began answering these questions for Starowicz with "these incredible stories of people," the executive producer knew he had something the public would want to see.

Which is why Starowicz wasn't surprised when *Canada: A People's History* proved an immediate success, drawing an average of 2.3 million English and French viewers in its first season. People always reach out to the past when they're troubled by the future, he says.

Ranging from 15,000 BC to the 1990s, the millennial series (2000-2001) brought events in our history alive in ways we'd never seen before. For the 1759 siege of Quebec City, researchers found a two-hundred-year-old British magazine containing an interview with a French soldier who had fought on the Plains of Abraham. We also heard a diary account of the decisive struggle from a seventeen-year-old British militiaman, who told us, "A man could not stand erect without being hit, any more than he could stand in a shower without having rain fall on him."

And if the concerns of contemporary Canadian society made us reach out for the past, modern technology also helped the series' filmmakers recreate pivotal scenes from distant centuries. To show the British fleet gathering below Quebec City prior to the battle of the Plains of Abraham, filmmakers digitally transformed a single, intricately detailed, five-foot replica of a period British battleship into a hundred-mile-long armada. The battle itself, which was shot in a farmer's field in North Gower, near Ottawa, was staged with ninety-eight re-enactors who portrayed Wolfe's and Montcalm's troops. Their efforts were then cloned by the series' graphics project leader, Stephen Dutcheshen, into a battle involving thousands of soldiers.

With the battle sequence completed, Dutcheshen's team then merged an image of London's skyline after a Second World War air raid with a Quebec City skyline (that had

already been pruned of modern buildings) to recreate the charred capital of New France.

What gave meaning to all this robust, digitally enhanced action were the brief, telling biographical sketches of the combatants underscoring each scene. These weren't armies. They were soldiers. People. We came to know the displaced Irish and Highlanders fighting for Wolfe, as well as the homegrown militia fighting for their homes and the imported French soldiers who were battling only to stay alive.

"By focusing on ordinary people at the mercy of great historical forces," Brian Bethune observed in *Maclean's*, "the series

Ontario demonstrators burn Métis leader Louis Riel in effigy in A People's History *simulation of the 1885 Northwest Rebellion.*

turns them — and by extension all Canadians — into participants of an epic battle."

Canada: A People's History was adapted into a best-selling book, and has accumulated more than 150,000 DVD and video sales. But before it aired there were many who felt that Starowicz's $25-million project, which required the cooperation of both French and English filmmakers and historians, was folly. (Of course, Starowicz had heard that kind of doomsaying before, when he created *The Journal*.)

For one thing, the producer was told that the much-valued eighteen- to thirty-two-year-old demographic wasn't interested in history. Starowicz figured that was bunk when he saw how interested his computer design unit was in the project. "The graphic compositing department at CBC is full of kids with green hair," he laughs.

And while the CBC hoped to line up five corporate sponsors for the series, in the beginning only Sun Life Financial agreed to participate. (Bell Canada Enterprises came on board before the second season went to air in the fall of 2001.) Even then, the network ran the series without advertising spots.

"The CBC, God bless it, decided not to commercialize the history of Canada," Starowicz comments. "We didn't use the series to sell doughnuts and hamburgers. It's disheartening that some people think that the history of Canada will only be produced if it is deemed an appropriate vehicle for selling soda pop. That's why we have a public broadcaster."

Thesaurus Rex

Rex Murphy is a frequent visitor to *The National*, where he holds forth on a variety of subjects with the music and argumentative wit of the best saloon lawyers. Here are excerpts from two of his "Point of View" pieces:

On the death of Pierre Elliott Trudeau, September 29, 2000

He walked outside the boundaries of expectation in almost everything he did. He was intense, private, and reserved and gave himself to the one profession, the one vocation, that most depends on exhibition, attention, and continuous display.

He paid the country the deepest tribute a real politician can: he believed in it with his brain and his heart, and gave the wit of the one and the heat of the other to enlarging and enlivening its possibilities and our citizenship.

On MP pay raises, June 5, 2001

Einstein claimed that nothing could move faster than light. But then Einstein never saw Canadian Members of Parliament when they decided to give themselves a raise.

The speed, in parliamentary terms, with which the raise is moving through the House of Commons may undermine our entire understanding of modern science. After Don "Make-It-So" Boudria, the House leader, gets this raise through the Commons in three days, I expect to head down to NASA and let them in on the secrets of intergalactic travel.

Has anything else been proposed, debated, and passed the Canadian House of Commons in three days? Tom Wappel can't post a letter in three days. The Endangered Species Act was first proposed in 1996, and this law on which the fate of whole species depends was proposed again in 2000 and again in 2001. That's five years. And still no bill. If they could've linked the fate of the bald eagle or the platypus duck to the hourly rate of MPs, I dare say by now this whole country would be one gigantic national park and nature preserve from sea to sea and baby seals and aardvarks would be on the new Canadian flag.

Wendy Mesley joined CBC in 1981, became national affairs correspondent ten years later, and was host of the acclaimed *Undercurrents* for six seasons. She is now co-host, with Diana Swain, of *CBC News: Disclosure*.

"*Full disclosure*"

UNDERCURRENTS CAME OUT of my increasing frustration with political reporting. In the early '90s civil servants were being laid off while communications firms were exploding. And it had become difficult to have a real conversation with anyone in Ottawa because of all the PR armour and the media training politicians had been given.

Rather than covering the schmuck cabinet minister who is really just the puppet, in many cases, of the great PR, behind-the-scenes manipulators, I wanted to expose some of what I knew was happening behind the scenes. That small idea became firmer over the years under the guidance of our executive producer, FM Morrison. We lasted almost seven years. And I think the spirit of *Undercurrents* remains intact in *Disclosure*.

The story I'm proudest of so far on *Disclosure* was exposing how a number of business shows are actually glorified infomercials where companies pay for the story and provide questions. That has profound implications when you consider that the viewers watching might be making investment decisions.

One of the first shows we did on *Undercurrents* was about marketing disguised as journalism. The makers of Tylenol hired a pollster to do a poll, then hired a PR company to release the findings as news and basically managed to conscript everybody into treating it as news when it was really advertising.

We continue doing so many stories on media and marketing on *Disclosure* because I believe that's where the power is these days. There's a lot more power in Hollywood and Wall Street than on Capitol Hill. The same thing is true in Canada.

The best compliment I ever received came from Larry Zolf, who told me he thought *Undercurrents* carried on the spirit of *This Hour Has Seven Days*. That meant a lot to me.

One thing *Undercurrents* taught me and *Disclosure* is confirming is that — and I know this sounds sucky but it's true — nobody but CBC would ever put those shows on the air. When *Undercurrents* was cancelled I went to all the people [from other networks] who had said, "Oh, it's such a great show, let me know if you ever want to come do it at our network." And what did they say to me then? They said, "You've got to be nuts, you're taking on advertisers and corporations, and you want time to research...." And I really realized CBC is the only place that would invest in doing the kind of important investigative work that we're trying to do.

Ten, nine ... ten

Like clocks in fall, *The National* turned back an hour in 1993 and for a time was called *Prime Time News*, with co-hosts Peter Mansbridge and Pamela Wallin. Ratings plummeted because viewers hated the time slot, and the show's format — a mix of news and current affairs — failed to come together. Wallin was dismissed in 1995 amid great controversy.

"It's pretty simple. We tried a show; it didn't work," Mansbridge once told the *National Post*. "The audience hated it and the network forced it upon us in a very short period of time. There were a lot of emotions through a lot of things that happened around here. [Barbara Frum died in 1992.] And then suddenly, in the middle of that, there was a new direction, new management, a new show. We were given three months to put it on. One month before the show started, there was a national referendum which took up a lot of my time ... I remember Wallin and I sitting there and the guys were still building the set around us, one hour before we went to air. The show never had a chance."

After veteran producer/journalist Tony Burman became head of news in 1995, *Prime Time News* and the 9 p.m. time slot were scrapped and *The National* at 10 was born again. Wallin later formed her own successful production company.

Above: Peter Mansbridge talks to Prime Minister Jean Chrétien in a 1996 town hall meeting at the University of Ottawa. CP (FRED CHARTRAND)

Right: Ian Hanomansing, host of Canada Now, *the national supper-hour news.*

"*The art of news*"

I WAS WORKING at the Churchill, Manitoba, airport and a CBC manager heard my voice and offered me a position as a radio DJ.

Churchill didn't have live TV in 1966. Programming came on a train. The whole town would conspire *not* to know what had happened on *Hockey Night in Canada*. We'd wait and all get together to watch taped games.

At the time, Churchill was the only northern CBC radio station without a newscast. So I started one. My model was *Radio Free Friday*, with Peter Gzowski, which was a forerunner to *As It Happens*. It was a Mark Starowicz show. Our first newscast was two minutes. (Churchill was a small town.) And I did interviews, edited tape, everything.

We also started an openline show, *Words with Peter Mansbridge*. In those days, you were supposed to have delays so people couldn't swear. We didn't have one, but figured out a crude tape loop that gave us leeway. So we were ready for anything that first day, but didn't get a single call. Not one. I talked the whole time.

Next day, we did the show again, but called it *Words and Music with Peter Mansbridge!* But that's where I learned to think and talk on my feet, in Churchill.

My other training was the years I spent as a reporter and correspondent. This would have been in the '70s when I graduated from a series of Prairie bureaus to Parliament Hill. By then I'd become a political junkie.

I'd been part of election coverage in 1979, but in 1981 I was asked to fill in for George McLean, anchor of the weekend *National*. It was a huge moment for me. Here I was, this kid who had been working at an airport thirteen years earlier, and to have worked my way up to sitting in that chair, well that meant something to me. My heart was pounding through my jacket. I still have a bit of that feeling every night. There is a responsibility to this job and I never ever forget that.

In 1981 I was brought in from Ottawa to do a number of things: I anchored weekends and filled in as Washington and London correspondent. The first time I ever got an earlymorning panic call — "Come to work *now*" — was when Ronald Reagan was shot. Shortly after that there was an assassination attempt on the pope. Then, not long after, another call: Anwar Sadat had been assassinated. I learned an important lesson during those crises. You get a lot of information on days like that, but much of it is wrong. So you have to be a filter.

With September 11, 2001, we knew almost immediately what had happened — terrorists had attacked the World Trade Center and the Pentagon — we just didn't know why. Everything I ever did, every story or broadcast I worked on, prepared me for that awful day. The same was true of our team. To do what we did — forty-four straight hours of live broadcasting — called upon our collective expertise.

We had to know about airlines and aircraft, about terrorism and Middle East politics. We had more than two hundred years of accumulated knowledge working for us that day — with David Halton, Don Newman, Don Murray, Neil MacDonald, Brian Stewart, and Patrick Brown participating in the coverage.

And those are just on-air people. The live news specials crew — Dave Knapp, Mark Bulgutch, Fred Parker, Yvonne Berry, Paul Mountsteven, Nilesh Hathi — were extraordinary. Arnold Amber developed that group, and we're like a hockey team that's been through the wars. We know each other's strengths. The viewer only sees me, not this wall of people behind me. But they're there.

TV isn't magic, it's expertise. This core group has been together a long time and we have a belief in and understanding of each other. That's what really separates us from other networks on days like that. Fifty years of tradition has allowed us to make news a fine art.

Battle fatigue

BRIAN MCKENNA, producer-director of the Second World War documentary trilogy *The Valour and the Horror: Canada and the Second World War*, met author-refugee Salman Rushdie at a PEN benefit shortly after McKenna's 1992 TV series created a national controversy.

"Welcome to the club," Rushdie said.

"Well, maybe same club, different week," McKenna responded.

Canadian veteran groups who sued Brian and Terence McKenna for libel wouldn't appreciate the comparison to Rushdie. The Montreal brothers, many veterans felt, defamed them with an "inaccurate and biased" account of the war. (The libel suit was later disallowed by the Supreme Court.) The veterans' fury quickly spread to an angry debate in the House of Commons.

A stylish collage of newsreel footage, dramatizations, and first-person accounts of Canadians at war, *The Valour and the Horror* consists of three segments: *Savage Christmas: Hong Kong, 1941* told how Canadian soldiers were sent on a suicide mission to defend Hong Kong. *Death by Moonlight: Bomber Command* presented a controversial account of the bombing of German cities. And the final episode, *In Desperate Battle: Normandy, 1944*, suggested that the enormous Canadian losses at Normandy were due to incompetent military leadership.

Response to the series was swift and varied.

The *Globe and Mail* called the trilogy "an invaluable and engrossing series of quasi-historical documents with enormous value as revisionist history."

The Valour and the Horror Revisited, a collection of essays by five historians, concluded that the McKennas distorted history by not conducting archival research in Germany. "No professional historian questions that Bomber Command targeted civilians with area bombing," co-editor David Bercuson declared. "What the film leaves out is that the Nazis used area bombing first, the Allied campaign skewed the German war effort, and the cities targeted were major producers of munitions."

Then-CBC chairman Patrick Watson, who had been singed by the *This Hour Has Seven Days* furor in the '60s, publicly defended the McKennas' trilogy but had lingering reservations about the work.

"I thought the documentary portions of the film were brilliant," he says. "On the other hand, some of the dramatizations sickened me. But I defended the film because I felt, especially given what had happened to us on *Seven Days*, it was important to defend the process that brought the film to air."

The documentary series also provoked difference of opinion when it reached broadcasting courts of appeal. CBC ombudsman Bill Morgan described the trilogy as "flawed" and containing "errors or confusions of fact." The CRTC concluded that "parts of the films may have been incorrect. [But] the filmmakers too appear to have reasonable grounds for the assertions made in the series.... The Commission considers that, generally speaking, both the supporters and detractors of the series appear to be able to marshal at least an arguable case for their claims. In the Commission's view, history cannot be considered as a single, immutable truth; to some extent, history depends on one's perspective."

Here are the McKennas' accounts of the making of the series, which won a Gemini for outstanding documentary series in 1993:

TERENCE MCKENNA:
"All worthwhile history is revisionist. This term is thrown around loosely; generally, traditional historians use it to refute history they don't like. What we did was apply the same journalistic principles we employed when Brian was a producer at *the fifth estate* and I was producing at *The Journal*.

"Where we thought we could say something new, we did. And obviously when you're dealing with journalistic principles you're often looking for controversy and points of dispute. So we had that in the back of our minds as we approached the material. In the segment *Death by Moonlight*, we went back to Europe with air force veterans and relived their training procedures in Britain. Then we brought them to their targets in Germany. The most interesting stuff in the film was these two pilots interacting not only with the fighter pilots who were trying to shoot them down, but also with the victims of their bombing.

"Two women who lived through the firestorm described what it was like on the ground. And it was an incredible moment because our pilots could appreciate the humanity of the German civilians who were the targets of firestorms that killed tens of thousands of people."

BRIAN MCKENNA:
"I knew this story was going to be explosive. It was clear to me that our veterans, pilots Doug Harvey and Ken Brown, didn't know the real story of their mission.

"I'll never forget, we were in London, in the Cabinet War Room where Churchill and his military chiefs made the decision to change from bombing military targets to bombing civilians. And as we read Doug and Ken the orders, they just blanched! And I remember Harvey said, 'Where did you get that?' And we showed them the documents. They were shell-shocked and you could see the gears turning.

"Orwell says that if you don't give something a name, it doesn't exist. Maybe we'd never given what we were doing there a name.

"Another bit of research brought out this story of a guy out of college, signing up for Bomber Command. This will be easy, we'll be above the battle, not in the trenches like our fathers in WWI, he thought. And he goes out on his first mission. They send out fifty planes, forty-two come back. Second mission, forty-two go out, thirty-eight return. He does the math and realizes his odds of surviving thirty missions were one in three. He goes to the base intelligence office and says, 'Show me where I'm wrong here.' And the intelligence officer says, 'Have you showed this to anyone else?' 'No.' 'Don't,' he says. 'You shouldn't have gone to university. Have a drink.'

"Attacking Canada's military historians as a group was probably not the wisest decision. We had no idea. Peter Trueman, writing in the *Toronto Star*, said, 'If there still is an Establishment in this country, the McKennas are going to hear from them.' And we discovered he was absolutely right. There was an Establishment in this country and we woke it up."

Sandy Cushon joined CBC in 1972 as an agricultural commentator and went on to host CBC Winnipeg's *Points West*. He began hosting CBC-TV's longest-running program, *Country Canada*, in 1975, stepping down twenty-five years later. Reg Sherren now hosts the program.

"*A fifty-year calendar*"

I WAS RAISED on a farm in Oxbow, Saskatchewan. My brother still runs the place, although it's different from when I grew up. A lot has changed over the years. When Murray Creed started *Country Calendar* in 1954 we were a rural nation. Sure, lots of us lived in cities, but our values were rural. But by the '70s, farmers and fishermen had become a small rump of the population. The old ways were disappearing.

I started hosting the show in 1975. We'd changed the name to *Country Canada* by then, but it was the same half-hour show out of Winnipeg, with reports from all over. First story I did, I went to Washington and saw Earl Butts fire up a crowd talking about agri-power and a new deal that would make the hewers of wood and drawers of water rich. I came home all excited. Of course, that didn't happen. Agriculture started to slide and has never recovered.

Life became cruel for lots of people, and here at *Country Canada* we couldn't do much except tell their stories. Every year it seemed we'd do a big feature on farmers who were forced out. What was difficult about these stories was that agriculture was said to be booming. It was farming that was dying. Well, the world was changing. Just as TV was going from film to tape, farmers were going from 150- to 500- to 1,000-acre ranches. Unfortunately, a lot of people didn't make it.

The image of Grandma and Grandpa on the farm wasn't accurate anymore. We had to tell new stories. What we did

was go to a half-hour profile format for a number of years. We wanted to tell the incredible stories of the people who were making it. We visited a modern cash-crop farm, a ranch, a modern dairy farm. One of the most memorable visits was to Bob Walker's farm, near Creemore, Ontario. It was the most beautiful farm I'd ever seen. He was a sheep man who was losing sheep to coyotes. He had these incredible sheepdogs, which I could relate to because we had sheepdogs on our farm in Oxbow. Bob walked five dogs at once. But you know, he eventually had to sell. So we went back to do another show on him. That was a tough one to make. Real tough. Bob has another farm now, though.

The reward of doing the show all these years is meeting the people we profile. Wonderful people. I've been in every obscure place you can name — and some you can't. I was in Joe Batt's Arm, on Fogo Island, just before the moratorium on cod. I got to try jigging for cod and met some of the best people of Canada — the Newfoundlanders. The decline of the cod fishery is just one example of the pressures and changes we've documented over the years.

In every part of the world, you have cities and then you have places many people consider the backwater. Generally that's a derogatory term. But you know, it's in the backwater where you meet real people, the people who strip away all the crap and corruption and tell it like it is. In all the places I went on *Country Canada* I didn't find too many I wouldn't want to go back and visit.

Scene from a 1958 Winnipeg Country Calendar. *Regional editions of the agricultural show were produced in Winnipeg, Edmonton, Vancouver, and the Maritimes. Host Johnny Moles is second from right.*

Country Calendar *co-host Norm Garriock (left) takes a really close look at the dairy industry in 1954. Garriock discussed agriculture in the first fifteen minutes of the Sunday afternoon show, while partner Earl Cox (right) offered gardening advice in the last half.*

Country Canada *host Sandy Cushon and sound technician Ed Chong talk to Rudy Usick, head of the Manitoba Beef Marketing Commission, in 1982. In 2002 the series became a marquee show for the CBC digital channel, Country Canada.*

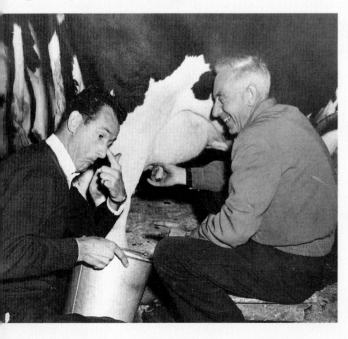

Right on the money

AN INTERVIEWER ONCE asked Jonathan Torrens, former host of *Street Cents* and *Jonovision*, what it was like to be the sexiest man on Canadian television.

"I don't know," Torrens replied. "Let me ask Knowlton Nash and I'll get right back to you."

It should come as no surprise that Torrens can fire back a media-celebrity punchline. *Jonovision* and *Street Cents* radiate pop-culture smarts. And both shows enjoy reputations for being faster than a kid's thumb on a TV remote.

The sneaky charm of the Emmy Award-winning *Streets Cents* lies in its ability to send up TV while it goes about its job of investigating consumer goods. For instance, a kid who e-mailed the show in 1996, asking what brand of tent to buy for a camping trip, was rewarded with a parody of the then-popular and extremely intense American domestic drama, *Party of Five.*

The skit takes place under canvas and revolves around how *Party of Five* little sister Claudia (played by *Street Cents* host Rachel Clark) bought a tent that wasn't big enough for a quintet. This leads to an emotionally draining screaming match between elder siblings Bailey and Julia that consists entirely of information on tent manufacturing:

"How was she supposed to know that with a low-end camping tent they don't give you as much room per person, and that's how they keep the prices down?" cries Julia (host Anna Dirksen tossing her hair around like Neve Campbell).

"She's old enough to learn that there is no industry standard for the amount of room a person needs," a properly grim Bailey (Torrens) responds from underneath a Scott Wolf wig.

(What makes this lunatic visual pun — *intense kids in tents!* — all the more fun is knowing that *Street Cents* is shot out of the old *Don Messer's Jubilee* studio in Halifax.)

Since 1989, *Street Cents* has tested just about

The Halifax Street Cents *cast in their fifth season (1993-94), from left to right: Brian Heighton (standing), Anna Dirksen, Jonathan Torrens, Benita Ha, and Moui the pig.*

Coming to a bathtub near you

The preferred mode of TV transportation for preschoolers from Monday to Thursday for nine seasons, *Theodore Tugboat* (1993-2001) was the story of the most conscientious boat in the Great Ocean Tug and Salvage Company fleet at Big Harbour.

As introduced and narrated by Haligonian Denny Doherty, formerly of the Mamas and Papas, Theodore cooperated with, helped, and taught important life lessons to other members of the fleet, particularly best friends Emily, Hank, and Foduck.

The animated series dealt with the three "F's" of children's programming — feelings, friendship, and fairness — in a manner that was applauded by various parental groups. And kids loved the spinoff tug toys, which howling moms and dads stepped on in the shower first thing in the morning.

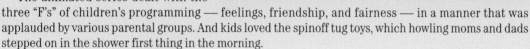

Theodore and Hank head up the coast.
ANDREW COCHRAN ASSOCIATES

everything kids and teenagers buy, from pizza and hamburgers to electronics equipment, running shoes, and cars. Part of the fun here is that kids are finally allowed to comment on goods dangled before them by advertisers. And products that don't make the grade are tossed into "the Pit" and "blown up real good," as John Candy used to say on *SCTV*.

All this roughhousing might make the show sound a little cavalier. But if you watch closely you'll appreciate that *Street Cents* takes its consumer watchdog job seriously (if not in an altogether sober fashion). The show has no commercials. Hosts don't wear brand-name clothes. "And we just don't pick a product and say, 'I wanna put it in the Pit,'" executive producer Barbara Kennedy once said. "A product has to be thoroughly researched and then it has to go through CBC lawyers, who are tough."

Besides, *Street Cents* is just too smart about pop culture to get all morally indignant. Anna Dirksen once went on a tirade about commercials, screaming:

"All I ask is to be entertained without the constant interruption of commercial advertising. I mean why do we mindlessly subject ourselves to the stupidity of cold sufferers with giant noses for heads; of frogs croaking the brand names of beer?"

"Because," Clark told her, "that way TV's free."

"Oh."

Jonovision (1996-2001), starring Torrens again, was an after-school talk show that felt like a play date with the smartest kid in class. The series was always issue oriented, but after that it was anything goes. "What I didn't want was something earnest," Torrens says. "You know, kids sitting around in beanbag chairs saying, 'Let's rap!'"

The series changed formats about as often as blonder-than-blond Torrens changed hairstyles. (His 1997 two-storey Jerry Lee Lewis pompadour remains the definitive *Jono*-do.) Sometimes it was a talk show. Other times a game show. Occasionally a sketch and variety show. There were also heavy metal band competitions. (Torrens promised that his first album would be called *Guitarded*.)

For all the show's restlessness and raw wit, *Jonovision* remained a warm and courteous, teen-friendly show. The nerviest jokes were always on Jono. Like the skit about the n-n-nervous suitor who pre-recorded then lip-synched his pitch for a date with a girl, only to have the tape cough into a French lesson — "Le pamplemousse est délicieux" — mid-spiel.

But then what else do you expect from a guy who, when asked the teen-beat question "Which Disney character do you most closely resemble?" answered "Michael Eisner."

251

Jonathan Torrens was host of the award-winning Halifax-based co-production *Street Cents* and the comedy/talk show for teenagers, *Jonovision*. He also had a recurring role as the town doctor in *Pit Pony*.

"*Jonoaudio*"

MY FIRST TV gig was playing one-half of a horse in a commercial and, no, I wasn't the lead. So you could say I was typecast early.

I auditioned for *Street Cents* in Halifax at age fifteen. They wanted teenaged boys. And I thought, *Hey you're obnoxious, why not?* I had to eat hamburgers for a week then come back and tell everyone how I felt. I must have done okay because they made me host a few shows later.

Looking back, I think people responded to my blind naiveté. I wasn't a child actor. My voice hadn't changed. I was a kid tossed into a giant electronic salad. One moment I'm at a Cineplex telling kids that when they buy popcorn they're paying for ambiance not butter, next I'm a squirrel in a comedy sketch.

Frankly, I graduated high school by the skin of my behind. But it was worth it to be involved in the first wave of kids' shows that tried to educate without preaching. The idea of a consumer show for kids with a bit of attitude — you know, blowing up bad products in the Pit — was brilliant. But we never told kids what to do. We let them make up their own minds.

The show was never work. A friend called TV production "fifty people trying to draw a straight line with a pencil." But I was fascinated by television. I worked long hours, participating wherever I could, so that when the carpet of national stardom was pulled out, I had options.

I decided it was time to go when we got, for the fourth time I think, a letter from a kid wanting to know why there was so much air in chip bags. *So they won't break, okay?* But you can't stay on a kids' show too long because you'll lose credibility. You don't want them saying, "Hey, whose dad's hosting the show?"

Jonovision started as a talk show, like *Ricki Lake*, but because it was Canadian we couldn't bus in overweight people from Buffalo, and there was no bitch-slapping. We tried to get into issues relevant to teens. You know — "*I know you stole my lip balm from my locker.*" "*I did it to get Cory to notice me*" — that kind of thing. As talk shows waned, so did our interest. Then it evolved into a game show-variety show. I loved *Kids in the Hall*. At its best, I don't think anybody knew what to expect when they turned *Jonovision* on.

Left: Guest Albert Schultz (Street Legal, Side Effects, Jake and Jill) is king for a day on Sesame Park.
CHILDREN'S TELEVISION NETWORK

Below (left to right): Basil, Louis, the Barbara Frum muppet, Dodi, a Mountie muppet, and Katie.
CHILDREN'S TELEVISION NETWORK

Park it right here

A REZONING BYLAW came into effect in 1996, turning *Sesame Street* into a park.

The beloved PBS preschooler kids' show, which started to be broadcast on CBC in 1970 and began including Canadian segments in 1973, was originally designed to reach an American inner-city audience (hence all the trash cans and tenements). Early Canadian *Sesame Streeters* included Louis, a bilingual otter, and frequent guest musicians Raffi and Fred Penner. (Alas, a proposed Canadian Muppet folksinger, Gordon Brightfoot, never passed the audition with a tyke test audience.)

By the early '90s, the show's pleasant jumble of skits, songs, puppetry, and animation was half-Canadian. Then *Sesame Park* went to air. "Instead of the urbanized, Americanized world of Sesame Street," a press release announced, "preschoolers will visit an ecologically friendly Canadian park, with Canadian Muppets embracing Canadian values and mores."

A few of the old *Sesame Street* regulars,

including Bert and Ernie, Grover, and Big Bird, stuck around to join Louis, Basil, Dodi, and Katie, along with special guests like Peter Mansbridge and Albert Schultz in their new, piney-fresh surroundings.

20 YEARS CANADIAN SESAME STREET

Our favourite corner

Opposite:
Hockey Night in
Canada*'s Danny
Gallivan (left),
Don Cherry
(centre), and Ron
MacLean (right).*

*Below: Don and
Ron. "We're like
Frick and Frack,"
MacLean says,
"we just seem to
play off each other
in a naturally …
comic way."*

THEY ARE DEFINITELY an odd pair of socks. The first time Don Cherry put on a headset to cover hockey for U.S. TV, the former Boston Bruin coach got into trouble with his producer.

"Who's gonna win the game?" his on-air partner asked.

"Well, I'll tell ya if this guy quits yelling in my ear," Cherry groused.

By comparison, Ron MacLean was a broadcast veteran before he started shaving. He had a CBC radio show in Red Deer, Alberta, at age fifteen. Ten years later, as a TV weatherman in Calgary, he gained renown for being able to ad lib his way out of any broadcast storm. The hockey addict jumped at the chance to join *Hockey Night in Canada* in 1986.

By then Cherry had made TV history as a commentator on *HNIC'*s *Coach's Corner.* Shouting to be heard over a deafening, Edwardian car-dealer wardrobe, Cherry was an almost immediate sensation. All he needed was one TV lesson from boss Ralph Mellanby.

"First game here, this was in 1980, someone asked me something, I go, 'Well, I think such and such …'" Cherry recalls. "Ralph came in all mad later and said, 'You don't think, you *know*! Give it to 'em straight.'"

Weeks later, Cherry was on air with Danny Gallivan. "What do you think, Don?" Gallivan asked during what was a particularly listless affair.

"Keeps going like this, the Zamboni driver is gonna be first star," Cherry replied.

Sartorial overkill only made Cherry's plain virtues more apparent. Here was an authentic, rarely heard TV voice whose thunderous exclamations and beery complaints transported us to Thunder Bay and Moose Jaw taprooms, hockey's parish churches.

But maybe it took the arrival of MacLean, who replaced host Dave Hodge in 1986, to make *Coach's Corner* a national institution. For if the essence of drama is conflict, here was a partnership capable of generating at least twenty years of creative tension.

Sitting down with Cherry in *HNIC'*s green room after *Coach's Corner,* just ten minutes go by before the coach shows you how to take a guy out in a hockey fight. "Punch below the eyebrow," Cherry says. "Skin's easy to cut there, eh? They bleed, you win."

MacLean later acknowledges that backing down from a midget fight ended his hockey career. "I'd hurt my thumb playing football," he remembers. "But I didn't really want to fight. I was in the wrong place at the wrong time. The '70s was the era of the Broad Street Bullies and Alberta was the roughest junior hockey in Canada."

In addition to differing views on hockey, the two men have opposing temperaments and speaking styles. ("He's Archie Bunker and I'm Meathead," MacLean says.)

"How come, you go in a supermarket, you're looking for hamburger, it's in metric or something," Don once told us. "But then say a killer is loose, *oh yeah,* then it's okay for

Sandra

Saskatchewan's Sandra Schmirler, who died in 2000, was the most accomplished and best-loved women's curler in the '90s. In addition to taking three Canadian and World Championships, along with an Olympic gold medal, she won millions of fans to her sport. "Because the mikes were on, women got to know us," says teammate and CBC commentator Joan McCusker. "They saw we were working gals and moms like themselves who were trying to keep life in balance. Sandra was fun and down to earth and let it all out in competition. People saw themselves in her. They wanted to be like her. They loved her."

McCusker, who joined the network's broadcast booth in 2001, has enjoyed her years in the limelight, although the mother of three (and wife of curler Brian McCusker) reports that fans always seem to notice her at inopportune times. "It usually happens when you're in the grocery store and the two-year-old is having a tantrum because you won't buy a chocolate bar," she says. "Just when the kids begin screaming, someone will go, 'Look, there's one of the curling girls.'"

The Canadian women's curling team after winning the gold medal at the 1998 Nagano Olympic Games. From left to right: Marcia Gudereit, current CBC curling commentator Joan McCusker, Jan Betker, and Sandra Schmirler. CP/COA

the press to say he's six-foot-two, two hundred pounds. That metric stuff drives me nuts."

MacLean meanwhile enjoys alliterative puns and, unlike his partner, is a staunch advocate of a modern, pluralistic Canada. His closing words to banquet crowds are always, "We're not here to see through each other, we're here to see each other through."

So how is it Don never tried to give Ron a poke in the eyebrow?

"Well, we've been through so much, fought so many wars together, we're friends," MacLean says. "And I love so much about Don. His mischief and the way he punches holes through pomposity. We get into fights on air; off air, too. And Don always seems to be in trouble. But, you know, maybe that keeps the show going."

The two men have been partners and friends for so long now that MacLean admits he sometimes has to remind himself not to let their TV work become too private and self-referential. That must be hard — off air, in *HNIC*'s green room, the two men carry on as if they were still on camera.

"Hey," Cherry says to an assistant while munching on a cookie. "When you send out promo shots of me and Ron, use last year's shots, eh? Look at him here in his white jacket — *gyanahh*."

"Ron said it's easy to autograph in the white," the publicist says.

"But he looks like a waiter!"

MacLean pops in. Cherry grows more animated. "Hey, you seen out there when we were doing autographs after the opening?" he asks.

"Yeah," MacLean says, stealing a cookie.

"There was a blind guy. You give him an autograph?"

"Nah," MacLean says. "Just pretended."

Cherry lets out a delighted howl and pours the remainder of his dessert into an unused ashtray.

"I'll tell the producer you just spilled your cookies," MacLean says, leaving.

Cherry bites his lip, trying not to smile. "You wonder I'm the way I am, working with a guy like that," he says.

Gold medallist Donovan Bailey in Atlanta in 1996. "There were three false starts," recalls Olympic commentator Don Wittman. "It felt unreal when Donovan finally won."

CP/COA (CLAUS ANDERSEN)

Warming up to the ice age

Above: Toller Cranston.

Right: And the cow skated over the moon. Olympic champion Elizabeth Manley with Loretta the Cow in a production of Back to the Beanstalk.

THE MODERN SKATING spectacular on television began with Toller Cranston's 1982 ice ballet *Strawberry Ice*, which was actually shot on a black surface and involved erotic dream sequences, tumbling animals, and Broadway legend Chita Rivera singing "Fever" dressed in a wreath of flames.

"My jaw hung open when I saw it," remembers Joan Tosoni, former director of *The Tommy Hunter Show* and director of many music specials and award shows. "I was wowed."

No one should ever try to out-fantasize Toller Cranston on ice, but producer/director Sandra Bezic and Tosoni's '90s skating specials with Kurt Browning, *Tall in the Saddle* and *You Must Remember This*, were also ambitious, imaginative (and difficult to achieve) productions.

Shot in Browning's hometown of Rocky Mountain House, Alberta, *Tall in the Saddle* featured a routine where Browning skated down a street that had been flooded and turned into a sheet of ice. "Except it was so cold Kurt's blades literally wouldn't glide on the ice," Tosoni remembers. "His skates would go *kkkrickk!* then stop."

In Bezic and Tosoni's next Browning special, *You Must Remember This*, the skater danced through raindrops in a memorable interpretation of "Singin' in the Rain." But only for short intervals. "We couldn't rain on the ice for longer than thirty seconds," Tosoni says. "Then we had to let it freeze again."

Skating specials are laborious work. Elvis Stojko spent five days choreographing the opening Elvis Presley parody on his 1997 special, *Elvis: Incognito*. "Then we started shooting," he says. "That three minutes you saw took two days to shoot."

But professional skaters are accustomed to marathon training sessions. "I'll put in a thousand hours of training on ice for the World Championships," Stojko says.

Above: Kurt Browning skating in the rain. DINO RICCI Below left: A chevron of Elvises led by Elvis Stojko. Below right: Gold medal winners Jamie Salé and David Pelletier at the 2002 Salt Lake City Olympics. CP (PAUL CHIASSON)

Hockey afternoon
in Utah

IT WAS ONE of those clement, late-winter afternoons that take us out of our homes for a post-hibernation stroll, but Staff Sergeant Carl Morgan of the Royal Newfoundland Constabulary told a reporter that the streets of St. John's were empty.

"It's eerie," is how Morgan described the third Sunday in February 2002.

Just about then CBC cameras cut to downtown Toronto, which also had the *something happened!* deserted-city look you see in apocalyptic sci-fi movies.

Where was everyone? Well, more than ten million of us were at home, hoping to witness our men's hockey team win a gold medal for the first time in fifty years. (The last time a Canadian men's squad, the Edmonton Mercurys, won Olympic gold, at Oslo in 1952, we didn't even have television.)

Hockey Night in Canada had become *Hockey Afternoon in Utah*. And few of us could resist the lure of an epic contest that, thanks to satellite technology, we could witness *together*, no matter where we were.

In addition to providing a glimpse of Toronto's barren Yonge Street, network cameras stationed in Vancouver, Edmonton, Regina, and Halifax bars gave us crowd reaction shots to goals by Paul Kariya, Jarome Iginla, and Joe Sakic that provided Canada with a 3-2 lead over the United States going into the third period of the gold medal game.

Canadian soldiers watching the contest in a mess tent in Kandahar also celebrated those goals (even though the game ended at 3 a.m. in Afghanistan). As did Kyle Ferguson and Bryan Allemang of Flamboro, Ontario, and friend Brad Kuntz of nearby Waterloo, who drove thirty-one hours, stopping only for gas, to watch the final at the Canadian Olympic Lodge in Salt Lake City.

Elsewhere in Canada, we congregated in tens and tens of thousands to watch history being made. In Vancouver close to twenty thousand gathered in front of a jumbo screen in GM Place. And in Russell, a Manitoba town of eighteen hundred, two hundred citizens packed the Yellowhead Room of the Russell Inn, some standing on chairs, to watch hometown hero Theoren Fleury.

Canada controlled play, but still enjoyed only a 3-2 lead with a little over four minutes remaining. When asked later why he kept reminding us of the slender lead, *HNIC* play-by-play man Bob Cole chuckles. "You never let the audience off the hook. You've got to know when to tighten the screws."

And when to loosen them. This is how Cole, who had been taught by Foster Hewitt in the '50s to save his most passionate delivery for the game's climax, called the second in a pair of late Canadian goals:

"Joe Sakic COMING RIGHT IN. **SCORES!** *JOE SAAAKICCC* scores. And that makes it 5-2, Canada. Surely that's gotta be it."

Cole quietened down and allowed the Canadian portion of the Utah crowd's singing of "O Canada" to fill the last minute. Afterwards, he turned to partner Harry Neale with a deadpan query that ushered us into the easy-feeling national celebration that followed.

"So Harry, glad you came?"

A few minutes later, Phil Esposito, our hero in the 1972 Canada-Soviet Union series, finally joined the celebration. Before the game, Esposito, who had worked in the U.S. his entire life, professed it didn't matter to him who won. Holidaying in Florida, he advised reporters he was hitting the beach instead of watching the game. But something got him in front of a TV to watch the final two periods and the gold medal ceremony.

"When the [Canadian] flag went up," he said, "that's when I realized I cared."

Other Canadians were more demonstrative. "Prime Minister Chrétien phoned right away and asked to speak to [Team Canada general manager] Wayne Gretzky," *HNIC*'s Ron MacLean remembers. "He was in great spirits.

Fans keep one eye on the gold medal men's hockey game and another on the Scott Tournament of Hearts in Brandon, Manitoba.
CP (CHUCK STOODY)

Graduation speech

One of the best TV moments at the 2002 Olympics — watched by 6.2 million people — came after the women's gold medal game, a match that saw Team Canada upset an American team that had beaten them eight straight by a score of 31-13. Huddled with her flushed, triumphant players, coach Daniele Sauvageau offered a stirring graduation speech: "You're going to go through tough times in life. Come back with responsibility, determination, and courage. And don't ever, *ever* give up on [yourself]."

Canadian women's hockey team coach Daniele Sauvageau (centre) and the triumphant team at Salt Lake City, February 21, 2002. CP/COA (MIKE RIDEWOOD)

He told Wayne that he and [his wife] Aline were jumping up and down. He was really 'in the moment' as they say. But we had a sound glitch, so that interview never played. He was a little more subdued when he and Wayne finally talked on air."

In Montreal, dozens of overly patriotic, flag-waving fans kidnapped a bus. Traffic died and an impromptu hockey game broke out on Robson Street in Vancouver, with players using empty Tim Hortons coffee cups for nets. Four provinces east, another game started up on Yonge Street in Toronto.

Nobody wanted the game to end. In fact, hours after the Olympic closing ceremony, *HNIC*'s MacLean and Cherry returned to their hotel with nothing to do, so decided to watch the game all over again in Ron's room.

"Ordinarily, Don is very disciplined — three beers each, and lite beers at that, is all we're allowed," MacLean says. "That night I had a few more."

Above: Team Canada's Theo Fleury and Mario Lemieux after the gold medal ceremony.
CP (TOM HANSON)

Left: Josie Daub (left) and Christian Hrab (right) react to Canada's win. More than five hundred fans watched the game on a giant-screen TV at the Canada Olympic Park in Calgary.
CP (JEFF MCINTOSH)

CBC-TV MILESTONES

1952: CBFT Montreal goes to air September 6, CBLT Toronto on September 8.

The first CBC-TV NHL hockey game (Canadiens versus Detroit Red Wings) is broadcast from Montreal on October 11.

The Toronto Maple Leafs make their home TV debut (against Boston Bruins) on November 1.

1953: CBOT Ottawa begins broadcasting, joining Montreal and Toronto via microwave links and thereby establishing a three-station network.

CKSO Sudbury, Canada's first private TV station and CBC-TV's first affiliate, is born. Later that year, CBUT Vancouver begins operation.

CBC scoops U.S. networks with footage of Queen Elizabeth's coronation on June 2. This marks the first time a televised event is shown on the same day in the U.K. and North America.

1954: *Country Calendar* goes to air on October 31. The ongoing show is renamed *Country Canada* in 1970.

CBWT Winnipeg and CBHT Halifax go to air.

The Plouffe Family begins broadcasting in both English and French.

1955: First telecast of the opening of Parliament.

1956: *Juliette* debuts on October 27.

The National News goes to air.

1957: *Front Page Challenge* premieres on June 24.

The first episode of *The Wayne and Shuster Show* is broadcast on October 16.

1958: The first coast-to-coast live TV broadcast, *Memo to Champlain*, airs on July 1, marking the completion of a microwave network that extends from Nova Scotia to British Columbia.

The Friendly Giant premieres on September 30.

1959: *Don Messer's Jubilee* debuts on August 7.

The microwave network is extended to Newfoundland.

1960: *The Nature of Things* debuts on November 6.

1962: *Take 30* goes to air on September 17.

1964: *This Hour Has Seven Days* debuts on October 4.

1965: *The Tommy Hunter Show* premieres on September 17.

The first trans-Atlantic TV newscast is shown via the Early Bird satellite.

1966: Canada is the third country (after the U.S. and Japan) to introduce colour television.

The CBC-TV technical department in Toronto develops instant replay for *Hockey Night in Canada*.

1967: Television comes to the North when CBC establishes a transmitter and playback machine in Yellowknife.

1968: The first televised debate among Canadian political party leaders airs on June 9.

1969: On April 14 CBC-TV airs the first major league baseball game (Montreal Expos versus St. Louis Cardinals) played outside the U.S.

1972: Game eight of the Canada-Soviet Union hockey series in Moscow. *Hockey Night in Canada*'s Foster Hewitt calls Paul Henderson's game- and series-winning goal.

The Beachcombers premieres on October 1. *Marketplace* debuts on October 5.

1973: The first live TV broadcast beams to the North via the Anik satellite.

1974: CBC's accelerated coverage plan leads to hundreds of TV transmitters being built in small, previously unserved communities.

1975: *The fifth estate* debuts on September 16.

1976: As host broadcaster of the Montreal Olympics, CBC revolutionizes Games coverage by providing live, all-day coverage of events.

1979: Live coverage of the House of Commons begins.

David Suzuki becomes host of *The Nature of Things*.

1981: CBC introduces closed captioning.

1982: In January *The National* moves to 10 p.m. in tandem with a new public affairs show, *The Journal*.

1984: The CBC-TV English all-news channel, *Newsworld*, is launched on July 31.

1993: *Royal Canadian Air Farce* and *This Hour Has 22 Minutes* debut on CBC-TV.

1997: CBC-TV adopts an all-Canadian prime-time schedule.

1998: CBC provides seven hundred hours of programming for the Nagano Olympics and is awarded broadcast rights for the next five Olympic Games.

2000: CBC goes live on January 1 for twenty-four hours of millennial-celebration coverage.

Canada: A People's History is launched on October 22.

2001: Launch of the new national supper-hour news program, *Canada Now*.

2002: Coverage of the Salt Lake City, Utah Olympics. Team Canada's February 24 gold medal-winning game against the U.S. draws over ten million viewers.

CBC celebrates its fiftieth anniversary with special broadcasts and events.

ACKNOWLEDGMENTS

Here's Looking at Us could not have been realized without the determination, resourcefulness, and enthusiasm of project coordinator and all-around marvel, Shelley Ambrose. I am also deeply indebted to editor Laurie Coulter for bringing her much-valued industry and skill to what was very much a collective enterprise.

In addition to the more than one hundred entertainers, broadcast journalists, and behind-the-scene talents who took time to share their CBC-TV memories with us, I would like to acknowledge several authors whose work I profited from in the creation of this book. In particular, Mavor Moore's *Reinventing Myself*, Knowlton Nash's *Cue the Elephant* and *The Microphone Wars*, Peter Kenter's *TV North*, Paul Rutherford's *When Television Was Young*, and Geoff Pevere and Greig Dymond's *Mondo Canuck* were all invaluable references.

Many thanks also to the many critics and journalists who have written on Canadian television in the last half century. Frank Penn (*The Ottawa Citizen*), Bill Anderson (*Canadian Press* and *TV Guide*), John Haslett Cuff, and John Allemang (*The Globe and Mail*) are just four critics whom I've admired over the years (and leaned on occasionally here).

Researcher-interviewer Sue Grimbly also deserves credit for her help with the '80s and '90s chapters.

Finally, I would like to express a heartfelt thanks to the creative talent who made the last half-century of CBC television such a compelling journey. So many talented individuals have made so many programs and events happen over the past fifty years that it was impossible to mention every one of them. This collection, though, sets out to capture the spirit of all of their achievements, and the highlights mentioned here are representative of a much longer list of people and programs that deserve recognition and celebration.

STEPHEN COLE

PHOTO CREDITS

All the photographs in this book, unless otherwise noted after the captions, have been provided courtesy of the CBC Still Photo Collection in the Design Library and the CBC Museum.

We would like to thank the following photographers: Bouthillier Photographie, 115; Norman Chamberlin, 102, 146 (top); Henry Fox, 8 (left), 49, 106; Elizabeth Frey, 13; David Hasten, 131; Lautre Photographers & Artists, 107 (top); Joseph Lederer, 133; Gilbert A. Milne, 11, 12; Herb Nott, 21, 36; Greg Pacek, 199; Brooke Palmer, 241; Fred Phipps, 8 (top), 39 (top), 148 (top), 164; David Portigal, 135; Robert Ragsdale, 17, 72, 73, 82 (bottom), 86 (top), 92, 93, 96, 107 (bottom, right), 116, 117 (bottom), 148 (bottom), 153 (top), 155; Dave Roels, 132; Paul Smith, 134; John Steele, 91 (middle); and Harold Whyte, 143.

We would also like to thank the Provincial Archives of Manitoba/CBC Communications Department Collection for providing the photographs on pages 7 (bottom), 23, 44 (bottom), 69 (middle), 82 (bottom), 127, 170 (left), 249 (bottom, right), the National Archives of Canada for the CBC photographs from their collection on pages 26 and 70, and the Canada Science and Technology Museum for the main photograph on the title page.

In addition, we would like to thank Joyce Davidson, David Knapp, Shelagh Rogers, and Joe Schlesinger for providing photographs.

INDEX

271

CANADIAN BROADCASTING CORPORATION

Project Director, 50th Anniversary Celebration:
Pia Maria Marquard

Project Manager: Shelley Ambrose

Research: Leone Earls and the
CBC Reference Library staff

Visual Research: Lynda Barnett and the staff
of the CBC Design Library

McCLELLAND & STEWART LTD.

President and Publisher: Douglas Gibson

Senior Editor: Dinah Forbes

Managing Editor: Jonathan Webb

Project Editor: Laurie Coulter

Copy Editor: Karen Alliston

Editorial Assistant: Jenny Bradshaw

Project Design: PageWave Graphics Inc.

Art Director: Kong Njo

Production Manager: Vicki Black

WITH THE ASSISTANCE OF:

Don Adams
Robert Albota
Ian Alexander
Jennifer Allan
Michael Allder
George Anthony
Gino Apponi
Jesse Barnett
Rosemary Bergeron
Deborah Bernstein
Faye Blum
Cathie Bolstad
Rikki Bote
Karen Bower
Nancy Boyle
Mike Brannagan
Jean Brazeau
Bonnie Bryan
Judy Campbell
Norman Campbell
Sandi Cameron
CBC Museum
CBC Radio Archives
CBC Regional
  Communications
CBC Talent Bank
CBC Television
  Communications

Alan Chan
Brien Christie
Lisa Clarkson
Ron Crocker
Eva Czigler
Dan Diamond & Assoc.
Joel Darling
Jill Delaney
Michelle Demeyere
Mary DePoe
Ernie Dick
Christine Donaghy
Gail Donald
Greig Dymond
Darlene Ebert
George Einarson
Heather Elliott
Anne Emin
Janet Evans
Cathy Forrest
Daniel Gelfant
Sheila Gervais
Steve Glassman
Louise Goldberg
David Goorevitch
Sue Grimbly
Alan Habbick
Graham Hall
Bill Harper

Ivan Harris
Roy Harris
Christian Hasse
Peter Herrndorf
Hockey Hall of Fame
Bridget Hoffer
Joanne Hoppe
Chris Howden
Rae Hull
Liliane Hunkeler
Doug Ianson
Imperial Oil Archives
Sian Jones
Carl Karp
Doug Kirby
David Knapp
Maria Knight
Phillip Kusie
Slawko Klymkiw
Duncan Lamb
Linda Lambe
Nancy Lee
Frank Machovec
Tamara MacKeigan
Pauline Malley
Rose Mangone
Peter Mansbridge
Trish Marek
David Masse

David McCaughna
Dawn-Rae McLaren
Jacquie McNish
Michele Melady
Anne Mercer
Mavor Moore
Terry Mosher
Knowlton Nash
National Archives
  of Canada
Janet Pacey
Rochelle Porter
Colin Preston
Provincial Archives
  of Manitoba
Lynn Raineault
Kathryn Rawson
Wendy Robbins
Jess Ruge
Joe Schlesinger
Adrian Shuman
Melissa Sinclair
Ruth-Ellen Soles
Gabrielle Spitzer
Lorraine Thomson
Bob Wakeham
Kealy Wilkinson
Jim Williamson
Laurie Wood